William Belsham

Memoirs of the reign of George III. to the session of Parliament

ending A.D. 1793

William Belsham

Memoirs of the reign of George III. to the session of Parliament ending A.D. 1793

ISBN/EAN: 9783337150358

Printed in Europe, USA, Canada, Australia, Japan

Cover: Foto ©ninafisch / pixelio.de

More available books at **www.hansebooks.com**

MEMOIRS

OF

THE REIGN OF

GEORGE III.

MEMOIRS

OF

THE REIGN OF

GEORGE III.

TO

THE SESSION OF PARLIAMENT

ENDING A.D. 1793.

BY W. BELSHAM.

VOL. III.

THIRD EDITION.

Beneficio quàm metu obligare homines malit; exterasque gentes fidae ac focietate junctas habere, quàm tristi subjectas servitio.   Liv. lib. 26.

LONDON:

PRINTED FOR G. G. AND J. ROBINSON, PATERNOSTER-ROW.

1796.

CONTENTS

OF THE

THIRD VOLUME.

1779.

	Page
SESSION of Parliament—Lord Rockingham's spirited Amendment to the Address	2
Earl of Ossory's Motion respecting Ireland	3
Humiliating Confession of Earl Gower	5
Lord North's Propositions respecting Ireland	5
Estimate of the National Force	6

1780.

Petitions to Parliament on the Subject of Public Oeconomy	7
Reform Bills introduced by Mr. Burke	8
Commission of Accounts instituted	9
Earl of Shelburne's Motion of Reform	9
Famous Motion of Mr. Dunning, affirming the Increase of Regal Influence	13
Other Motions carried in Opposition to the Court	16

VOL. III.   A   *Illness*

CONTENTS.

	Page
Illness of the Speaker—The Efforts of the Patriots prove finally abortive	17
Riots in London excited by the Catholic Act	18
Sanguinary Severities of Lord Loughborough	23
Laudable Conduct of the King	23
Alliance with Holland dissolved	26
Armed Neutrality	27
Victory by Sir Geo. Rodney over the Spanish Fleet off Cape St. Vincent's	29
Indecisive Engagement in the West Indies, between Sir Geo. Rodney and the Count de Guichen	30
West Florida conquered by the Spaniards	31
Fortress of Omoa captured by the English	31
East and West India Fleets taken by the Spaniards	31
Military Operations in America	31
Philanthropic Act passed by the Legislature of Pennsylvania	32
Defection of General Arnold	34
Victory gained by Lord Cornwallis at Camden	36
Defeat of Major Ferguson at King's Mountain	37
Extravagant Exultation of the Court Faction in England	38
Rupture with Holland	41
Dissolution of Parliament—Remarkable Address of Sir Geo. Saville	43

Meeting

CONTENTS.

	Page
Meeting of the New Parliament—Mr. Cornwall Speaker	46

1781.

Debates on the Declaration of War against Holland	52
Reform Bill of Mr. Burke revived, and again rejected	53
Corrupt and extravagant Loan of Lord North	55
Pacificatory Motion of Mr. Fox	58
Review of the Administration of Mr. Hastings in India	58
Ravages of Hyder Ally in the Carnatic	176
Naval Encounters in the East Indies	177
Parliamentary Proceedings against Sir Thomas Rumbold	179
Sir Elijah Impey recalled from India	179
Ineffectual Resolutions of the House of Commons, and of the Court of Directors, for the Recall of Mr. Hastings from India	180
Military Operations in India	181
Resignation of Mr. Hastings—His Character	197
Attempt on the Isle of Jersey	204
Capture of St. Eustatia	205
Tobago taken by the French	208
Eustatia retaken by the French	208
Naval and Military Operations in America	209
Colonel Tarleton defeated at the Cowpens	211
Victory of Lord Cornwallis at Guildford	214
General Green's masterly Conduct	215

CONTENTS

	Page
Lord Cornwallis's Successes in Virginia	218
Reverse of Fortune—Lord Cornwallis and his Army made Prisoners of War	224
Triumph of the Americans on the Capture of a Second Royal Army	226
Commodore Johnstone's Expedition to the Cape of Good Hope	227
Obstinate Engagement between the English and Dutch Fleets off the Dogger Bank	228
Spirited Proceedings of the Parliament and People of Ireland	230
Session of Parliament—Infatuation of Ministers	232
Motion condemnatory of the American War by Sir James Lowther	237
Remarkable Debate on the Army Estimates	241

1782.

Mr. Fox renews his Motion of Censure upon Lord Sandwich	244
Lord George Germaine advanced to the Peerage under Circumstances of unprecedented Indignity and Disgrace	245
Two hundred and seventeen Members of the House of Commons concur in Mr. Fox's reiterated Motion of Censure on Lord Sandwich	247
General Conway's Motion against the American War negatived by a Majority of One Voice only	249

General

CONTENTS,

	Page
General Conway's Second Motion carried by a Majority of Nineteen Voices	250
Successive Motions of Censure on the Ministers	252
Entire Change of Administration—Marquis of Rockingham a Second Time Minister	255
High and peremptory Claims of the Irish Parliament	262
Repeal of the Irish Declaratory Act	263
Mr. Burke's Reform Bill a Third Time introduced, and passed	265
King's Debts a Third Time discharged	266
Resolution respecting the Middlesex Election rescinded	267
Mr. Pitt's Motion of Enquiry into the State of the Representation	268
Death of the Marquis of Rockingham	276
Advancement of Earl Shelburne—Fatal Divisions amongst the Whigs	277
Minorca conquered by the Spaniards	284
Island of St. Christopher, &c. captured by the French	285
The Bahamas taken by the Spaniards	285
Decisive Victory of Sir George Rodney over the French off Dominique	286
Glorious Defence and final Relief of Gibraltar	290
Provisional Articles of Peace with America, signed at Paris, Nov. 1782	295
General Washington resigns his Commission	297

Session

CONTENTS.

	Page
Session of Parliament—Strength of the New Ministry	301

1783.

Preliminaries of Peace with France and Spain signed	301
Debates on the Peace—Terms of it disapproved by the Commons	312
Coalition between Mr. Fox and Lord North	313
Change of Ministry—Duke of Portland First Minister	313
Extreme Unpopularity of the Coalition Administration	317
Act of Renunciation of the Authority of Great Britain over Ireland	317
Embarrassments of the East India Company	318
Mr. Pitt's Plan of Parliamentary Reform	319
Remarkable Petition of the Quakers	321
Order of Council for the Regulation of Commerce between the Continent of America and the West Indies	322
Treaty of Peace signed between England and Holland	323
State of Europe	323
Mr. Fox's India Bill moved	336
Passes the Commons, but is rejected by the Lords	344
Sudden Dismission of the Coalition Ministers	346
Mr. Pitt First Minister—His great Popularity	347

Political

CONTENTS.

	Page
Political Conflict between the Crown and the Commons	348

1784.

Mr. Pitt's India Bill rejected	351
The Nation declares in favor of the Crown	356
The Parliament dissolved	357
Meeting of the New Parliament—Triumph of the Minister	358

K. GEORGE III.

THE sixth Seffion of the prefent Parliament began at Weftminfter on the 25th of November, 1779. The King informed the two Houfes, in his fpeech from the throne, "that he had met them at a time when they were, in concert with him, called upon by every principle of duty, and every confideration of intereft, to exert their united efforts in the fupport and defence of their country, attacked by an unjuft and unprovoked war, and contending with one of the moft dangerous confederacies that ever was formed againft the Crown and People of Britain. In the midft of his care and folicitude for the fafety of this country, he had not been inattentive to the ftate of his loyal and faithful kingdom of Ireland; and, in confequence of the Addreffes prefented to him in the preceding Seffion, he had ordered fuch papers to be laid before them as might affift their deliberations, and he recommended it to them to confider what farther benefits and advantages might be extended

extended to that country." Echoes of the Speech in the ufual ftyle being propofed, Lord Rockingham moved in the Houfe of Peers a very fpirited amendment, " befeeching his Majefty to reflect upon the extent of territory, power, and opulence —of reputation abroad and concord at home, which diftinguifhed the opening of his Majefty's reign, and marked it as the moft fplendid and happy period in the hiftory of this nation; and to turn his eyes on the prefent endangered, impoverifhed, and diftracted ftate of the empire; and ftating to his Majefty, that if any thing can prevent the confummation of public ruin, it can be only new counfels and new counfellors, a real change from the conviction of paft errors, and not a mere palliation, which muft prove fruitlefs." This was negatived after a very warm debate by eighty-two voices to forty-one. A fimilar amendment was moved in the Houfe of Commons by Lord John Cavendifh, and occafioned a debate no lefs violent, in the courfe of which Mr. Fox particularly diftinguifhed himfelf by the boldnefs and energy of his obfervations. He faid, " that the plan of Government which had been in this reign invariably purfued, had been very early adopted. It was not the mere rumour of the ftreets that the King was his own Minifter, the fatal truth was evident; and though denied by the Members of the Adminiftration, it was propagated by their followers.

It

It was a doctrine in the highest degree dangerous, as tending to relieve Ministers from their responsibility, and to transfer it to a personage who could not by the principles of our Constitution be called to an account. But, he said, it should be a warning to Sovereigns, that though in general the evils of a reign were, according to the principles of our Government, ascribed to the wicked counsels of Ministers, yet when these evils reach to a certain height, Ministers are forgotten, and the Prince alone is punished. Thus it was with the Royal House of Stuart. CHARLES and JAMES had no doubt wicked Ministers, to whom the errors of their reign were justly in a great degree to be attributed; yet the one lost his life, and the other his crown. The patience of the people was not unlimited, and, however passive for a time, they would at last do themselves justice." The amendment was in the result negatived by two hundred and thirty-three voices to one hundred and thirty-four.

On the 6th of December a resolution of censure on the Ministers was moved in the House of Commons by the Earl of Upper Ossory, relative to the affairs of Ireland. This nobleman possessed large property in that kingdom, and was moreover distinguished by a general candor and liberality of conduct, which gave peculiar weight to his present animadversions. His Lordship observed,

"that

"that the Ministers seemed totally to have abandoned the government of that country to chance. They neither felt for its distresses, nor provided against its resentments: the present state of Ireland, his Lordship said, was truly alarming, and seemed to portend a sudden dissolution of the constitutional connection which had so long subsisted between the two countries. To the shameful inattention and criminal neglect of the Ministry, who might in the early stages of the miseries of that kingdom have granted the Irish nation substantial relief, was the present spirit of resistance wholly imputable. To what had the conduct of Ministers led? Either to an unreserved acquiescence in every proposition which Ireland in her present distempered state might think proper to demand, or the horrible alternative of a civil war while engaged in the present unequal contest with France, Spain, and America." This motion was powerfully supported by Mr. Fox, Mr. Burke, and Mr. Dunning, a lawyer and speaker of great eminence both in the House and at the Bar; and opposed in an elaborate speech by Lord North, who declared his intention to bring forward certain resolutions respecting Ireland in a few days. It was negatived by one hundred and seventy-three voices to one hundred. A similar motion of censure in the House of Peers by the Earl of Shelburne was negatived by eighty-two to thirty-seven

seven voices. In the course of the debate which arose on this occasion, the late Lord President Gower asserted his entire conviction that the censure now moved had a just and adequate foundation. "He had presided," his Lordship said, "some years at the council table, where HE HAD SEEN SUCH THINGS PASS, THAT NO MAN OF HONOR OR CONSCIENCE COULD ANY LONGER SIT THERE. The times were such as called upon every man to speak out; sincerity and activity in our councils could alone restore energy and effect to our Government." On the day previously fixed Lord North brought forward his propositions respecting Ireland, which were substantially the same with those originally moved by Lord Nugent in the Session of 1778, but accompanied with several additional concessions, particularly the very important one that Ireland should be allowed the free exportation of her woollens. These resolutions passed unanimously, and were received in Ireland not only with satisfaction but exultation, from the flattering and delusive expectation of deriving from them an effectual and immediate relief to her distresses.

The attention of the public in England was not a little attracted by the Estimates of the Army and Navy, which were about this time laid before Parliament. Eighty-five thousand men had been at an early period of the Session voted for the sea service,

vice, and before the recefs the Secretary at War moved, " that one hundred and eleven thoufand men be voted for the land fervice, exclufive of militia, amounting with the additional volunteer companies to forty-two thoufand. The foreign troops in Britifh pay were calculated at twenty-four thoufand, and the artillery at fix thoufand. The entire aggregate of this formidable force, therefore, fell little fhort of two hundred and feventy thoufand men, without including the troops ferving upon the Irifh or Indian eftablifhments. To fupport this vaft force twelve millions were raifed by way of loan, in addition to the permanent means of fupply; and thofe who moft deplored the incredible and enormous folly which had reduced the nation to a fituation fo critical and dangerous, could not but view with pleafure and aftonifhment the power, the riches, and the fpirit, now difplayed in defence of all that was dear and valuable to a free and independent people. The Oppofition in Parliament had been for fome time paft gradually acquiring ftrength; and the nation at large, notwithftanding their original predilection for the war, began at length to be ferioufly alarmed at the magnitude of the conteft, and the prodigious and ruinous expence with which it was attended. The undifguifed and unexampled profufion which pervaded every department of Government, could not but
strike

ſtrike the moſt careleſs obſerver; and, on a ſudden, OECONOMY became the prevailing and popular cry throughout the kingdom.

Early in the new year, 1780, public meetings were convened in moſt of the principal counties, and Petitions to Parliament were framed, with the laudable and expreſs view of eſtabliſhing a ſyſtem founded upon principles of ſtrict and diſintereſted frugality. The County of York, with great propriety and effect, took the lead on this occaſion. In their petition to the Houſe of Commons they earneſtly requeſted, " that, before any new burdens were laid upon this country, effectual meaſures might be taken by that Houſe to enquire into and correct the groſs abuſes in the expenditure of the public money; to reduce all exorbitant emoluments; to reſcind and aboliſh all ſinecure places and unmerited penſions; and to appropriate the produce to the neceſſities of the State in ſuch manner as to the wiſdom of Parliament ſhould ſeem meet." This petition was preſented to the Houſe on the 8th of February 1780, by Sir George Saville, Member for the county, who ſtated, " that it was ſigned by above eight thouſand freeholders. This petition, he ſaid, had been procured by no underhand arts or public canvaſs; it was firſt moved in a meeting of ſix hundred Gentlemen; and there was, he believed, more property in the hall where it was agreed to, than was contained

tained within the walls of the Houſe of Commons. It was a petition, he ſaid, to which the Adminiſtration would not DARE to refuſe a hearing, however the arts of miniſterial artifice and fineſſe might be employed to defeat the purpoſe of it." A number of other petitions of ſimilar import being preſented, Mr. Burke at length brought forward a ſpecific Plan of Reform, profeſſedly aiming at two grand objects: " firſt, the reduction of the national expenditure; ſecond, the diminution of regal influence—that influence which took away all vigor from our arms, wiſdom from our councils, and every ſhadow of authority and credit from the moſt venerable parts of the Conſtitution."—. To effect theſe purpoſes, Mr. Burke moved for leave to bring in certain bills for the better regulation of his Majeſty's civil eſtabliſhments, for the ſale of foreſt and other crown lands, for more perfectly uniting to the Crown the principality of Wales, the counties palatine of Cheſter and Lancaſter, and the duchy of Cornwall. But theſe bills, after a violent conflict, in the courſe of which the Miniſter was more than once left in a minority, were finally loſt.

A notice given by Col. Barré of an intention to move for the appointment of a Select Committee to inſpect the public accounts, ſeemed, however, to meet with univerſal approbation. It was for that reaſon, therefore, artfully and unfairly

fairly taken up by the Minister himself, who abruptly brought in a bill, contrary to the remonstrances of Col. Barré, and the concurring resentment of a large proportion of the House, for instituting a Commission of Accounts, consisting of persons *not Members* of the House of Commons. This was deemed unparliamentary, and in strong language opposed as an abdication of the rights and privileges of the House. But it passed into a law by a considerable majority; and the successive Reports of the Commissioners appointed in virtue of this Act, form, by their accuracy, ability, and impartiality, the best reply to the various objections urged against it.

The House of Peers in the mean time were far from being indolent or inattentive spectators of the interesting scenes now passing. On the very day that the Petition of the County of York was presented to the House of Commons, the Earl of Shelburne moved, in the House of Peers, " for the appointment of a Committee of Members of both Houses of Parliament, possessing neither employments nor pensions, to examine into the public expenditure, and the mode of accounting for the same." This motion was supported by his Lordship in a very able speech, in which he declared " that the great point to which his wishes tended, and to effect which his motion was chiefly framed, was to annihilate that undue influence operating upon both Houses of Parliament, which, if not eradicated,

cated, would prove the destruction of this country. To restore to Parliament its constitutional independence, and to place Government upon its true foundations, wisdom, justice, and public virtue, was, the noble Earl said, his most earnest desire, and this could not be effected without striking at the root of parliamentary corruption. Exclusive of this great and primary object, his Lordship shewed, that the most shameful waste of the public money had taken place in every branch of the national expenditure. To support a most ruinous and disgraceful war, a wicked, bloody, and unjust war! the Minister had borrowed year after year upon fictitious and unproductive taxes, and anticipated the produce of the Sinking Fund to answer his own views. Solely intent upon BORROWING, he appeared to have lost sight of every idea of decreasing the debt. It was the uncontrolled possession of the public purse which created that corrupt and dangerous influence in Parliament, of which such fatal use had been made; which put into the Minister's hands the means of delusion, which served to fortify him in his mad career, and which left no hope or prospect of punishing him for the enormity of his crimes. Influence so employed his Lordship declared to be a curse far greater, and more to be deprecated, than pestilence or famine. The present motion, the noble Earl observed, was not of a nature novel to Parliament; in former times, pa'ticularly in the years 1702, 1703,

1703, and 1717, there had been Commiffioners of Accounts appointed by Act of Parliament. The object of the propofition now before the Houfe was of a nature exactly fimilar, and it went to the abolition of all offices, whatever their falaries or appointments, that anfwered no other end but that of increafing the undue and unconftitutional influence of the Crown." In fupport of the motion, the Duke of Grafton declared, " that from his own knowledge and immediate obfervation, he could affert with confidence that the fpirit of difcontent and diffatisfaction was almoft univerfally gone forth, and that the Petitions recently prefented expreffed the genuine fenfe of the People." On the other hand, Lord Chefterfield, a young man not AS YET diftinguifhed by the eminence either of his knowledge or talents, and who had lately taken his feat in the Houfe on the deceafe of his illuftrious relation, the famous Earl of Chefterfield, affirmed, with fingular temerity, that " the majority of the people were well contented under the prefent Government, and that the County Petitions and Affociations were the laft ftruggles of an EXPIRING FACTION." The Lords Stormont, Mansfield, and the Lord Chancellor, maintained, with far more plaufibility, " that the prefent motion was a violation of the inherent excluſive privilege of the other Houfe to control the public expenditure, which no compofition, compromife,

or

or compact, would induce them to part with. They insisted that the motion was brought forward to embarrass Government, and to throw an odium upon his Majesty's confidential advisers; and that the petitions with which the motion was connected were filled with absurd and impracticable notions of public reform, and specious theories calculated to mislead the nation, and to introduce universal confusion." The Marquis of Rockingham distinguished himself in the debate by an animated speech in defence of the motion. His Lordship said, " that a system had been formed at the accession of his present Majesty to govern this country under the *forms of Law*, but in reality through the immediate influence of the Crown. This was the origin of all our national misfortunes; the measures of the present reign wore every internal and external evidence of that dangerous and alarming origin; and, when combined, they presented such a system of corruption, venality, and despotism, as had never perhaps been known under any *form* of free and limited Government. This system he had for seventeen years uniformly and vigorously opposed, and particularly during the short time he had presided at the head of the Treasury, but to very little purpose. As he had come into office at his Majesty's desire, so he had quitted it in obedience to his authority. His Lordship implored the Ministry not to persist in that blind and hitherto invincible spirit

of

of obstinacy, which had brought the nation into its present calamitous situation, but to pay some attention to the voice of the people, and the interests of their country." On the division the numbers were, NON CONTENTS 101, CONTENTS 55, five-and-thirty of whom entered their protest on the Journals. This was the largest minority that had for many years been known in the House of Peers in opposition to the Court; and, exclusive of Placemen, Pensioners, and Bishops, this expiring Faction constituted a clear and decisive majority of the Lords present at this interesting discussion.

On the 6th of April the House of Commons resolved itself, on the motion of Mr. Dunning, into a grand Committee, in order to take the petitions of the people into consideration, and on this occasion a most extraordinary and memorable debate arose. " The first object, Mr. Dunning said, which he meant to submit to the House, was a proposition collected from the several petitions, which, if agreed to, would establish the grounds of their prayer for redress. His second proposition should include the means of that redress. Should the House concur in his propositions, he meant to follow them up with real, substantial, and practicable measures. But, should they dissent from them, or endeavour to evade or procrastinate, there would be at once an end of the petitions and a full answer to the petitioners. His first motion was, that it should be resolved by this House, "that the
INFLUENCE

INFLUENCE of the CROWN had increased, was increasing, and ought to be diminished." This motion was, by a singular fortune, warmly supported by the Speaker of the House, who, though rarely accustomed to take part in their debates, declared, " that, on an occasion like the present, he should deem himself criminal in remaining silent; the resolution proposed contained an allegation which was too notorious to require proof—which in its full extent did not admit of proof. It could be known only to the Members of that House, as they were the only persons competent to resolve it; they were bound as jurors by the conviction arising in their own minds, and were obliged to determine accordingly. The powers constitutionally vested in the executive part of the Government were, he said, amply sufficient for all the purposes of good government, but its undue influence had increased to a degree absolutely incompatible with every just idea of a limited monarchy. What the petitioners demanded should have originated within those walls; they were sitting as the Representatives of the People, solely for their advantage and benefit, and were pledged to them for the faithful discharge of their trust." Notwithstanding the determined opposition of the Minister and of the Courtiers in general, particularly of the Lord Advocate of Scotland, Henry Dundas, who moved, as an amendment, to prefix the words, " it is now necessary to declare," it appeared on the division, which took place

place at midnight, on the amended resolution, that the numbers were in favour of the motion two hundred and thirty-three, against it two hundred and fifteen; so that the Court was left in a minority of eighteen. Mr. Dunning then moved, "that it was competent to that House to examine into and to correct abuses in the expenditure of the Civil List, as well as in every other branch of the public revenue, whenever it shall seem expedient to the House to do so." This was again opposed by Lord North, who, in the strongest terms, expressed his wishes that the Committee would not proceed. The motion was nevertheless agreed to by the House. Mr. Thomas Pitt then moved, " that it was the duty of that House to provide, as far as might be, an immediate and effectual redress of the abuses complained of in the petitions presented to the House from the different counties, cities, and towns, in this kingdom." The Minister once more earnestly implored the Committee to desist, but with no effect; the motion was agreed to. It was lastly moved by Mr. Fox, " that the resolutions should be immediately reported to the House;" which was deprecated and protested against by Lord North, as violent, arbitrary, and contrary to the established usage of Parliament. The motion, however, was carried; and the Chairman reporting the resolutions accordingly, they were severally agreed to by the House.

On the 10th of April, the Committee being resumed,

resumed, Mr. Dunning congratulated the House upon the late decisions, which he however said could avail little unless the House proceeded effectually to remedy the grievances complained of by the people. The alarming and increasing influence of the Crown being now admitted by a solemn decision of that House, it was incumbent upon them to go from generals to particulars. With a view therefore of extirpating that corrupt influence, he should move, " that there be laid before the House every Session, within seven days after the meeting of Parliament, an account of all monies paid out of the civil revenue to, or for the use of, or in trust for, any Member of Parliament since the last recess." This was objected to by Lord North, the Lord Advocate of Scotland, the Attorney General Wedderburne, &c. but was carried without a division. Mr. Dunning then moved, " that the persons holding the offices of Treasurer of the Chamber, Treasurer of the Household, Cofferer of the Household, Comptroller of the Household, Master of the Household, Clerks of the Green Cloth, and their Deputies, should be rendered incapable of a seat in that House." This was again opposed, and by the same persons as before; but on a division was carried by a majority of two hundred and fifteen to two hundred and thirteen voices. So far the patriotic party in Parliament had triumphantly proceeded, to the infinite joy of the disinterested and independent part of the public, when the sudden

den illnefs of the Speaker obliged the Houfe to adjourn to the 24th of April; on which day, the Committee being refumed, Mr. Dunning moved for an Addrefs, " that his Majefty would be pleafed not to diffolve the Parliament or prorogue the prefent Seffion until the objects of the petitions were anfwered." When the Houfe, after a vehement debate, came to a divifion on this important queftion, it was at once difcovered that the unfortunate illnefs of the Speaker, " whofe health was never " better worth than now," had infected " the very " life-blood of their enterprife;"—the motion being rejected by a majority of 254 to 203.

During the recefs, a fudden and fatal change had taken place in the temper and difpofition of the Houfe, and that influence of the Crown which the Parliament had determined *ought to be diminifhed*, was, as it now appeared, too firmly eftablifhed to be in danger of diminution. Mr. Fox rofe after the divifion, and in the moft poignant language reprobated the conduct of thofe men who had thus receded from the folemn engagements they had fo recently entered into; and Mr. Dunning fcrupled not to charge thefe Members with direct treachery to the Nation, confidering this refolution as an effectual bar to all future means and efforts of redrefs. So indeed it proved; for when, on a fubfequent refumption of the fubject, he moved, " that the two refolutions paffed on the 10th of April be reported," a motion was made from the oppofite side of the House, " that the Chairman leave the chair," which, on a division, was carried by a majority of 177 to 134 voices:—and thus miserably ended those deliberations, which once displayed so fair and flattering a prospect of political reform; and thus contemptuously were the petitions of more than one hundred thousand electors consigned to everlasting oblivion.

It is necessary to recall to our recollection, that an Act of Parliament had passed in the course of the Session of 1778, relieving the Roman Catholics from some of the heavier penalties inflicted upon them in the last century. This act seemed to be well-approved in England; but the fanatical spirit, unextinguished since the days of Knox, and which at the present period discovered itself by unequivocal symptoms in Scotland, prevented the extension of this very defective and imperfect toleration to that kingdom. On the bare suspicion of the intended indulgence, great tumults took place at Edinburgh and Glasgow, the Popish Chapel in the Metropolis was destroyed, and the houses of the principal Catholics attacked and plundered; on which the Lord Provost published a singular Proclamation, ascribing the riots to the " apprehensions, fears, and distressed minds of well-meaning people, and assuring them that no repeal of the Penal Statutes would take place." Encouraged by this wretched pusillanimity, the fanatics formed themselves into a society, styled the " Protestant Association," to

oppose

oppose any remission of the present persecuting laws against the Papists, and of this Association Lord George Gordon was chosen President, a man in the highest degree wild, eccentric, and enthusiastical. This Association was gradually extended to England, and much pains were taken by inflammatory harangues and pamphlets to prejudice the minds of the vulgar against the late wise and salutary relaxation of the penal code. It was at length determined to prepare a petition for a repeal of the law in question, which is affirmed to have obtained one hundred and twenty thousand signatures, *or marks*, of men of the lowest orders of society, whose excess of zeal could be equalled only by the grossness of their ignorance;—a combination of qualities at once ridiculous and terrible. Lord George Gordon, who was himself a member of the House of Commons, declined to present this petition, unless he were accompanied to the House by at least twenty thousand men.

A Public Meeting of the Association was, in consequence, convened in St. George's Fields, on June 2, 1780, whence it was supposed that not less than fifty thousand persons proceeded in regular divisions, with Lord George Gordon at their head, to the House of Commons, where their petition was presented by their president. Towards evening this multitude began to grow very tumultuous, and grosly insulted various Members of both Houses, compelling them in passing to and from the Houfe to cry, No Popery! and to wear blue cockades. During the debates on the petition, Lord George Gordon frequently addreffed the mob without, in terms calculated to inflame their paffions, and exprefsly ftating to them, " that the people of Scotland had no redrefs till they pulled down the Popifh chapels." After the adjournment of the Houfe, the mob, on this fuggeftion, immediately proceeded to the demolition of the chapels of the Sardinian and Bavarian ambaffadors. The military being ordered out could not prevent the mifchief, but apprehended various of the ringleaders.

The next day, Saturday, paffed quietly; but on Sunday the rioters re-affembled in vaft numbers, and deftroyed the chapels and private dwellings belonging to the principal Catholics in the vicinity of Moorfields.

On Monday they extended their devaftations to other parts of the town; and Sir George Savile's houfe, in Leicefter Fields, was totally demolifhed by thefe blind and barbarous bigots—that diftinguifhed fenator and patriot having had the honor to be the firft mover of the bill.

On Tuefday, the day appointed for taking the petition into confideration, the mob again furrounded the Parliament Houfe, and renewed their outrages and infults. The Houfe, after paffing fome refolutions adapted to the occafion, and expreffive of their juft indignation, immediately adjourned.

In

In the evening the populace, now grown more daring than ever, attacked the prison of Newgate, where their comrades were confined, with astonishing resolution; and, setting the building in flames, liberated more than three hundred felons and debtors resident within its walls. Encouraged by the impunity with which they had hitherto acted, they now proceeded to Lord Mansfield's house in Bloomsbury Square, which they totally demolished, his Lordship escaping not without difficulty. The prisons of Clerkenwell were also forced, many private houses plundered or destroyed, and scarcely did the night afford any cessation of the riots.

On the succeeding day, the mob, rendered more desperate by the mischiefs and villanies they had already perpetrated, attacked with incredible fury the houses of various individuals, chiefly Catholics, which they had previously marked for destruction. In the evening the King's Bench, the Fleet Prison, and the New Compter, were set on fire, and, with a prodigious number of private dwellings in different parts of the town burning at the same time, formed a tremendous scene of conflagration, to which London, since the great fire of 1666, had seen nothing parallel or similar.

The same day attempts were made by the rioters on the Bank and Pay-Office; but these, being strongly guarded, happily escaped that destruction which must have involved the whole nation in irrepa-

irreparable diftrefs and ruin. What appeared moft to excite the public indignation was the criminal fupinenefs of the Magiftracy of London * during thefe horrible commotions, apparently threatening to lay the metropolis of the empire level with the ground, and which actually prefented in many parts the image of a city ftormed and facked.

At length the King himfelf declared, with laudable refolution, in Council, " that, although the Magiftrates had not done their duty, he would not be deficient in his;" and general orders were immediately tranfmitted to the military to fire upon the rioters, without waiting for directions from the Civil Magiftrate, in confequence of which the flaughter was terrible; but in a fhort time the commotions were effectually fuppreffed, and by Thurfday noon order and tranquillity were perfectly reftored.

On that day Lord George Gordon was taken into cuftody, and, after a ftrict examination before the Privy Council, committed clofe prifoner to the Tower on a charge of HIGH TREASON, for which

* It moft affuredly was not forgotten that Mr. Gillam, an excellent Magiftrate of the county of Surry, was tried at the Old Bailey for his life, in confequence of the order given by him at the riots in St. George's Fields, A. D. 1768, for the military to fire, after long and patiently enduring the fevereft provocations from the rioters, and twice reading the riot act. Such a precedent could not but tend, in fimilar emergencies, moft dangeroufly to enfeeble the power of the executive government.

there

there does not appear to have been sufficient ground, and on his trial he was subsequently acquitted. An impeachment by the House of Commons for High Crimes and Misdemeanors would have been a mode of procedure far more eligible and efficacious, and would indubitably have insured that punishment which his rash and insolent conduct so justly merited.

A Special Commission was issued for the trial of the rioters, of whom a very great number, consisting of men very opposite in description and character, were apprehended. Lord Chief Justice De Grey, whose mild and benignant disposition, as well as his infirm health, was ill-suited to this painful task, willingly resigning his office; the Attorney-General Wedderburne was advanced to the Chief Justiceship, under the title of Lord Loughborough. The multiplicity combined with the precipitate and indiscriminate severity of the sentences, passed in his judicial capacity by this magistrate upon the rioters, far exceeded any thing known in this country since the days of Judge Jefferies: such indeed as left the memory of these transactions impressed upon the public mind in indelible characters of blood.

On the 19th of June the Parliament met pursuant to their adjournment; and the King, going in state to the House of Peers, made a very judicious speech, " lamenting the necessity which had obliged him, by every tie of duty and affection to his people, to employ the force entrusted to him for the suppression of those acts of felony and treason, which had overborne all civil authority, and threatened the immediate subversion of all legal power, the destruction of all property, and the confusion of every order in the state;—at the same time renewing his assurances, that he had no other object than to make the laws of the realm, and the principles of the constitution, the rule and measure of his conduct."

An address of thanks was deservedly voted in reply to this speech, without a single negative.— The general effect of these recent commotions was very favorable to Administration, by inspiring a too well founded dread of popular interposition in any shape or upon any occasion, however apparently tending to the accomplishment of the most desirable and salutary purposes. After this nothing of material import passed in either House of Parliament, and on the 8th of July 1780 an end was put to the present session.

The political alienation which had for some years taken place between England and Holland became daily more visible and notorious. A requisition had been made by the Court of London to the States General, soon after the declaration of war against Spain, for the succors stipulated by the treaty of 1678, confirmed by various subsequent agreements; but no answer could be obtained from their
High

High Mightinesses. On the contrary, loud complaints were made of the conduct of the English Court, which had caused to be seized, and carried into the different ports of Great Britain, ships belonging to the subjects of the Republic, navigated under the faith of treaties, and not laden with contraband goods:—this, no doubt, was in many instances, the fact. On the other hand, Great Britain complained, with equal truth, that France received from Holland continual supplies of naval and military stores, contrary to the faith of treaties; and that the principle of self-defence warranted the seizure and detention of all vessels laden with such exceptionable cargoes.

On the 1st of January, 1780, Commodore Fielding fell in with a fleet of Dutch merchant ships off Portland, convoyed by a small squadron of men of war, commanded by Count Byland. Captain Fielding desiring permission to visit the merchant ships, in order to ascertain whether they contained any contraband goods, was refused by the Dutch Admiral; on which he fired a shot a-head of the Count, who returned a broad-side: Commodore Fielding did the same, and then the Dutch immediately struck their colors. Such of the merchant ships as had naval stores on board were stopped, and the Dutch Admiral was informed that he was at liberty to hoist his colors and prosecute his voyage. But he refused to quit his
convoy,

convoy, and accompanied the Commodore to Portsmouth. A memorial in strong and resentful terms was presented by Count Welderen, by order of the States, in consequence of this transaction, which was represented as a direct attack upon the independence and sovereignty of their High Mightinesses, and a peremptory demand made of reparation and redress, to which no regard was paid. But on the 17th of April a declaration was published by the King of Great Britain, by which it was announced, " that repeated memorials having been presented by his Majesty's Ambassador to the States General, demanding the succors stipulated by treaty, to which requisition they had given no answer, nor signified any intention of compliance, his Majesty considered their High Mightinesses as having deserted the alliance that had so long subsisted between Great Britain and the Republic: and his Majesty from this time suspended, provisionally, all the stipulations of the several existing treaties, particularly of the Marine Treaty concluded at London A. D. 1674."

Holland was, however, far from being singular in her complaints respecting the violated rights of neutrality. The Powers of the Baltic, with a firmer tone, and in more decided language, declared their resolution to adopt such measures as were necessary for their own security. Early in the spring 1780 the Empress of Russia addressed a declaration to the

the Courts of London, Verfailles, and Madrid, containing an explicit ftatement of the principles on which fhe had determined to act for the removal of thofe moleftations which had interrupted the navigation of her fubjects, and for the protection of the liberty of commerce in general.

The radical principles here laid down were:—I. That neutral fhips fhould enjoy a free navigation even from port to port, and on the coafts of the Belligerent Powers.—II. That all effects belonging to the fubjects of the Belligerent Powers fhall be looked upon as free on board fuch neutral fhips, excepting only warlike ftores or ammunition—but neither the veffels, paffengers, or the reft of the goods, fhall be liable to feizure or detention. "To thefe principles" her Imperial Majefty declared "fhe was firmly refolved to adhere; and, for the honor of her flag, and the fecurity of her fubjects, fhe had ordered a confiderable part of her naval forces to be equipped, to act wherever her honor, intereft, or neceffity fhould require."

Denmark and Sweden acceding in form to this declaration of Ruffia, and ordering fimilar equipments of their marine, this confederacy of the Powers of the North acquired the appellation of "the Armed Neutrality;" and the bafis on which it was founded feemed to give univerfal fatisfaction throughout Europe—England alone, againft whom it was manifeftly levelled, excepted.

In

In the anſwer of the King of France it was ſaid, that what her Imperial Majeſty claimed from the Belligerent Powers was nothing elſe than the rules actually preſcribed to the French navy, and that ſolid advantages muſt reſult from this meaſure, not only to the ſubjects of Ruſſia, but to all nations." The reply of England was cold, and civilly evaſive; but this meaſure in reality excited ſo deep a reſentment, that the conduct of England reſpecting Ruſſia, for ſeveral years ſucceeding this period, may be aſcribed chiefly, or ſolely, to the alienation and hatred originating in the preſent obnoxious procedure.

The war between Great Britain and Spain had ſcarcely commenced when the blockade of Gibraltar was formed by ſea and land; and the hope of recovering that fortreſs probably operated as no inconſiderable inducement with Spain to engage in the preſent war.

Early in the year 1780 Sir George Rodney, an officer diſtinguiſhed by his gallant exertions in the late war, was appointed to the command of a powerful fleet, deſtined for the relief of that place, having on board Prince William Henry, the third ſon of his Majeſty. On the northern coaſt of Spain, he fell in with a convoy of twenty-two merchant-ſhips, richly laden, under the protection of a ſquadron of ſeven ſhips of war; to which he immediately gave chace, and in a few hours the whole were

were taken. This success was, however, only the prelude to another and much greater.

On the 16th of January, off Cape St. Vincent, he descried a Spanish squadron, consisting of fourteen sail of the line, which he directly bore down upon, and, notwithstanding the storminess incident to the season, taking the lee-gage, in order to prevent the enemy from retreating into their own ports; at four in the afternoon the action began, and in little more than half an hour one of the Spanish ships blew up with a dreadful explosion. The engagement nevertheless continued with unabating fury in the midst of darkness and confusion, and, before morning, the Phœnix of 80 guns, Don Juan de Langara, the Spanish Admiral's own ship; the Monarca, the Princessa, the Diligenti, of 70 guns each, struck their colors; the St. Julien and St. Eugenio were also captured, but through the violence of the tempest were afterwards driven on shore and lost. The others escaped in a very shattered condition; and the whole squadron, as to any immediate capability of service, might be considered as annihilated. Though the force of Admiral Rodney was greatly superior, his skill and courage were fully apparent in the mode of conducting the attack, which the violence of the storm, the darkness of the night, and the vicinity of a lee-shore, every where encircled with shoals and breakers, rendered very dangerous; the Admiral's own ship, the Sandwich, and several others, were in extreme hazard

of

of being loft on the fhoals of St. Lucar, and did not get into deep water till the next day.

After effecting the primary object of his commiffion, the relief of Gibraltar, Sir George Rodney proceeded to the Weft Indies, fending home his prizes under the care of Admiral Digby, who, on his paffage, captured the Prothée, a French fhip of 64 guns, and part of her convoy of merchant fhips.

No fooner had Admiral Rodney taken upon him the command in the Weft Indies, than every poffible exertion was made to bring on a general action, which Count de Guichen, who commanded the French fleet, cautioufly avoided ; but intelligence being received that in the night of the 15th of April, 1780, they had put to fea with their whole force, Admiral Rodney, who was ftationed at St. Lucie, immediately followed, and early on the morning of the 17th came in fight of the enemy; at noon the Admiral made the fignal for a general and clofe engagement, fetting himfelf a noble example of courage to the fleet by bearing down upon the French Admiral, whom he fought with unremitting fury till the enemy bore away, leaving the Sandwich, which from caufes not eafily or clearly afcertainable was very ill fupported in this action, a mere wreck upon the water. Other partial and indecifive encounters alfo took place, in which little inferiority of fkill or courage was difcernible on the part of the French officers or feamen.

During

During thefe tranfactions in the Weft Indies Don Galvez, the Spanifh Governor of Louifiana, reduced the Britifh fettlements on the Miffiffipi, and had made great progrefs in the conqueft of the province of Weft Florida, though Penfacola held out to the next year.

As a very inadequate counterbalance to thefe fucceffes, an expedition had been undertaken from Jamaica to the Spanifh main; and the fortrefs of Omoa, which contained a confiderable booty in fpecie and merchandife, was taken by ftorm, but foon afterwards evacuated. A very heavy misfortune in the autumn of this year took place, in the entire capture of the outward bound Eaft and Weft India fleets in the Bay of Bifcay by the Spaniards, —a lofs which had no parallel in the naval and commercial hiftory of Great Britain, fince the famous capture of the Smyrna fleet in the reign of King WILLIAM.

The war in the northern provinces of America feemed throughout the whole of the fummer of 1780 to be almoft at a ftand. On the 10th of July a large body of French troops commanded by the Comte de Rochambeau, under convoy of a confiderable fleet, arrived at Rhode-Ifland. This the Comte affured the States was only the vanguard of a much greater force deftined by the King, his Sovereign, to their aid. A fcheme was foon after formed by Sir Henry Clinton and Admiral Arbuthnot, of a

combined

combined attack against the French and Americans at Rhode-Island; and a large proportion of the forces stationed at New York were embarked for that purpose; but General Washington, by a rapid movement passing the North River, and advancing to New York, compelled them to desist from their purpose.

It affords a grateful relief from the sensations which oppress the mind in listening to the tale of human folly and wretchedness, to revert to an act of the most exalted philanthropy passed about this period by the Legislature of Pennsylvania, to the following purport : " When we contemplate our abhorrence of the condition to which the arms and tyranny of Great Britain were exerted to reduce us—when we look back on the variety of dangers to which we have been exposed, and the deliverances wrought when hope and fortitude have become unequal to the contest,—we conceive it to be our duty, and rejoice that it is in our power, to extend a portion of that freedom to others which hath been extended to us,—to add one more step to universal civilization, by removing, as much as possible, the sorrows of those who have lived in undeserved bondage. Weaned by a long course of experience from those narrow prejudices and partialities we had imbibed, we conceive ourselves, at this particular period, called upon, by the blessings we have received, to manifest the sincerity of our profession. In justice, therefore, to persons who having no prospect before them

them whereon they may reſt their ſorrows and their hopes, have no reaſonable inducement to render that ſervice to ſociety which otherwiſe they might; and alſo in grateful commemoration of our own happy deliverance from the ſtate of UNCONDITIONAL SUBMISSION to which we were doomed by the tyranny of Britain: BE IT ENACTED, That no child born hereafter ſhall be a SLAVE; that Negro and Mulatto children ſhall be ſervants only till twenty-eight years of age; that all ſlaves ſhall be regiſtered before the firſt of November next; that they ſhall be tried like other inhabitants; and that no Negroes or Mulattoes, other than infants, ſhall be bound for longer than ſeven years."—Such were the ſentiments and ſuch the conduct of a people once attached to Britain by every civil and ſocial tie, by which either dignity or advantage could be derived, or durability be hoped—but whom Britain, in the hour of her inſolence and infatuation, firſt attempted to treat as ſlaves, and then to puniſh as rebels.

Towards the autumn of the preſent year, a remarkable event took place in the defection of General Arnold, who commanded a conſiderable body of troops at Weſt Point on the North River, and who had entered into a ſecret correſpondence with Sir Henry Clinton to betray into his hands that important poſt, and the whole of the troops entruſted to him. The military talents and ſucceſſes of

VOL. III.   D   Arnold

Arnold had raised his reputation so high, that the danger of placing confidence in a man wholly destitute of honor and probity in private life was not sufficiently adverted to. The intercourse between the American and English Generals was carried on through the medium of Major André, a young man of singular accomplishments, who had passed up the river unknown and unsuspected from the head quarters at New York to the post of West Point. But on his return by land, September 23d, after eluding the vigilance of the regular patroles, he was apprehended in disguise, and with a false passport, by three American privates, to whom he in vain offered great rewards if they would suffer him to escape. On examination, the papers found upon him, and which he had no opportunity to destroy, discovered all the particulars of the conspiracy. His case being referred to a board of General Officers, of which the Marquis de la Fayette was one, they unanimously determined that he came under the denomination of a spy; and that, agreeably to the law and usage of nations, he ought to suffer death; which, notwithstanding the urgent solicitations and the impotent and injudicious menaces of Sir Henry Clinton, was, on the 2d of October, inflicted upon him in that degrading mode "which gives the brave the keenest wound." Such was the noble candor and magnanimity of his conduct consequent on the discovery, that the high

character

character of the American Commander would have derived additional luftre from indulging the earneft and fole requeft of Major André, to be permitted to die as a foldier, not as a felon. General Arnold, with great difficulty, on the apprehenfion of Major André, made his efcape to New-York, and was immediately promoted to the rank of Brigadier General in the King's fervice.

In the fouthern provinces the events of the war were of a nature more important and interefting. After the departure of Sir Henry Clinton from Carolina, Lord Cornwallis was left with a force apparently very inadequate to maintain poffeffion of the province againft the increafing armies of the Americans, of which General Gates, the conqueror of Burgoyne, had now taken the command. The Britifh forces, having advanced towards the north frontier of the province, found their farther progrefs intercepted by the enemy, who with far fuperior numbers were pofted near the town of Camden. Lord Cornwallis, fenfible that a retreat would be equivalent to an abandonment of the recent conquefts, determined to rifk an engagement; and in the night of the 15th of Auguft, 1780, the troops were put in motion, in hope of furprifing General Gates in his camp. That commander, with a view likewife to the furprifal of Lord Cornwallis, had marched his troops during the night to the attack of the Britifh camp, and the advanced parties of the two armies unexpectedly met in a wood near Camden. A fort of truce was obferved till day-light appeared, when the action commenced on the part of the Britifh General, who was well pleafed to obferve that the American Commander had been under the neceffity of taking a very difadvantageous and confined pofition, bounded by fwamps on both fides, which prevented his making any efficacious ufe of his great fuperiority of numbers. The militia, of whom General Gates's army chiefly confifted, unable to refift the new and formidable attack of the bayonet, fled at the firft onfet. The continental troops maintained, neverthelefs, their ground with great refolution; but finding themfelves totally deferted by the militia, who could never be brought to rally, were compelled to retreat, leaving behind them their cannon, camp equipage, and ftores. This victory feems to have been the moft complete which was obtained in the whole courfe of the war. The purfuit continued for more than twenty miles; and Colonel Tarleton coming up with a detached corps at the Catawba fords under General Sumpter, charged them with fuch vigor that they were inftantly broken, and the greater part either cut to pieces or taken prifoners.

General Gates, who thus unfortunately at Camden faw thofe laurels fade which he had fo glorioufly acquired at Saratoga, now, with little apparent

parent attention to the point of honor, left the shattered remains of his army to the care of a General Smallwood, and retired into North Carolina to consult with the Government of that province upon the means of future resistance and defence.

Lord Cornwallis, eager to improve his victory to the utmost, advanced, as soon as the excessive heats incident to the climate and season would permit, to the vicinity of Salisbury, on the frontier of North Carolina, having first detached Major Ferguson to the western side of the province to collect and arm the Royalists in that quarter. No sooner was the communication of this officer with Lord Cornwallis interrupted by the extension of the distance, than a plan was formed to surround and cut him entirely off. Divers corps of the provincial militia effected a rapid junction with the mountaineers of the western districts, under the command of Colonels Williams and Cleveland, to the amount of several thousand men, and, marching in quest of Ferguson, soon discovered his encampment on an eminence known by the name of King's Mountain. The Americans, dividing their force into different columns, ascended the hill in various directions, and attacked the Royalists with great fury. Major Ferguson was successful on whichever side he directed his efforts; but no sooner was one division driven back, than the former resumed its station, so that his exertions were entirely unavailing. But his

his unconquerable spirit disdained all ideas of surrender; and the unequal conflict continued till this officer received a mortal wound; and no chance of escape being left, nor prospect of successful resistance remaining, the second in command sued for quarter, which was granted, and more than eight hundred men laid down their arms, about three hundred being killed or wounded in the action.

This disaster was in its consequences almost as fatal to Lord Cornwallis as the affair of Trenton to General Howe. On the first intelligence of it, his Lordship retreated to Wynnesborough, where he was much harassed by the irregular but continual attacks of the Provincials: and General Gates was enabled to write to the President of the Congress, " The enemy have so far the worst of the campaign, having lost considerably more men, officers, and arms than your army; and even lost ground, as they had several posts at the beginning of the campaign on the Pedee, all of which are now evacuated." But the exultation of the Court faction in England, on the intelligence of Lord Cornwallis's victory at Camden, was extreme. Untaught by former disappointments, all the flattering and favorite ideas of absolute conquest and unconditional submission seemed for a time to be revived. " I have not the least doubt," said the American Secretary of State to Lord Cornwallis in his dispatch of November 9th, " from your Lordship's vigorous and

and alert movements, that the whole country south of the Delawar will be restored to the King's obedience in the course of the next campaign." It is even possible that the animation inspired by this success contributed to the adoption of the violent counsels, by which at this period matters were brought to the last extremity with the States General.

On the 3d of September, the Mercury, a Congress packet, was taken by the Vestal frigate off the banks of Newfoundland. On board this packet was Mr. Laurens, late President of the Congress, charged with a commission to Holland. On being brought to England, he was examined by the Privy Council, and committed close prisoner to the Tower, on an accusation of high treason. His papers, which had been thrown overboard, and by great dexterity and diligence recovered and deciphered, were found to contain the sketch of a treaty of amity and commerce between the Republic of Holland and the States of America. This treaty appeared to be in a train of negotiation, and to have received the sanction and approbation of M. Van Berkel, Counsellor and Pensionary of Amsterdam. Such was the high offence taken by the Court of London at this discovery, that immediate orders were transmitted to Sir Joseph Yorke, to represent to the Sates General, that the States of Amsterdam, as appeared from the papers of the Sieur Laurens, calling himself President of the pretended Congress, had entered into a clandestine correspondence with the American rebels, and that instructions and powers had been given by them for the purpose of concluding a treaty of indissoluble friendship with the said rebels. His Britannic Majesty, therefore, required not only a formal disavowal of so irregular a conduct, but also insisted on speedy satisfaction adequate to the offence; and the exemplary punishment of the Pensionary Van Berkel and his accomplices, as disturbers of the public peace and violators of the rights of nations; otherwise the King would be obliged to take such steps as became his dignity and the interests of his subjects. The States General, though they passed without difficulty resolutions of disavowal and enquiry, delaying to give a formal and explicit answer to this declaration, a second memorial was presented by Sir Joseph Yorke on the 12th of December, in which the Ambassador requires an immediate and satisfactory answer from the States. "The King," he says, "has never imagined that your High Mightinesses had approved of a treaty with his rebellious subjects. That had been raising the buckler on your part. But the offence has been committed by a city which makes a considerable part of the State, and it belongs to the Sovereign Power to punish and give satisfaction for it: and it will not be till the last extremity, in case of denial or silence, that the King will take them upon himself." The Ambassador was

now

now informed that the memorial would be taken *ad referendum* by the Deputies of the refpective provinces, according to the received cuftom and conftitution of their government. This being regarded as a palpable evafion, the Ambaffador received orders immediately to leave the Hague, and a Declaration of War was publifhed againft Holland on the 20th of December 1780. This was a meafure totally unexpected on the part of the States General, who were ill-prepared for fuch a rupture. Before the departure of Count Welderen, he delivered, by order of the States, a letter to Lord Stormont, which his Lordfhip returned unopened.

However unjuft and indefenfible had been the policy of the Britifh Government, the hoftile conduct of the Dutch, apparently proceeding lefs from a fpirit of generous attachment to the caufe of violated freedom, than from a fordid and avaricious felfifhnefs, had rendered them the objects of the national refentment and averfion. The declaration of war, therefore, which carried with it a refemblance of vigor, and even of magnanimity, was received with a great fhare of approbation and applaufe. There were not, however, wanting thofe who, without any prejudice in favor of Holland, hefitated not to affirm that this laft act of the Britifh Miniftry filled up the meafure of their iniquity and abfurdity. " Where," faid they, " could be the civil or political

tical offence for the subjects of a foreign state to enter into provisional agreements with the Americans, which were not, and could not be supposed valid, till the recognition of American independence had taken place, and which, in the very words of the instrument itself, professed to be merely " outlines of a Treaty of Commerce, such as *might be concluded hereafter*, between their High Mightinesses and the United States of America?"

If to maintain an amicable intercourse of this indefinite nature with the Americans was criminal in the Dutch, Holland could be regarded in no other light than as a province of England. The King of England seemed not to recollect, that the subjects of the States General were not his subjects, or accountable to him for their actions. They farther affirmed, that a provisional treaty, or speculative project, for it was no more, of peace and amity with America, did by no means necessarily imply enmity or ill-will to England:—that this treaty, whether it boded good or ill to England, had been already publicly and unreservedly disavowed by the Dutch Government; and that nothing less than a direct and positive injury could, in the eye of reason, justify a denunciation of hostility.

As to the insolent requisition of exemplary punishment on the person of Van Berkel, who might, for any thing that appeared, be actuated by motives the most upright and patriotic; the King of England

England ought to have reflected, that the laws of England, in similar circumstances, would not have authorised him to have inflicted the slightest punishment on even the meanest of his subjects, who should have formed the plan of a mere contingent agreement with the revolted provinces of another power, to take effect only when their claim of sovereignty should be actually recognised, and when the conditions should be approved and ratified by the Government to which alone they owed allegiance.

On the whole, it may safely be affirmed, that a more frivolous and invalid plea or pretext of national hostility has seldom been urged, even by Royal logicians. The folly of the measure also was no less obvious than its injustice: for, though Holland was attacked thus suddenly and unprepared, there could be no doubt but that she would, in a short time, become a potent accession to the strength of that formidable confederacy which seemed already to threaten the very existence of Britain.

The FOURTEENTH PARLIAMENT of Great Britain was dissolved by proclamation on the 1st of September, and a new Parliament convened, which met on the 31st of October 1780.

On the event of this dissolution, amidst the multiplicity of election advertisements usual on such occasions, a very remarkable address from Sir George Saville, member for the county of York,

to

to his constituents, was published, well deserving
the notice of history, as exhibiting the sentiments,
not merely of that eminently distinguished patriot,
but of all intelligent, reflecting, and disinterested
persons, at this alarming period. In renewing the
tender of his services, he confesses, that " it has
not been without much serious consideration, and
more than common hesitation, that he determined
upon it. The satisfaction and honor," says this
Aristides of Britain, " of attending your business
have ever over-balanced the labor. But my attendance during the last Parliament has been something
worse than laborious—it has been discouraging,
grievous, painful. Look back for a moment upon
the things which have been done, or, being done,
have been approved of by that body of which I
have been a constituent part. In comparing the
present with the past situation of public affairs, one
consolation only remains, that of being able to assert
that there has been no measure of all those, that
have proved so ruinous and fatal, which I have not,
as an individual, resisted to the utmost of my power:
—a poor, barren, ineffectual negative is indeed
all the claim I can plead to your favor; and truth
obliges me to add, that I at length return to you
with hardly a ray of hope of seeing any change in
the miserable course of public calamities.

" On this melancholy day of account, in rendering up to you my trust, I deliver to you your share

of a country maimed and weakened—its treasure lavished and mis-spent, its honors faded, and its conduct the laughing-stock of Europe;—our nation in a manner without allies or friends, except such as we have hired to destroy our fellow-subjects, and to ravage a country in which we once claimed an invaluable share.—Forbearing as well the forward promises as the superficial humbleness of phrase in use on these occasions, I make it a solemn duty to lay before you, without disguise or palliation, the present state of your concerns, as they appear to me, and the gloomy prospect which lies before us. Some have been accused of exaggerating the public misfortunes—nay, of having endeavored to help forward the mischief, that they might afterwards raise discontents. I am willing to hope that neither my temper nor my situation in life will be thought naturally to urge me to promote misery, discord, or confusion, or to exult in the subversion of order, or the ruin of property. Trust not, however, to my report: reflect, compare, and judge for yourselves. But, under all these disheartening circumstances, I could yet entertain a cheerful hope, and undertake again the commission with alacrity as well as zeal, if I could see any effectual steps taken to remove the *original cause* of the mischief: THEN THERE WOULD BE A HOPE. Till the purity of the constituent body, and thereby that of the representative, be restored, THERE IS NONE. I look upon restoring election and representation

in

in fome degree—for I expect no miracles—to their original purity, to be that without which all other efforts will be vain and ridiculous."

For the accomplifhment of this moft important purpofe, he concludes with expreffing his earneft wifh, " that whatever is thought of may be purfued with that true fpirit of firmnefs and moderation which belongs to the caufe of juftice; and above all, that by every means that can be devifed, a good underftanding and union may be infured amongft refpectable men of all ranks and defcriptions, who agree in the main principles of liberty, whatever differences may fubfift in fmaller points, or in matters not calling for immediate difcuffion."

At the meeting of the new Parliament, Mr. Cornwall was, for reafons which require no comment, chofen Speaker of the Houfe of Commons in the room of Sir Fletcher Norton, on a divifion of 203 voices to 134. The KING, in his opening speech, declared " his fatisfaction in having an opportunity, by the recent election, of receiving the moft certain information of the difpofition and *wifhes of his people*, to which he was ALWAYS *inclined to pay the* UTMOST ATTENTION! He acknowledged the arduous fituation of public affairs; but the late fignal fucceffes of his arms in Georgia and Carolina would, he trufted, have important confequences, in bringing the war to a happy conclufion." An amendment to the addrefs, confifting in the omiffion of feveral complimentary paragraphs,

graphs, was moved in the House of Commons by Mr. Thomas Grenville.

The BLESSINGS of his Majesty's reign being recognised in the proposed address, in high-flown terms, as inspiring sentiments of reverence and gratitude, Mr. Fox declared, " that in this part of the address he could not concur, as he was yet to learn what those BLESSINGS were. The present reign had been one continued tissue of disgrace, misfortune, and calamity. As to the honorable mention made of the late successes in America, and of the gallant officers by whom they had been obtained, he should answer, that he would not concur in applauding his own brother, who was now serving in America, for any success he might obtain. He never had joined, and as long as he lived he never would join, in a vote of thanks to any officer, whose laurels were gathered in the American war; for he regarded that war as the fountain-head of all the mischief and misery under which this country now labored: and he was well convinced that the ministerial prospects of success, however transiently flattering, would be closed in disappointment and delusion." The address, as originally moved, was at length carried by a majority of 69 voices, which, when compared with the majorities of former times, afforded some faint gleam of hope that better days were gradually, though slowly, approaching.

Nothing

Nothing meriting specific notice passed in either House previous to the recess of Parliament; but on the 25th of January 1781, two days only after they had re-assembled, Lord North delivered to the House of Commons a message from the King, in which his Majesty acquainted them, " that, during the recess of Parliament, he had been obliged to direct letters of marque and general reprisal to be issued against the States General of the United Provinces. For the causes and motives of his conduct he referred to his public manifesto, which, with various other papers, he had ordered to be laid before the House." At the close of a long speech, justificatory of the late measures of Government, Lord North moved, " That an address be presented to his Majesty, assuring him that the House would, with a firm and determined resolution, support the just and necessary war against Holland, for the maintenance of the honor of his Crown, and the rights and interests of his People." This motion was seconded by Lord Lewisham; but it was not carried without a long and animated debate, in which Mr. Thomas Townshend, afterwards created Lord Sydney, particularly distinguished himself. He severely censured " the late long adjournment, which was only calculated to free the Executive Government from the control and inspection of Parliament, who had now only to ratify what the rashness of Ministers had most

unad-

unadvisedly done. In this manner had the House been led into the American war, that fatal source of all our calamities. In this manner had the French rescript been announced; and afterwards the Spanish rescript; and at length the declaration of war against Holland, our antient and natural ally. Year after year had the Minister acquainted the House with a new enemy, but never had he yet brought them the welcome information of a new friend. Much had been said of the provocations we had received from Holland, and the predominance of a French interest in that country—but had Holland received no provocation from us? The infolence of the British memorial presented to the States in 1777, contributed more than any thing else to the prevalence of the French faction in Holland. It had been stated, as a serious ground of offence, that Holland had not complied with the requisition of troops, which, by treaty, she had engaged to furnish. But it was notorious, that, in the event of this compliance, Holland would have been immediately invaded by France; and, in conformity with the same treaties, we must then have sent a much greater aid to the assistance of the Republic. If the Dutch at the present period had changed their political system respecting this country, it was owing to the criminal conduct of an Administration, who had precipitated us into a war, whence all our misfortunes had arisen. In consequence

quence of that war, our American commerce was loft; and could it be a matter of furprife that the Dutch, a people who exifted by commerce, fhould be defirous to fecure a fhare of it? We were abandoned, not by the Dutch only, but by all the Powers of Europe, who were all equally convinced, that, under the prefent wretched adminiftration of affairs, whoever became the ally of Great Britain would only fhare in her difgrace and her misfortunes."

In the Houfe of Lords, the Duke of Richmond, Lord Shelburne, and Lord Camden inculcated the fame ideas with great animation and ability. "As to what was called *the treaty* between Holland and America," Lord Camden faid, "it was the mere unauthorifed act of Van Berkel, and betrayed neither directly nor indirectly any intention in the States General of an hoftile nature. It did not even appear that they knew any thing of this man or his colleagues; and much lefs that they had determined to ratify this pretended treaty, or project of a treaty, by which no one was bound, and no one could be injured."

His Lordfhip contrafted the conduct of the prefent Minifters to the States General, with that of Lord Chatham, who, in the zenith of his victories, had never deviated from the line of refpect and moderation. "He was too wife and magnanimous, whatever might be the caufes of complaint, to adopt the ftyle and language of that provoking,

provoking, arrogant, and indecent memorial, to which, more than to any other circumftance whatever, the fubfequent conduct of the Republic might be attributed. His Lordfhip was of opinion, that the manifefto againft Holland ought not to receive the fanction of their Lordfhips, till ftronger evidence were produced of the neceffity, juftice, and policy of that meafure; and, if no better grounds of hoftility fhould be the refult of a more particular enquiry, Parliament would be bound to order immediate reparation and fatisfaction to be given for the injury already fuftained by Holland ; and an end would be of courfe put to the farther profecution of hoftilities."

In both Houfes, neverthelefs, the addreffes were carried by great majorities; but the diffentient Peers recorded their objections in a ftrong and vigorous proteft. Their Lordfhips declare, "that they can never believe a rupture fo contrary to the uniform and approved policy of our ableft ftatefmen can have become neceffary, on our part, without grofs mifmanagement in our councils ; and that honeft and able Minifters might have prevented *this*, amongft other wretched confequences of the unfortunate American war." The States General themfelves, in their counter-memorial, affirm, "that the plan or project of a treaty with America, which had excited, to fuch a degree, the difpleafure of

the

the King of England, although it depended altogether on the anterior recognition of American independence, had been, however, without hesitation, disavowed by them. But the punishment insisted upon was not within their power, and they could not assent to it, without striking at the root of the fundamental constitution of the State. That, obliged by what is held most sacred to defend the rights and privileges of their subjects, the Republic could not forget itself so far as to submit to the will of his Britannic Majesty, by attempting to overturn those rights and privileges, and exceeding the limits prescribed by the fundamental laws of its government. Those laws required the intervention of the judicial department, and those were the means which the States of Holland, to whose peculiar cognizance it belonged, had resolved to use, by requiring on this subject the advice of the Court of Justice established in their province. Of this the Chevalier Yorke had been formally apprised :— but what was the astonishment of their High Mightinesses, when the said Ambassador, calling the said resolve *illusive*, flatly refused to transmit it to his Court ! This obliged their High Mightinesses to send it to Count Welderen, their Minister in London, with orders to lay it before his Britannic Majesty, whose Ministers had nevertheless returned it unopened to the Ambassador."

The

The war, thus rashly and haughtily commenced, was conducted in the bitter spirit of animosity and revenge*. But before the military operations of the year are entered upon, it will be proper to terminate the Civil and Parliamentary History of the present Session.

The famous Reform Bill of Mr. Burke was revived soon after the recess: but, on the motion for the second reading, it was rejected, *in toto*, by a majority of 233 voices to 190; though ably and powerfully supported by many of the most eminent Members of the House.

Amongst the speeches which attracted most strongly the public attention was that delivered with much grace and energy by Mr. William Pitt,

---

* It is a remarkable fact, positively affirmed by Rendorp, burgomaster of Amsterdam, in a political publication, called *Memorien dienende tot Opheldering*, and still uncontradicted, that Sir Joseph Yorke, when he left the Hague, went to Antwerp, and instigated the inhabitants of that city to petition the Emperor to insist on the free navigation of the Scheldt. And it is notorious, that when this demand was, some years afterwards, actually made by the Emperor, England, far from taking any alarm, looked on with calm indifference, or rather with pleasure. But when the same thing was, more recently, attempted by France; the balance of Europe was discovered to be in imminent danger of subversion: and England and Holland, without allowing any time or opportunity for explanation or retractation, were plunged into a most ruinous and destuctive war, under the pretext of defending the violated rights of the Treaty of Westphalia.

second son of the late Earl of Chatham, who in very early youth had been elected a Member of the present Parliament, and who now exhibited himself to an admiring nation as equally the heir of his talents and virtues. "One great object," Mr. Pitt said, " of all the petitions which had been presented, was a recommendation of œconomy in the public expenditure; and the design of the present bill was, to carry into effect the wishes of the people, by introducing a substantial system of œconomy. Besides the benefits which would result from the bill in this respect, it had another object still more important, and that was the reduction of the influence of the Crown—an influence which was the more to be dreaded, because more secret in its attacks, and more concealed in its operations, than the power of prerogative." Mr. Pitt adverted to the extraordinary objections which had been made to the bill; it proposed to bring no more than 200,000l. per ann. into the public coffers, and that sum was insignificant, in comparison of the millions annually expended. " What then is the conclusion we are left to deduce? The calamities of the present crisis are too great to be benefited by œconomy. Our expences are so enormous, that it is useless to give ourselves any concern about them; we have spent, and are spending, so much, that it is foolish to think of saving any thing. Such is the language which the

opponents

opponents of this bill have virtually employed. It had also been said, that the King's Civil List was an irresumable parliamentary grant; and it had been even compared to a private freehold. The weakness of such arguments was their best refutation. The Civil List revenue was granted to his Majesty, not for his private use, but for the support of the Executive Government of the State. His Majesty, in fact, was the trustee of the public, subject to parliamentary revision. The Parliament made the grant, and undoubtedly had a right to resume it when the pressure of the times rendered such resumption necessary. Upon the whole, he considered the present bill as essential to the being and independence of this country, and he would give it his most determined support."

Early in March, the Minister, Lord North, brought forward the annual statement of the Public Account. The entire expenditure of the year his Lordship calculated at twenty-one millions, twelve of which it would be necessary to raise by a public loan: as to the terms of which, his Lordship had contracted with the subscribers, to grant 150l. capital stock at three per cent. and 25l. capital stock at four per cent. for every 100l. in money; thus creating a new capital of eighteen millions three per cent. and three millions four per cent. being nine millions more than the sum actually paid

paid into the Exchequer. To defray the interest of this loan, new taxes would be wanting to the amount of 660,000l. annually, i. e. 60,000l. more than the legal established interest of five per cent.: exclusive of which, as the subscription to the loan bore a premium of ten per cent. the farther sum of 1,200,000l. was lost to the nation. The terms of this extraordinary contract were, even by several of the friends of the Minister, declared to be extravagantly high; and it was by Mr. Fox reprobated in the most indignant expressions of severity, as " the most corrupt in its origin, the most shameful in its progress, and the most injurious in its consequences, that ever came under the contemplation of that House. In order to carry on a wicked, impolitic, and bloody war, the Minister would not scruple," said this formidable speaker, " to extort the last guinea from the pockets of the people. The noble Lord stands convicted of having made, in the character of agent and trustee for the nation, an improvident, scandalous, and profligate bargain, for which he deserves public execration and exemplary punishment." On a division, the motion of the Minister was carried by a majority of 169 to 111 voices.

In the House of Lords, it was again vigorously opposed by Lord Rockingham, the Duke of Portland, and other Peers, who, in a joint protest, recorded their names, to adopt the language of their Lordships,

ships, "in testimony of their strongest condemnation of the terms of this loan, and of the MOTIVES which they conceive dictated terms so very disadvantageous to the Crown and Nation." All the influence and all the activity of the Ministers of the Crown were now indeed obviously necessary to prevent a parliamentary abandonment of the present system. Some weeks afterwards, the subject was again revived in the House of Commons, by a motion of Sir George Saville, that a Select Committee be appointed, to enquire into the circumstances of the last loan, to make an estimate of its terms, and report the same to the House. "Though the bargain of the Minister had been irrevocably ratified by the House, this distinguished patriot observed, that it was not yet too late, on discovering the shameless prodigality of the terms on which it was concluded, to pass a vote of censure, or even of impeachment, on the man who had sacrificed the public in so gross and daring a manner." This gave rise to a vehement debate, at the conclusion of which the motion was rejected by a majority of 46 only, in a House consisting of near 400 Members. And thus were the loud calls of the nation, for an œconomical reform in the public expenditure, set at contemptuous defiance by the unprincipled effrontery of the Ministers.

Towards the end of the session, Mr. Fox moved the House, to resolve itself into a Committee, to

consider

consider of the American war, for the purpose of devising some means of accommodation. This motion was supported in an animated speech by Mr. Pitt, who expressed his utter abhorrence of a war, "which was conceived," he said, " in injustice, nurtured in folly, and whose footsteps were marked with slaughter and devastation. It exhibited the height of moral depravity and human turpitude. The nation was drained of its best blood and its vital resources, for which nothing was received in return but a series of inefficient victories or disgraceful defeats,—victories obtained over men struggling in the holy cause of liberty,—or defeats which filled the land with mourning for the loss of dear and valuable relatives, slain in a detested and impious quarrel." The motion was rejected by a majority of 73 voices.

A very considerable proportion of the present session was occupied in the consideration of the affairs of India, of which the interval between the civil and military transactions of the present year affords a proper opportunity to take a general review, from the period in which the memorable bill of regulation framed by the Minister, Lord North, A. D. 1773, passed into a law.

In the month of April 1772, took place, in consequence of the removal of Governor Cartier, the memorable appointment of Warren Hastings, Esq. as Governor-General of India; a man, whose conduct

conduct throughout all the inferior gradations of office stood confessedly unimpeached *. The members of the Supreme Council appointed under the new Act were, Sir John Clavering, Colonel Monson, and Philip Francis, Esq. than whom persons of more inflexible probity and enlightened beneficence could not have been selected by the wisdom of Parliament, for the purpose of stemming that tide of corruption and rapacity which inundated the government of India throughout all its departments and ramifications; and which, when opportunities and temptations arise to a certain height, shall cease to " overleap the mounds of right" when the Ganges shall cease to flow. It

---

* When Lord Clive embarked for Europe, February 1760, he left the government in the hands of Mr. Holwell *pro tempore;* Mr. Vansittart being then actually appointed, and arriving at Calcutta in the month of July. Mr. Vansittart remained in Bengal till the beginning of 1764, and was succeeded by Mr. Spencer, who was quickly superseded by Lord Clive. On the second resignation of Lord Clive, Mr. Verelst was advanced to the government of Bengal. To him succeeded Mr. Cartier. Both these gentlemen entered into the views, and acted upon the system established by Lord Clive. At length the Sullivan party prevailing in the Direction, Mr. Hastings was, in opposition to the influence of his Lordship, appointed Governor of Bengal; and the more secret transactions, with the concomitant intrigues and cabals, which distinguished his administration, can be perfectly understood only by those who have wasted their time in developing the complex and clashing interests, and never-ceasing contentions and animosities, of the Clive and Sullivan factions.

is remarkable, that these three gentlemen were impressed with so high an idea of the merits of Mr. Hastings, upon whose powerful aid and local experience they depended to give efficacy to their exertions in the public service, that Sir John Clavering, with the approbation of his co-adjutors, had actually addressed the King, previous to their departure from England, to bestow upon the Governor some distinguished mark of his royal favor, with a view to induce him to relinquish the intention which he was supposed to entertain of resigning the government.

On the arrival of the new Counsellors in India, in the autumn of 1774, their astonishment was great to find the whole system and policy of Mr. Hastings diametrically contrary to their pre-conceived ideas of his character. His manners also were marked by a coldness and *hauteur*, wholly incompatible with the cordiality of friendship; and they had the chagrin to perceive, that they were regarded by him not as associates in the great and necessary work of reform, but in the odious light of detectors, spies, and rivals. The project so universally and justly execrated in England, of setting up the lands of the Zemindars, Polygars, &c. to public auction, appeared, from the immediate and unqualified adoption of this odious system by the new Governor, to be the favorite policy of Mr. Hastings himself. In the space of about 200 years, during which the kingdom of Bengal and its appendages

pendages had been under the Mahomedan government, the original ground rents or heriots, *auſſil jumma*, of the Zemindars, and other great hereditary landholders who held under the government, had never been raiſed; and a permanent intereſt being thus created in the land, the Talookdars, Polygars, and Ryots, who poſſeſſed the ſubordinate rights of property under the Zemindars, were neither themſelves oppreſſed, nor allowed to oppreſs the actual occupants and cultivators of the ſoil. But from the fatal period that Bengal fell into the hands of the Engliſh, the ſecurity of property was no more *. After being ſubject for a ſucceſſion of years to every depredation and invaſion, Mr. Haſtings, amongſt the firſt acts of his government, inſtituted a COMMITTEE of CIRCUIT, inveſted with the tranſcendent power to diſpoſe of all the lands in the kingdom,

---

* In the reign of the Emperor Akber, famed for the wiſdom and equity of his government throughout Hindoſtan, a general and regular aſſeſſment of revenue was formed in Bengal, and the quotas payable by each diſtrict of the province, and each village of the diſtrict, clearly and ſpecifically aſcertained. No deviation from the eſtabliſhed rule and mode of aſſeſſment, as we are aſſured, took place from the reign of Akber to the elevation of Jaffier Ali Khan, who, in order to raiſe the ſum which he had ſtipulated as a reward to the authors of the revolution of 1757, departing wholly from the fundamental Conſtitutions of Akber, multiplied exactions, and introduced that ſyſtem of oppreſſion, which under the ſubſequent government of the Engliſh produced univerſal conſternation, calamity, and ruin.

from

from the highest Zemindar down to the lowest Ryot, by public auction, or farm for the term of five years. The pretext for this enormous outrage was the decay of the public revenue, of which, in consequence of this measure, Mr. Hastings had the courage to promise the Court of Directors an immediate and progressive augmentation; acknowledging, nevertheless, the country at the same time to be in a very languishing state, and that the population had decreased in the proportion of ONE THIRD since the grant of the Dewannee from the Emperor. The most dreadful confusion, as might well be imagined, instantly ensued; and Mr. Hastings, in his minute of April 1773, confesses, " that the expected improvement had not taken place, being obstructed by a circumstance which COULD NOT BE FORESEEN, viz. the farmers having engaged for a higher revenue than their districts could afford. It is true, says he, that the lands were almost all over-bid for; and many let to indigent and desperate adventurers; but this was UNAVOIDABLE IN SUCH A MODE." But this consequence being *confessedly unavoidable*, candor would degenerate into folly, to credit the declaration that it was not *foreseen*. The deficiency in the revenue was in fact enormous, falling, in five years, no less than two millions and a half short of the settlement. But the subsequent conduct of Mr. Hastings furnished the most satisfactory

clue

clue to this bufinefs. The lands being on all hands admitted to be partially over-rated, the Governor and Council were of courfe called upon to exercife a difcretionary power of remiffion. This opened an immenfe field of fraud and peculation, and could not fail to prove to individuals in certain fituations an exhauftlefs fource of wealth. The Court of Directors declared themfelves, in the fequel, " fully aware of the duplicity which had been practifed in the letting of the lands in Bengal; that flagrant corruption and great oppreffions had been committed;" and they ordered a profecution to be commenced againft the perfons who compofed the Committee of Circuit. But after long and ftudied delays, Mr. Haftings ultimately propofed, and carried his propofition in Council, " that orders fhould be given for withdrawing the faid profecution." It is worthy of remark, that the *banyan* or black fteward of Mr. Haftings, Cantoo Baboo, rented, under the new tenure, lands to the value of 150,000l. per annum; and remiffions to a very great amount were granted to this man, as well as to all thofe whofe reafons appeared to the Governor and Council equally valid. The Zemindary of Baharbund, taken from the Rannee of Radfhi, was alfo given in perpetuity to Cantoo Baboo, at a rent of 82,000 rupees, although the value of it was rated at 350,000. The fame

Cantoo

Cantoo Baboo was also permitted to contract largely for the provision of the Company's investments; "but this," the Court of Directors, in their general letter of December 1776, say, "we positively forbid in future." The astonishment into which Sir John Clavering and his colleagues were thrown, on being apprized of this extraordinary state of things in Bengal, was much increased by the alarming information of a war, into which the Governor General had recently entered in conjunction with the Vizier Sujah ul Dowla, Nabob of Oude, for the absolute conquest and EXTIRPATION of the nation of the Rohillas, inhabiting the fertile and beautiful province of Rohilcund, situated to the northward of the dominions of the Vizier, and bounded by the high range of mountains dividing Hindostan from Tartary. It was not pretended by Mr. Hastings, that the Company had received any injury whatever from the Rohilla nation; but that we engaged in the war solely as allies of the Nabob Vizier. The causes or pretexts of the quarrel, with respect to the Vizier himself, were of a nature palpably unreasonable and unjust. The Rohilla nation, being involved in hostilities with the Mahrattas, had applied to the Vizier for assistance, who agreed to furnish them with a large body of troops for an equivalent in money. But, through the dilatory, or perhaps insidious, policy of the Vizier, the
auxiliary

auxiliary troops did not arrive till the enemy were repulsed. The Rohilla Government, therefore, objected to the payment of the promised stipend; on which the Vizier, with the previous and eager concurrence of Mr. Hastings, determined to declare war against the Rohillas *, a brave, free, and generous people, for the purpose of adding so desirable a territory to his dominions. The Rohillas, in the highest degree alarmed at this confederacy, offered to submit the whole cause of dispute to the arbitration of the English; but this was peremptorily refused by Mr. Hastings, who urged the Vizier, already wavering in his purpose, in strong terms to the execution of his design, declaring to him, " that it would be absolutely necessary to persevere in it until it should be accomplished; and that he could not hazard or answer for the displeasure of the Company, if they should find themselves engaged in a fruitless war, or in a ruinous expence for prosecuting it." This apprehen-

---

* This is the Rohilla statement of the case. Nevertheless it must be acknowledged that Sir Robert Barker and the other officers employed in this expedition strongly attest the performance of the service contracted for by the Vizier, in their respective examinations at the bar of the House of Commons. But if the object of the Rohilla War had been merely the recovery of a sum of money, whether justly or unjustly claimed, it would, in a moral and political view, have been a trifle light as air and spotless as innocence in comparison of that blackness of darkness in which it is now enveloped.

fion was founded on very reasonable grounds; for the Court of Directors, in their instructions to the Supreme Council, had laid it down as an unalterable maxim, "that they were to avoid taking part in the political schemes of any of the Country Princes, *particularly* of the Nabob of Oude, of whose ambitious disposition they were well apprised." A considerable body of troops under Colonel Champion, being detached to the aid of the Vizier, entered the province of Rohilcund, and a pitched battle took place, in which Hafiz Rhamel, the principal leader of the Rohillas, and many other of their chieftains were slain. The whole country, described as "a garden not having one spot in it of uncultivated ground," was, in consequence of this victory, converted into a frightful waste, and in a great measure depopulated, either by the rigors of military execution, or by forcing the wretched inhabitants beyond the mountains, to wander and perish in the Tartarian deserts. For this service, the Vizier had agreed to pay into the treasury of Calcutta the sum of forty lacks of rupees; and Mr. Hastings, in vindication of his conduct, alleged, and in his subsequent memorable PARLIAMENTARY DEFENCE entered upon record, the following very extraordinary reasons: " The acquisition of this sum to the Company, and of so much specie added to the exhausted currency of our provinces; that it would

give

give wealth to the Nabob of Oude, of which we should participate; that he should be always ready to profess, that he did reckon the probable acquisition of wealth among his reasons for taking up arms against his neighbors; that it would ease the Company of a considerable part of their military expence, and preserve their troops from inactivity and relaxation of discipline; that the Rohillas are not a *nation*, but a body of foreign adventurers, who had made a conquest of the country about sixty years before; that this province would be a most commodious acquisition, and the weakness of the Rohillas, with the open and defenceless state of the country, promised an easy conquest; and finally, that such was his idea of the Company's distress at home, added to his knowledge of their wants abroad, that he should have been glad of *any occasion* to employ their forces which saved so much of their pay and expences." The principal of the Rohilla Chieftains, who escaped from the decisive battle of St. George, was Fyzoola Khan, who retired to a remote part of the country with his treasures, and the shattered remains of the Rohilla army; and after the death of Hafiz, renowned throughout the East for the superiority of his intellectual talents and personal accomplishments, Fyzoola Khan was very generally acknowledged as the head of this unfortunate and devoted nation. Finding his utter inability to continue the war, he sued in very submissive terms for peace which the Vizier, through the intercession of Colonel Champion, thought proper to grant; and a treaty was accordingly signed at Lall-Dang, October 1774, agreeably to which Fyzoola Khan was confirmed in the possession of Rampore, Shawabad, and some adjoining districts; on condition of giving up half his treasure, and of furnishing a certain stipulated quota of troops when called upon. This indulgence was, however, little to the satisfaction of Mr. Hastings, who had previously declared with respect to Fyzoola Khan, " that he appeared not to merit *any* consideration. The petty sovereign of a country estimated at six or eight lacks, ought not *for a moment* to prove an impediment to any of our measures, or to affect the CONSISTENCY of our conduct." The Rohilla war was subsequently condemned in decisive terms by a formal resolution of the Court of Directors, passed November 1775, " as contrary to the express and repeated orders of the Court, and inconsistent with the principles both of policy and justice;" and this resolve was, with the singularly complaisant omission of the last word, confirmed by a vote of the Court of Proprietors. But this extraordinary transaction, ranking among the first and most important acts of Mr. Hastings's administration, and affording a decisive and infallible criterion of its general tenor and spirit, demands a yet farther and more distinct investigation.

After

After the conquest of Bengal, the Company at home seemed fully satisfied with the extent of their acquisitions; and the dispatches of the Court of Directors were from that period filled with rigorous injunctions to avoid all offensive wars, in which they appear with good reason perpetually apprehensive that the ambition, temerity, and avarice of their servants in INDIA would involve them. Nevertheless, at the distance of half the globe from the scene of action, it was impossible not to allow in the execution of their orders some latitude of discretion. "The situation of affairs, say they, in their general letter of the 30th of June 1769, may be varied by unforeseen events at the very moment we are writing;—whenever you think yourselves OBLIGED for our SECURITY upon EMERGENT OCCASIONS to adopt measures of a contrary, i. e. hostile, tendency, you are to give us very full reasons for such deviation." In another letter they say, "You must undoubtedly act according to the EMERGENCY of affairs:" and again in another dispatch, "As we know not what alliances may be formed to justify us in carrying our arms beyond the bounds of the provinces, we are prevented from proposing any PRECISE PLAN for your guidance in this respect."

These necessary though reluctant concessions on the part of the Directors, Mr. Hastings in his MINUTES of DEFENCE preposterously perverts into a justification of the Rohilla war; although the Rohillas were notoriously as unwilling as they were unable

unable to do any injury to the Company. The real grounds of the war appeared from the first sufficiently obvious. The pretext held out was, that the Vizier, as an ally of the Company, was entitled to our affistance; and that, as *guarantees* of the treaty between him and the Rohilla chiefs, we were bound to grant it. Without adverting to the justice or injustice of the Vizier's demand on the Rohillas, it is enough to say, that this pretended guarantee confisted only in the treaty being signed at the request of the Rohillas themselves, from their well-grounded distrust of the Vizier, in the *presence* of Sir Robert Barker, Commander in Chief of the Company's Forces, as a witness of the same. It is not pretended that Sir Robert Barker had authority to pledge the Company as guarantees of the treaty; and that he should take upon him to bind the Government by so serious and important an act, without special instruction and direction, is an incredible suppofition; and in fact, Sir Robert Barker, being interrogated at the bar of the House of Commons—" Whether he conceived that he had by any act of his bound the Company to a guarantee of the treaty by war?" answered positively, 'I DID NOT.' Also in a letter written even before the actual conclusion of the treaty, he declares, " that it was the farthest from his intention that the Company should in any respect whatever be mentioned in the agreement between the Vizier and the Rohillas."

From the first suggestion of this project of conquest

queft and extirpation by the Vizier, *if indeed the Vizier were the original projector*, it is evident that Mr. Haftings urged its profecution with an ardor far fuperior to that difcovered by the Nabob, whofe ambition was counteracted by his avarice, and who on cool reflection appears to have thought the prize fcarcely worth the purchafe. " I availed myfelf," fays Mr. Haftings, " of his eager folicitude for the attainment of this point, to engage his affent to another meafure of much greater value to the Company—that is to fay, the increafe of his annual payments or fubfidy to the amount of two hundred and ten thoufand rupees per month." But it is fufficiently evident, that when this conceffion was once extorted from the Vizier, his " eager folicitude" fubfided into a ftate of mind which the artifices of Mr. Haftings only prevented from finking into coldnefs and indifference; and when Mr. Haftings affirms, " that this war derived its *propriety* from circumftances of nice relation and various detail*," he undoubtedly confounds its *propriety* with its *exiftence*.

In a letter written by Mr. Haftings to the Vizier, April 21, 1773, he enlarges on the great advantage which would refult to the Vizier from the reduction of the Rohilla country, " becaufe, fays he, by that means the defenfive line of your dominions

* Minutes of Defence.

would be completed, by including within it all the land lying on that fide of the river Ganges."—
"The ALLUREMENT (to adopt the language of Mr. Haſtings in his Defence), thus held out to the Vizier, ſucceeded. He propoſed in reply a meeting with me at Benares. I found him ſtill equally bent on the deſign of reducing the Rohillas, which I ENCOURAGED as I had before done, by dwelling on the advantages which he would derive from its ſucceſs; by objecting with great force the ORDERS of the COMPANY reſtricting us from ſuch remote ſchemes of conqueſt, to which I therefore could not aſſent without ſuch conditions obtained in return for it as might obviate their diſpleaſure, and win their ſanction to ſo hazardous and UNAUTHORIZED a meaſure. Having at length obtained this point, viz. *the increaſe of the ſubſidy*, I eaſily yielded my *aſſent* to the Rohilla plan, i. e. to the plan which the Vizier had been thus *allured* and *encouraged* to undertake, on the ſtipulation of forty lacks for its accompliſhment. As a precaution againſt any effects which were to be apprehended *from the Vizier's* IRRESOLUTION, the conditions originally accepted were dictated to him in the form of a letter, to be written by him, in which a clauſe was inſerted, ' that whether the country was conquered, or a peace concluded between him and the enemy, the ſtipulation for the forty lacks ſhould

become

become EQUALLY DUE.' Thus at laſt, ſays Mr. Haſtings exultingly, an occaſion took place, when, by a *ſlight deviation* from the defenſive plan, our alliance with the Vizier might be converted into ſolid advantages. In effect, the ſame reaſons which before urged us to ſhun every military expedition, now operated in the contrary direction, and recommended the employment of our army for the purpoſe of REDUCING our EXPENCES, and ADDING to our CURRENCY."

Surely the public accuſers of Mr. Haſtings would not wiſh to heighten the colors of the picture he has here drawn of himſelf! As to the mode in which this WAR of EXTIRPATION, or, to uſe that more ſoft and gentle phraſeology which gives a ſpecious gloſs to deeds of the blackeſt villany, " this ſlight deviation from the general plan of defence," was conducted, we are well aſſured that Colonel Champion never mentioned the ſervice on which he was employed without the deepeſt expreſſions of grief and abhorrence. " Whilſt all ASIA knows, ſays this commander, that the Engliſh gave him, i. e. the Nabob Vizier, the rod, will they not reaſonably conclude that the ſcourges which the agent gives are connived at ?—will they not ſay every Engliſh chief is another Sujah ?"—" The authority given to the Vizier over the army, ſays the Colonel in a letter to Mr. Haſtings, dated May 10, 1774, has totally abſorbed that degree of conſequence

consequence due to my station. My hands have been tied up from giving protection or asylum to the miserable. I have been obliged to give a deaf ear to the lamentable cries of the widow and the fatherless, and shut my eyes against a wanton display of violence and oppression, of inhumanity and cruelty. The Company's interest constrained me in public to stifle the workings of my feelings, but I *must* give way to them in private—it would affect your SENSIBILITY too much, were I to descend to particulars. The family of Hafiz, the Begums included, have been driven to the necessity of making supplications for a little rice and water; and of the prisoners, many have died for want of sustenance. I wish to leave scenes which none but the merciless Sujah can bear without heart-bleeding pain—relieve me therefore as soon as possible."

In a moving representation to the Colonel from the sons of Hafiz, of their manifold distresses, they say of the Vizier, " He has deprived us of our country, of our riches, and even of our HONOR; and not satisfied with that, he is going to send us prisoners to Fyzabad. We desire no country, no riches, no palaces; but at Bissoulee are the tombs of our noble ancestors—near them, under some shade, we beg permission to spend the remainder of our days as Faquiers." These things the Colonel says he is compelled to state, although the ungracious reception of his former representations

gave

gave him but little encouragement to plead the cause of the unhappy.

In a subsequent letter, dated June 15, 1774, the Colonel desires that he may be empowered to withdraw the English troops, in case the Vizier will not otherwise be prevailed upon to desist from his enormities; but this Mr. Hastings, in his reply, declares to be "obviously inadmissible. Where, said he, is our authority to judge or control the conduct of the Vizier, farther than respects his engagement with us? Even granting we had an authority to control the Vizier's conduct in the manner you propose, we must have demonstration of the *infallibility* of the person we entrusted with such an authority before we could be vindicated in the delegation of it. All the country subdued becomes absolutely the Vizier's. On the terms you propose, the English commander would supersede his authority in the government of his new possessions." In lieu therefore of the expedient suggested by the good sense and humanity of Colonel Champion, the Governor General ordered his Resident Mr. Middleton, in whom fortunately " no demonstration of infallibility was required," to *remonstrate* and *expostulate* with the Vizier concerning his conduct towards the Rohillas, " in order to exculpate the English Government from the IMPUTATION, as Mr. Hastings well expresses it, of assenting to such a procedure." But so little
did

did the Vizier regard thefe feeble and formal remonftrances, that in the fequel the family of Hafiz, after fuffering the moft dreadful and fhocking indignities, were carried in captivity to Fyzabad.

In a fubfequent letter from the Nabob Mahub Ulla Khan, eldeft fon of Hafiz, he moft earneftly fupplicates, in the name of GOD and Chrift, the interpofition of the Englifh commander for their releafe. "O my guardian," fays he, "turn your face to the bufinefs of a flave, and have us enlarged, and it will not go unrewarded." As to the extravagant plea fet up by Mr. Haftings in defence of this moft infamous and unprovoked invafion, "that the Rohillas were not a nation, but a body of foreign adventurers, who poffeffed the country by a prefcription of *only* fixty years," it is furely fufficient to reply, that the inhabitants of Rohilcund under their prefent government enjoyed peace and profperity—that thefe people, whom he will not allow to be a nation, were able to bring an army of fifty or fixty thoufand men into the field; and that it might with infinitely more force be retorted on the Englifh themfelves—that THEY were a body of "foreign adventurers," who had been at this time fcarcely feven fummers in poffeffion of the country they occupied. With equal feeling and animation it has been faid in relation to the general merits of the Rohilla war, "There is no power in this world that can annihilate fuch a queftion—THOUGH IT

WERE

WERE DEAD, YET SHALL IT LIVE. The cause by its own energy shall turn upon the force that oppresses it, and sting to destruction the vulnerable heel that endeavours to keep it down."

Another very important transaction, of which the new Counsellors were also for the first time apprized at their arrival in India, left no room for doubt, if doubt could otherwise have subsisted, as to the real character and systematic policy of the Governor General. In the solemn treaty of peace concluded August 1765 at Illahabad, between the Nabob Vizier of Oude and the East India Company, it is stipulated that the Emperor Sha Allum shall remain under the guarantee of the Company in full possession of the provinces of Corah and Illahabad, as a royal demesne; in consideration of which the *dewannee* of Bengal was granted by the Emperor in perpetuity to the Company.

About the year 1772 the Emperor, who had hitherto resided at Illahabad, removed to the antient capital of Dehli; but engaging soon after this period in unsuccessful hostilities with the Mahrattas, this people compelled him while in their power to grant *sunnuds* for the surrender of Corah and Illahabad to them. But Mr. Hastings, in his letter of March 1773 to the Court of Directors, says, " In no shape can this compulsatory cession by the KING release us from the obligation we are under to defend the provinces which we have so particularly

larly guarantied to him;" and they were accordingly occupied by the troops of the Company; and taken under its immediate and avowed protection. In a short time however the ideas of Mr. Hastings suffered a total change; for by an act of the Governor and Council, passed in *June following*, the engagements between the Company and the Emperor are declared to be DISSOLVED by his alienation from them and their interests, manifested by his removal to Dehli. Nevertheless, " if the KING should make overtures to renew his former connection, his right to reclaim the districts of Corah and Illahabad could not, say they, be disputed; and the Governor is authorised to restore them to him, on condition that he should RENOUNCE his CLAIM to the ANNUAL TRIBUTE of twenty-six lacks of rupees, reserved to the Emperor out of the revenues of Bengal, and to the arrears which might be due." Yet in the treaty concluded in person by the Governor General with the Vizier, in *September* 1773, it is asserted, " that his Majesty, having abandoned the districts of Corah and Illahabad, and given a *sunnud* for Corah and Currah to the Mahrattas, had thereby *forfeited* his right to the said districts." And in his subsequent report of this interview and negotiation with Sujah ul Dowla, the Governor declared, " that the Administration would have been culpable in the highest degree for retaining possession feffion of Corah and Illahabad for any other purpofe than that of making an advantage by the difpofal of them, and therefore he had ceded them to the Vizier for fifty lacks of rupees—the nett annual revenue of thefe provinces being eftimated at twenty-five lacks." At the fame time the Governor and Council determined to withhold the tribute of twenty-fix lacks of rupees from the Emperor, pretending, " that they were not fatisfied of his amicable intentions, and that the reduced ftate of the treafury rendered fuch payment impracticable."

Such was the treatment which the Emperor of Hindoftan received from the fervants of a foreign mercantile company, although Mr. Haftings himfelf, in a minute recorded in the Council-book on another occafion, declared, " that fallen as the Houfe of TIMUR is, it is yet the relic of the moft illuftrious line of the caftern world—that its fovereignty is univerfally acknowledged, though the fubftance of it no longer exifts—aud that the Company itfelf derives its conftitutional dominion from its oftenfible bounty."

The difintereftednefs of Mr. Haftings in all points of pecuniary concern had in England been the theme of high panegyric; but certain facts which came to the knowledge of the new Counfellors on or foon after their arrival in India, fet this part of his character alfo in a light which could fcarcely be confidered as problematical. Of thefe these it will suffice to touch on two or three of the most conspicuous. By the regulating act of 1773, a salary of 25,000l. per annum was settled on the Governor, and he was in the most positive and peremptory manner prohibited from receiving any present or donation in any manner, or on any account whatever. And on his accession to the government, Mr. Hastings in the ostentation of his generosity had declared, " that this prohibition admitted neither of refinement nor misconstruction, and that in his opinion an opposition would be to incur the penalty."

On the 30th of March 1775, a petition was laid before the Board, setting forth, " that Khan Jehan Khan, then Phousdar of Houghley, had obtained that office from the Governor, with a salary of 72,000 sicca rupees per annum; and that the said Phousdar *had given a receipt of bribe to the patron of the city*, to pay him annually 36,000 rupees out of the salary above mentioned." It being moved, " that the petitioner should be ordered to attend the next day to make good his charge," Mr. Hastings objected to the motion; which being nevertheless carried, the Governor declared, " that he would not suffer a judicial enquiry into his conduct at the Board of which he was President," and pronounced the meeting of the Board dissolved. Other sums from various persons, arising in the aggregate to a vast amount, were acknowledged by Mr. Hastings

tings in his confidential difpatches, doubtlefs to guard againſt the effects of fimilar informations, to be *privately received*; but, as the Governor General *alleged*, fubfequently converted to the Company's ufe. This however did by no means fatisfactorily appear. As an apology for his original intention of concealment, he fays, " Having had occafion to difburfe from my own cafh many fums which, though required to enable me to execute the duties of my ftation, I have hitherto omitted to enter in my public accounts, and my own fortune being unequal to fo heavy a charge, I have refolved to reimburfe myfelf in a mode the moſt fuitable to the fituation of your affairs, by charging the fame in my Durbar account of the prefent year, and crediting them in a fum *privately received*." On the firſt fuggeſtion of fufpicion as to the motives of this conduct, he profeſſed to the Court of Directors, September 1775, " that it was his fixed determination moſt fully and liberally to explain every circumſtance." Being called upon by the Court, after a very long interval, for this promifed explanation, he declared, " that he had been prevented from the execution of this defign by a variety of *more important occupations*; and that the fubmiſſion which his refpect would have enjoined him to pay to the command impofed upon him was LOST to his RECOLLECTION." But by far the moſt remarkable accufation of this nature againſt Mr. Haſtings, was that preferred by the Rajah

Rajah Nund-comar to the Supreme Council, in the month of March 1775, of various sums amounting to many hundred thousand rupees, received by the Governor General for offices and employments corruptly disposed of by him; and of this the Rajah, who was a native Hindoo of the Brahman caste, and of the highest rank, offered to produce incontrovertible evidence. Instead of stating any thing in his defence, Mr. Hastings declared, "that he would not suffer Nund-comar to appear before the Board as his accuser, and dissolved the meeting *.

Soon after this an attempt was made by the Governor to indict the Rajah, before the Supreme Court of Judicature, for a conspiracy against the Government; but the Grand Jury refusing to find the bill, it was determined to proceed against the Rajah in a different mode: and while the charge against the Governor was yet pending before the Council, he was indicted, upon the English statute of forgery, for a certain counterfeit bond pretended

* The legality of the power, thus assumed by the Governor General, of dissolving the Council at pleasure, being deemed questionable, the Court of Directors thought proper, for satisfaction on this point, to take the opinion of a man very eminent in his profession, who, although he decided in favor of Mr. Hastings, at the same time remarked, "that he believed him to be the first Governor that ever dissolved a Council enquiring into his behaviour when he was innocent." And the Court of Directors, in the result, positively forbade the Governor General to dissolve any Council in future, against the consent of the majority of the Members actually present.

to have been issued by the Rajah many years before; and which, if the charge could be imagined to have any foundation, amounted, by the laws of India, only to a misdemeanor. On this accusation he was brought to trial before Sir Elijah Impey, Chief Justice of the Supreme Court, and condemned to suffer capital punishment. Being committed to close custody in the common gaol at Calcutta amidst a crowd of felons, a petition was presented from the Rajah to the Supreme Council, setting forth, " That after having been honored with the confidence of the Nabob Jaffier Ally Khan, and after having discharged the first office in the Subahdary, and being now ten years retired from public life, it might perhaps startle the Honorable Board to receive an address from him, dated from the common gaol at Calcutta, had he not prepared them for some fatal change in his situation, by the representation he had before made of the severe menaces thrown out against him by the Governor General. Should my life," said the Rajah, " be taken away by the flagitious charge now laid against me by men the most abandoned, the facts before alluded to will remain upon record; the witnesses will be ready, and the proofs producible whenever the Governor General has COURAGE sufficient to hear them. My only intention in setting forth the services I have done, and the character I have to an advanced age supported, is to introduce my request, that I

may

may not suffer, from the bare accusation, a punishment equal to that of death, the violation of the most sacred duties of my religion; the institutions of which strictly enjoin a number of ablutions, prayers, and other ceremonies to be performed by the sect of Brahmans before they can take any kind of food:—nothing of this can be performed in the place where I now am. I therefore humbly request that I may be permitted to reside, under as strict a guard as may be judged requisite, in some place where these objections may be obviated."

This petition being transmitted to the Chief Justice, and it being at the same time represented that the Rajah had remained for 80 hours without sustenance, permission was obtained to fix a tent on the outside of the prison-gate for the purpose of washing and eating. Mobaric ul Dowlah, Subah of Bengal, being apprised of the deplorable situation of the unfortunate Rajah, transmitted a letter to the Governor and Council, interceding in his favor.

" The affair of Maha Rajah Nund-comar," said the Subah, " is really hard and rigorous. The Maha Rajah has transacted affairs of the greatest importance. When Meer Coffim Ally Khan had taken the resolution to ruin and expel the English, the Maha Rajah exerted himself to the utmost in supplying them with grain and money. The services of the Maha Rajah are well known to the KING of Hindostan. Certainly he never could have committed

mitted fo contemptible a crime. People employed in important affairs will, undoubtedly, have many enemies; and thofe who have been active in the affair of Nund-comar have long been his declared foes. Taking therefore into confideration the welfare of the people, I beg, with refpect to this affair, that the Rajah's execution may be fufpended till the pleafure of his Majefty the King of England fhall be known."

This interceffion, however, proved wholly unavailing and ufelefs. In a paper written by Nund-comar, for the infpection of the Supreme Council, he fays, " Now that the hour of death approaches, I fhall not, for the fake of this world, be regardlefs of the next. The forgery of the bond, of which I am accufed, never proceeded from me. For the fault of reprefenting a juft fact, my enemies, having no other means to conceal their own actions, deeming my deftruction of the utmoft expediency for themfelves, revived an old affair of Mohun Perfaud, which had been formerly found to be falfe; and LORD IMPEY and the other Judges have tried me by the Englifh laws, which are contrary to the cuftoms of this country—and, taking the evidence of my enemies, have condemned me to death. In my laft moments I requeft, that you, General, will write my cafe to the juft King of England.—I fuffer, but my innocence will certainly be made known to him."

On the 5th August 1775, the day fixed for the execution of the Rajah, he appeared on the public fcaffold without difcovering the leaft fymptom of difcompofure. He defired the Sheriff to prefent his laft refpectful falutations to General Clavering, Colonel Monfon, and Mr. Francis; and pray for their protection of Rajah Gourdafs, and that they would pleafe to look on him now as Head of the Brahmans. When not engaged in converfation aloud, his lips continued moving as if engaged in prayer, his beads hanging in his hand. The Brahmans who attended him on this melancholy occafion were in agonies of grief and defpair; and the furrounding crowd teftified their horror and confternation at this event, by clamorous howlings and lamentations. The Rajah embraced the attending Brahmans clofely, and faid he was ready.. " My own fpirits funk," fays the Sheriff, Mr. Mac-Raby, in his interefting narrative of this extraordinary fcene, " and I ftepped into my palankeen; but before I was well feated he had given the fignal, and the ftage was removed. His fteadinefs, compofure, and refolution throughout the whole of the melancholy tranfaction, were equal to any examples of fortitude I have ever feen or read of. The body was taken down, after HANGING the ufual time, and delivered to the Brahmans for burning."—Thus miferably perifhed the moft diftinguifhed and illuftrious of the Hindoo inhabitants of Bengal: and in the fub-

fequent

sequent council minute of Sir John Clavering, Colonel Monson, and Mr. Francis, these Gentlemen with good reason say, " After the death of Nund-comar, the Governor we believe is well assured, that no man who regards his safety will venture to stand forth as his accuser;—and they remark, that in the interim which had elapsed since the alleged offence of the Rajah, he had been promoted and employed by the Governor General; that his son the Rajah Gourdass was appointed to one of the first offices in the Nabob's household;—and that the accusation, which ended in his destruction, was not produced till he came forward and brought a specific charge against the Governor General, of corruption in his office."

The conduct of the Governor General, in relation to Mahomed Reza Khan, a mussulman of the highest distinction, was scarcely less extraordinary; though to attempt to develop the secret motives which led to it, would open a scene of dark and complex intrigue, totally foreign to the purposes of general history*. This distinguished personage was, through the influence of the English Government, on the decease of the late Na-

* The true solution of Mr. Hastings's conduct respecting Mahomed Reza Khan is, that this Minister was elevated to the high station he occupied by the interest of Lord Clive; and that Mr. Hastings was, on the other hand, intimately connected with the Anti-Clive or Sullivan faction, to whom he owed his advancement.

bob Meer Jaffier Ally Khan, conftituted guardian of his children, and adminiftrator or regent of the Subahdary during the minority of his fon Nudjah ul Dowla. As to his general character, the late Prefident, Lord Clive, in his letter to the Supreme Council of July 3d, 1765, fays, " It is with pleafure I can acquaint you, that the more I fee of Mahomed Reza Khan, the ftronger is my conviction of his honor and moderation." Alfo the Prefident and Council, in their difpatch to the Court of Directors, June 1767, fay, " Mahomed Reza Khan has purfued the Company's intereft with fteadinefs and diligence; his abilities qualify him to perform the moft important fervices." And the Court of Directors, in their letter of February 1768, fay, " We muft, in juftice to Mahomed Reza Khan, exprefs the high fenfe we entertain of his abilities, and of the indefatigable attention he has fhewn in the execution of the important truft repofed in him." Neverthelefs, the cabals of his enemies after a time fo far prevailed, that the Court of Directors tranfmitted orders to deprive Mahomed Reza Khan of his office, and to inftitute an enquiry into his conduct. In conformity to his fecret inftructions, Mr. Haftings caufed this Minifter to be arrefted in the city of Moorfhedabad, and to be brought down to Calcutta, where he was, by various artifices of delay, kept in prifon for two years. At length being

brought

brought to trial, he was completely and honorably acquitted of the charges preferred against him: and the Court of Directors, in their subsequent dispatch, testify their satisfaction in the result of this enquiry; at the same time ordering him to be reinstated in the offices which he had heretofore held. This was accordingly done by General Clavering, Colonel Monson, and Mr. Francis, who now constituted the majority of the Council:—not, however, without a formal protest from the Governor General Hastings; though the Court of Directors again declared their high approbation of this reappointment, giving him an assurance of their favor and protection. This was, however, of little avail; for no sooner did Mr. Hastings obtain a majority in the Council, by the deaths, first of Colonel Monson (Sept. 1776), and in the following year of Sir John Clavering, than Mahomed Reza Khan was again removed from his offices, the principal of which was filled by Sudder ul Hock Khan, a man wholly devoted to the Governor, who wrote to the Nabob, that nothing could retrieve the confusion into which the country was thrown, but an unlimited power lodged in the hands of the Superintendant: to which the Nabob, now become, to use the words of Mr. Hastings, "a mere pageant without even the shadow of authority," his annual revenue also being arbitrarily reduced from 42 to 16 lacks—expressed

in

in abject terms his entire acquiescence and submission. The Court of Directors, on being informed of these proceedings, in a tone of high displeasure declared, "that NO DOUBT could be entertained of the true design of this extraordinary business," and positively commanded the immediate restoration of Mahomed Reza Khan to the office of Naib Soubadar. After much studied evasion and delay, this order was complied with. But, on the departure of Mr. Francis from India, Mahomed Reza Khan was a third time dismissed from his office, by Mr. Hastings, without any specific charge, trial, or enquiry whatsoever.—On a retrospective view of these transactions, it cannot but excite our astonishment to hear Mr. Hastings affirm, in his Minutes of Defence, respecting Mahomed Reza Khan, " I am sure his sentiments for me are those of GRATITUDE and AFFECTION." On the last dismission of Reza Khan, Sir John Doyley was placed near the person of the Nabob Mobaric ul Dowla, to superintend his expences, with a particular instruction to the Nabob, not to admit any English, but such as the said Sir John Doyley should approve, to his presence. SUCH was the spirit of Mr. Hastings's internal administration; the most remarkable events relating to his external policy yet remain to be investigated.

The MAHRATTA STATES are the only people of Hindostan who were not subdued by the
Moguls,

Moguls, or who never acknowledged allegiance to the Houſe of Timur. Secure amidſt their inacceſſible mountains, they preſerved, unimpaired, their liberty and independency, and were at all times regarded by the moſt powerful of the Mahomedan Emperors as very formidable adverſaries. This nation confiſted of a number of diſtinct tribes, governed by their reſpective chieftains, but who all recognized, as their ſupreme head, a Prince ſtyled the Sou or Ram Rajah, i. e. the Great Rajah, whoſe throne was eſtabliſhed at Setterah. Since the decline of the Mogul power, that of the Mahrattas had riſen rapidly on its ruins.

At this period their dominions extended from Travancore, near the ſouthern extremity of the peninſula, to the province of Guzzerat, northward, divided from the Perſian territories by the river Paddar, the Jumna ſeparating them from the empire of the Mogul. To the eaſt they ſtretch to the Carnatic and the dominions of the Nizam of the Decan, the province of Catac carrying their poſſeſſions irregularly acroſs the peninſula to the Bay of Bengal. Their revenues were computed to amount to more than twelve millions ſterling; and their military eſtabliſhment, which was compoſed chiefly of cavalry, to 300,000 men.

It is a ſingular circumſtance in this government, that the ſovereignty of the Sou or Ram Rajah exiſts at this day only in name. Nana Row,

Row, peifhwa or prime minifter of the country at a period not very remote, feizing the perfon of the Rajah, confined him in a fortrefs near Setterah; and, ufurping the powers of the government, continued to adminifter them in the name of the Sovereign. Nana Row, dying, left the fucceffion to his fon Mada Row, who finding a rival in the perfon of Ragonaut Row, his uncle, a man of an intriguing difpofition and moft flagitious character, kept him in clofe confinement till near the time of his own death; when, being anxioufly defirous to enfure the quiet fucceffion of the peifhwafhip to his brother Narrain Row, he became reconciled to Ragonaut, in confequence of the moft folemn promifes of the latter to affift the young Narrain Row with his moft tender care, protection, and advice. The credulous Mada Row fhed tears of joy and fatisfaction at this happy event, and clofed his eyes in peace. But the vile and unnatural wretch, thus generoufly liberated, immediately engaged in new plots againft his nephew Narrain; and in a few months after his acceffion, Sept. 1773, the young peifhwa was affaffinated by the villanous contrivance of his uncle, who expected to have fucceeded without difficulty to the government. But the horror and deteftation excited by a crime of this enormous magnitude occafioned an oppofition fo general, that the parricide Ragonaut was compelled to fly his country.

Unhap-

Unhappily he directed his course to the island of Bombay, the government of which not only granted him, without hesitation, their protection; but, affecting to admit the validity of his claims, they commenced open hostilities against the Mahrattas, indulging the most ambitious and sanguine hopes, if the restoration of Ragonaut Row could be accomplished by their aid, to rival Madras and Calcutta in opulence and power.

The island of Salsette, and the city of Baroach, were quickly reduced by the valor of the Company's troops; but it does not appear that at this period the Presidency of Bombay received any encouragement from Mr. Hastings to prosecute these nefarious projects of aggrandisement. On the contrary, the Governor joined with the new Counsellors, Clavering, Monson, and Francis, in reprobating these proceedings; declaring by an Act of Council, passed May 1775, that the measures adopted by the Presidency of Bombay had a tendency to a very extensive and indefinite scene of troubles; and that their conduct was unseasonable, impolitic, unjust, and unauthorised." And availing themselves of the superiority vested in them by the late act, Colonel Upton was sent on an embassy to the Mahratta Court, for the purpose of negotiating a peace, which was concluded at Poonah, and ratified March 1st, 1776, upon terms very honorable and advantageous. By this

this treaty Salfette, Baroach, and various adjoining diftricts in the Guzzerat provinces, were ceded to the Company, and the fum of twelve lacks of rupees allotted to them as an indemnification for the expences of the war.

On the other hand, it was ftipulated that Ragonaut Row fhould withdraw from Bombay, and that no protection or affiftance fhould be granted to him or any other fubject of the Mahratta State, who may caufe any difturbance or rebellion in that country. Notwithftanding the folemnity of this engagement, Ragonaut Row ftill continued at Bombay, and by means of his agents fomented parties and diffenfions in the Court of Poonah, until the Mahratta Government, jealous in the higheft degree of the defigns of the Englifh, were provoked to receive with marked diftinction the Chevalier de St. Lubin, Agent or Ambaffador from the French Prefidency of Pondicherry.

Mr. Haftings was now completely emancipated from the control of the new commiffion, by the fucceffive deaths of Colonel Monfon and General Clavering; and even previous to the deceafe of the latter, being affured of the invariable fupport of Mr. Barwell, his own cafting vote gave him on all occafions a decided majority.

It is very remarkable, that during the whole courfe of the contention between the Governor General

General and the new Counsellors, the proceedings of the Governor were, in almost every dispatch from England, censured and condemned in severe terms, while the conduct of his opponents was as uniformly applauded; yet the Governor General was unaccountably continued in office, and suffered ultimately to carry his romantic projects into unrestrained and ruinous execution. In their letter of April 1776, the Court of Directors highly commend the indefatigable assiduity which, they say, appears in the laborious researches of the *majority* of the Council, and their zeal for the interest of the Company, and the welfare of the inhabitants, as well Natives as Europeans. In a subsequent letter, addressed to Sir John Clavering, in the expectation of his speedy return to Europe, the Court express the deep sense they entertain of his singular services, and the great concern they felt at the prospect of losing so invaluable a servant. And in their general letter of May 7, 1778, they lament the death of Sir John Clavering in warm and affectionate terms, as a great and public loss to the East India Company and to his country. So indeed it proved: for the Governor General, no longer restrained by the presence of this inflexible CENSOR, fixing his eyes on the western side of the continent, perceived an immense field in which his ambitious and restless disposition
might

might find a boundlefs fcope of activity and exer-
tion*.   On

* Soon after the death of Sir John Clavering, Mr. Francis tranfmitted to the Minifter, Lord North, a letter or memorial, dated September 1777, excellently written, and ftating in the cleareft manner the nature and pernicious effects of the policy purfued by the Englifh Government in Bengal, and the meafures neceffary to eftablifh permanent peace and profperity in India. In difcuffing the interefting queftion—" To what extent, and in what form, the actual fovereignty of Great Britain over thofe provinces fhall be avowed ?" he obferves, " that the principal branches of the Sovereign Power are exercifed by the Eaft India Company, partly under the authority of the Subahdar, partly under that of the King of Great Britain. At the fame time, the natives in general acknowledge no King but the Mogul, in whofe name the revenues are collected, and the current money of Bengal coined. Hence arife all the evils which flow from a divided dominion. The fafeft, the moft fimple, and the leaft invidious principle on which this territory could be held, Mr. Francis pronounces to be that of a fixed tribute from the native Prince of the country, avoiding all interference with the internal government. Circumftances, fays this fagacious Counfellor, infeparable perhaps from the Conftitution of the Eaft India Company, difqualified them in every fenfe for the duty and office which the acquifition of a territory in India impofed upon them. A body of merchants had interefts to provide for, befides thofe which belonged to them in their affumed character of Sovereign. Profit, being the only object of a trading company, became the fole object of Government when the two characters were united. Commercial principles of the worft quality, as derived from the conftitution of an exclufive Company, were all the principles which the India Company brought with them into the government of a great kingdom, and IT HAS BEEN GOVERNED ACCORDINGLY.

                                                            " After

On the 28th of January, 1778, the Governor introduced the subject at the Supreme Board in a very

"After raising the revenues as nearly as possible to the level of the rents, for the support of their GOVERNMENT, they monopolized the produce and labor of the country for the support of their TRADE. To obtain the highest possible revenue from the land, they were obliged to avow, or countenance, a principle subversive of all national prosperity, and not less false in fact than absurd in theory and dangerous in practice—' that the ruling power was proprietor of the soil.' On this principle they universally dispossessed the hereditary and lawful owners, and farmed the country to strangers. In a few instances, where the proprietors were employed, it was not in their true character, but as farmers of Government. *There is* NO EXAMPLE, *I believe, of such an* ACT OF POWER *in the* HISTORY *of* HINDOSTAN. ' Of all despotic governments,' M. Montesquieu tells us, ' there is none more oppressive than that where the Prince declares himself proprietor of the soil, and heir of all his subjects. It always follows that the cultivation of the earth is abandoned; but if, besides this, the Prince is a merchant, every species of industry is ruined.'

"Your Lordship will soon perceive how much it is the general object of this representation to establish an opinion, that to make the possession of Bengal beneficial and permanent, we should revert to the antient institutions of the country, as far as we are acquainted with them, and present circumstances will permit. If it were not for the experience of some years past, it might be superfluous to say, that we provide for our interests when we consult the happiness and prosperity of the people who labor for us.

"It appears to have been the Company's original policy, or that of Lord Clive, to govern these provinces through the medium of the Subahdar, and the best they could adopt, supposing them

very long minute, unfolding in a sufficiently unequivocal manner his vast and daring projects.—

"If to interpose in any shape in the internal government. This system was soon violated in fact, and not long afterwards avowedly renounced. The predominant power of the Council at Calcutta necessarily reduced the Subahdar to a cipher, and left him and his subjects, as it always will do, a prey to individuals. Forms and appearances were, however, in some degree preserved till the death of Syef ul Dowla, in 1770. From that period we see nothing in the administration of public affairs, but enormous abuses on one side, and an absolute want of power or perseverance to correct them on the other. The Subahdar's authority, since the Company's acceptance of the Dewannee, has been gradually reduced under three successive Nabobs, and is now merely titular in the person of Mobarek ul Dowla. The administration of criminal justice is, however, still exercised in his name by the Naib Subah Mahomed Reza Khan, and we sometimes avail ourselves of the pretence of his authority in our differences with the foreign factories.

"The Company hold the Dewannee by grant of the Mogul, Sha Allum. The treaty concluded by Lord Clive, August 1765, not only acknowledges him as King of Bengal, but secures to him the full possession of Korah and Illahabad, as a royal demesne for the support of his dignity and expences; and by a particular agreement between him and the Company, of the same date, they engage themselves to be security for the payment of twenty-six lacks a year, out of the territorial revenue, *in consideration* of his Majesty's having been graciously pleased to grant them the Dewannee of Bengal. Your Lordship knows how little these treaties have been regarded. His tribute was stopped, and his country, though avowedly entrusted to our good faith, and accepted as a deposit, sold to Sujah ul Dowla.

"The

"If REPORT could be believed," Mr. Haſtings ſaid,
"written engagements had paſſed between the
Mahratta

"The Britiſh power is now unqueſtionably the firſt in India, at leaſt for defence. To make it reſpectable in itſelf, and beneficial to mankind, it muſt be guided by ſolid, judicious principles of policy, and they muſt be ſteadily purſued. Enough has been done to eſtabliſh the reputation of our arms. If we mean to keep what we have acquired, *ſome* care muſt be taken to eſtabliſh an opinion of our ſteadineſs and juſtice.

"With reſpect to the amount and collection of the revenues, the principal queſtions are—1ſt, Whether the lands ſhall be reſtored to the hereditary owners? 2dly, Whether the revenues payable to Government ſhall be fixed immutably at a certain ſum? and 3dly, By what rule or ſtandard ſhall that ſum be aſcertained? To the two firſt queſtions I have invariably given an affirmative anſwer, founded on reaſons which I deem incontrovertible. The third muſt be determined by the capacity of the country, eſtimated from an average of the actual collections, and combined with the indiſpenſable demands of Government. The *farming ſyſtem* was adopted as the act of a proprietor, with a profeſſed view of diſcovering the ultimate value of the eſtate, or the utmoſt that could be obtained from it. Your Lordſhip will judge how far the end, ſuppoſing it attainable, could juſtify the means. To General Clavering, Colonel Monſon, and myſelf, it always appeared an arbitrary, unexampled act of power, without a ſhadow of right to ſupport it. The principle on which it went annihilated every idea of private property, while in fact it has been ruinous to the country, for the ſole benefit of the Company's ſervants and their banyans. But even if the farms had, in every inſtance, been fairly allotted to the higheſt bidders, the meaſure could have produced no other conſequence than that of forcibly alienating the whole landed property of the

Mahratta Court and M. St. Lubin, the object of which, whatever it be, muſt, if attempted, prove deſtructive

country in favor of indigent ſtrangers and adventurers, equally ignorant of the value and circumſtances of the farm, and careleſs how much they offered for immediate poſſeſſion. The laſt ſettlement made by the COMMITTEE of CIRCUIT promiſed an immoderate increaſe of revenue, at a time when the famine had ſwept away ONE THIRD of the inhabitants, and when the country was repreſented to be in a general ſtate of decay. What the real object of the meaſure was, may be collected from the ſucceſs of it.

" The balances and remiſſions on the ſettlements of the laſt five years amount to the enormous ſum of two hundred and thirty lacks of Sicca rupees. The plain truth is, that over-ratement and remiſſion play into each other's hands. If the country be exorbitantly taxed, the Governor and Council *muſt* be truſted with a diſcretionary power to make remiſſions. This latitude once given, or aſſumed, it may be impoſſible to determine in what manner it is applied, or where the remiſſions centre at laſt, ſince the diſtribution may be ſo formed as to intereſt all parties in concealing it.

" If we had no facts or experience to guide our conjectures, it is apparent that a country expoſed to arbitrary variations in the annual aſſeſſments, at the diſcretion of a Council of State, eſpecially at this immenſe diſtance from the ſeat of empire, offers temptations which will not be ALWAYS reſiſted. Improvements in ſuch a ſtate of things are not to be expected, for who will employ his money or his labor in the cultivation of a ſoil that does not belong to him? or when he has no ſecurity that the whole produce may not be extorted from him by a new aſſeſſment?—The ſame ſyſtem of taxation which annihilates the property, attacks the induſtry of the ſubject, and invades the *ſources* of production.

" A NEW

structive to the British trade and influence in India. Although the Mahratta power, unallied with other states, was unable to cope with the Company, yet, sustained by the French, they are qualified to refuse acquiescence with our demands, which demands the island of Bassen offers as the only prospect of a security: that no obligation precludes us from demanding it, nor can any blame be imputed to us, if, as the superior power, we prescribe the terms of accommodation."

In addition to this demand, Mr. Hastings, in the plan subsequently laid by him before the Board, required " that the Mahratta Government give such security for the personal safety of Ragonaut Row as *he himself* shall require; that a specific sum be demanded to reimburse the Company for their late military charges; that a grant of territory be made contiguous to Basseen; and that no European settlement be allowed on the Mahratta coasts without consent of the Company." At the same time he communicated a plan formed by the Presidency of Bombay, to reinstate Ragonaut Row in the peithwaship by force of arms, being invited

---

" A NEW PRINCIPLE must be assumed for the government of the country, or it MUST FALL. The plain and simple remedy is, to oblige the Company to revert to their original principles, to renounce the unnatural character in which they have lately acted, and, if it be possible, to BECOME MERCHANTS AGAIN."

to this enterprife by fundry members of the Mahratta Government.

After much oppofition from Mr. Francis and Mr. Wheeler, who had recently fucceeded Sir John Clavering as a member of the Board, the Governor's propofals were carried in Council by his own cafting vote; and it was finally determined to fupport Ragonaut Row, in the event of the infraction of the Poonah or Poorunder Treaty, AS NOW EXPLAINED. Afferting that " the Prefidency of Bengal was in a condition to affift Bombay abundantly with men and money to carry on the Mahratta war," Mr. Haftings propofed to march a large detachment of the Company's troops acrofs the continent, for the purpofe of reinforcing the Bombay army. This alfo being carried in the fame manner, the deftined reinforcement under Colonel Leflie commenced this unprecedented march of 1100 miles early in May 1778.

Previous to this event, a letter was received from the Court of Directors, pofitively enjoining a ftrict adherence to the Treaty of Poorunder. But Mr. Haftings, in a haughty and peremptory tone, declared " his unalterable determination to profecute the meafures in which he had now engaged, to the utmoft of his power."

In order to promote and corroborate the fuccefs of his project, Mr. Haftings had for fome time

time paft moft affiduoufly courted the friendfhip and alliance of the Rajah of Berar, Moodajee Boofla, whofe dominions occupied the intermediate fpace between thofe of the Company and of the Mahratta States, inciting and urging that Prince, who was far advanced in years, and of a mild and pacific difpofition, openly to avow his claim to the fovereignty of the Mahrattas, to which the Rajah had fome obfcure and remote pretenfions. "In the whole of my conduct," fays the Governor General in a letter addreffed to the Prime Minifter of the Court of Naigpore (November 1778), "I have departed from the common line of policy, and have made advances when others in my fituation would have waited for folicitations; but I truft to the approved bravery and fpirit of the Maha-Rajah, that he will *ardently catch* at the objects prefented to his *ambition*."

Moodajee Boofla was, however, fo far from being willing to embark himfelf and his fortunes in the wild and crude projects of the Englifh Governor, that he wrote with his own hand a letter to Mr. Haftings, inculcating, in very refpectful terms, and in a manner which did equal honor to his head and his heart, the moft juft and falutary maxims of conduct both moral and political:—"Your friendly letter," fays the Rajah, "of the 19th Ramzan informs me that you have given directions to Colonel Leflie to co-operate with the forces which I shall unite with his; that as you offer me the forces of the Circar to promote my views, you in return request the assistance of mine to effect your purposes; that having thus explained to me your sentiments and views, you wait only to know mine.—The having caused a translation to be made into English of the Hindoo books called the Shasta, &c. and keeping the pictures of the former kings of Hindostan before your eyes; from their lifeless similitudes to discover which of them were worthy of rule and possessed of good faith—also the endeavor to preserve the blessing of peace till *forced* to relinquish it—the supporting of every one in his hereditary right, and revenging the breach of faith and engagements, but, on the submission of the offenders, the exercise of the virtues of clemency and generosity—the not suffering the intoxication of power to seduce you into a breach of faith, and the giving support to each illustrious house, in proportion to its respective merits—these are the sure means of exalting your greatness and prosperity to the highest pitch. The ALMIGHTY disposes of kingdoms, and places whomsoever he pleases on the seats of power and rule; but makes their stability to depend on their peaceable, just, and friendly conduct to others. My conduct is framed on these principles—I have not yet recovered the shock of Mr. Elliot's death: had he survived, such strokes of policy would have

have been employed, that the fufpicions of the Poonah Minifters, from apprehenfions of fupport being given to Ragonaut Row, which have caufed them great uneafinefs, would have been entirely removed."

Notwithftanding the failure of this negotiation, Mr. Haftings was not to be deterred from the profecution of his project. In proportion as difficulties prefented themfelves, his perfeverance and pertinacity feemed to increafe.

Colonel Leflie, who commanded the army now on its march to Bombay, dying October 1778, was fucceeded by Colonel Goddard. This able Officer, after furmounting great and various obftacles, reached the fouthern banks of the Narbudda, within the territory of Berar, January 1779; and immediately detached Lieutenant Wetherftone to the Court of Naigpore, again to urge the Rajah's acceffion to the propofed plan of operation. But the Lieutenant, in his letters to Colonel Goddard, declares that the Government of Berar were determined not to take any active part whatever with the Company's armies; that they had a thoufand arguments to oppofe to thofe he urged in favor of the plan for affuming the dignity of Ram Rajah of Setterah, *particularly* the faith pledged, and the alliance of friendfhip they had *fworn to;* with the prefent Peifhwa; that the afferting their pretenfions to the fovereignty would meet

meet with numberless oppositions; and that suc_cess could not be obtained without shedding much blood, and at the expence of violating the *sacred engagements* before entered into with them."

Mr. Wetherstone farther says, " that it seemed now to be the first wish of the Court of Berar to set aside our connection with Ragonaut Row, the supporting of whom they asserted to be highly impolitical, and that in the end it would be fully proved so; that this chief, Ragonaut Row, was held in universal abhorrence; and that the prejudices against him in the Decan would not easily, if ever, be removed. And the Rajah earnestly offered his mediation to make up all the existing differences."

About this period, likewise, letters were received by the Governor General from Siccaram Pundit, Prime Minister of the Poonah Government, containing heavy complaints of the conduct of the English since the conclusion of the treaty of Poorunder. " The Government of Bombay from that period has, in every instance, he asserts, excited troubles and commotions, in violation of the ties of friendship; and notwithstanding the express stipulation to expel Ragonaut Row from the dominions of the Company, they have performed nothing thereof. Out of regard to the friendship and alliance of the Company, I call God to witness that the Envoy of France was dismissed without

nego-

negotiating with him. It is mutually incumbent upon us to obferve the terms of the treaty."

And again, in a fubfequent difpatch, the fame Minifter fays, " Notwithftanding the conclufion of the treaty, the Bombay Government kept Ragonaut Row with them. It even appears to a conviction, that they *perfuaded* Ragoba, i. e. Ragonaut Row, to the meafures he has purfued. How then does the fupreme authority of the Council of Calcutta from the King of England appear, fince the Chiefs of the different fettlements do not regard engagements made by you as binding on them? And you, Sir, paying no regard to your own acts, take your meafures on the reprefentations of the Government of Bombay. This is indeed aftonifhing to the higheft degree! It is the dictate of found policy, that you withdraw your troops to your own territory. This will be a convincing proof of the fincerity of your friendfhip, and will fpread the fame of your good faith throughout the univerfe. From the commencement of the government of the family of the Peifhwa, they have entered into treaties with many of the Chiefs of the Eaft and Weft, *and have never before experienced fuch a want of faith from any one.*"

In the mean time, pending thefe negotiations and the march of the Bengal army, the Prefidency of Bombay, poffeffed with high ideas of their own ftrength, strength, confident of success, and jealous lest, by the arrival of the expected reinforcements, they should be obliged to divide the honor and profit of the expedition into the Mahratta country, with those of whose assistance they had no need, having made all the previous military preparations, and formally declared the treaty of Poorunder void, put their troops in motion November 1778.

The event of this expedition cannot be better related than in the words of Row Ghee, Resident at the Court of Poonah from the Nabob of Arcot: "The English *Surdars*," says this intelligent observer, in a letter to the Nabob, " with an army consisting of 700 Europeans, eight battalions of sepoys, and 40 pieces of cannon, marched, as I have already wrote to your Highness, from Bombay to the passes. Siccaram Pundit and Nana Furnese joined their forces, and satisfied the discontented chiefs, Scindia and Holkar, by giving them money, jaghires, and other presents. All the chiefs having met to consult, agreed unanimously ' not to receive Ragonaut Row, since he came with an army of English, who were of a different nation from them, and whose conduct in Sujah Dowla's country, the Rohilla country, Bengal, and the Carnatic, *they were well acquainted with*. Otherwise, in the end they would be obliged to forsake their religion, and become the SLAVES of EUROPEANS.' Upon this they exchanged oaths,

oaths, and a great army was sent to occupy the Ghaut, or pass of Tullicanoon. Mr. Martyn, the Bombay Resident at Poonah, had encouraged the English to believe, that as soon as their army should arrive at the Ghaut, Holkar would join them with all his forces. The English, trusting to this, waited there with impatience for a whole month, but no one appeared to join their standard. They then marched forward, although much harassed by the Mahrattas, who at length completely cut off their supplies of provisions.

"The English then determined upon retreating back to the Ghaut; but Siccaram, gaining intelligence of their march, detached a large body of troops to intercept them. An obstinate engagement ensued on the 13th of January 1779, in which the English, being surrounded and overpowered, lost 200 Europeans and 1200 sepoys. No possibility of escape now remained; and on the renewal of hostilities on the 15th, by a heavy cannonade from the Mahrattas, a gentleman, Mr. Farmer, advancing from the English camp, the firing ceased. The chiefs of the Mahrattas sent for him into their presence, and Mr. Farmer addressed them in the following words:—'We are only MERCHANTS—when disputes prevailed with you, Ragonaut Row came to us and demanded our protection. We thought he had a right to the government, and gave him our assistance.—
Nothing

Nothing but ill fortune attends him, and we have been brought to this miserable state by keeping him with us. You are masters to keep him from us. We shall henceforth adhere to the treaties that have formerly taken place between us; be pleased to forgive what has happened.'

" The Minister answered, ' Ragonaut Row is one of us—what right could you have to interfere in our concerns with him? We now desire you to give up Salsette and Basseen, and what other countries you have possessed yourselves of. Adhere to the treaty made in the time of Bajalee Row*, and ask nothing else.'

" Next day at noon Mr. Farmer returned, and told Scindia ' that he had brought a blank paper, signed and sealed, which the Mahratta Chiefs will fill up as they pleased.' Scindia told the Chiefs, ' that although they had it in their power to make any demands they pleased, it would not be advisable to do it at this time. For our making large demands would only sow resentment in their hearts, and we had better demand only what is necessary. Let Ragonaut Row be with us—let Salsette and the pergunnahs in Guzzerat be restored—let the Bengal army return back.'

" These articles being written out on paper, in Persian, Mahratta and English, sealed with the Company's

---

* This treaty was made in September 1761.

pany's feal, were figned at Worgaum by General Carnac and feven Officers. Hoftages were given for the due performance of them. After this the Mahratta furdars fent them victuals, which they needed much. The Englifh and fepoys, grounding their arms, marched out efcorted by 2000 Mahratta horfe."

Intelligence of this difaftrous event having reached Calcutta, Mr. Haftings declared in Council, that General Goddard, in cafe of the failure of the Poonah expedition from Bombay, had his exprefs orders to recur to his negotiations with Moodajee Boofla, which implied his return to Berar. But that Officer, regardlefs of this ftrange inftruction, proceeded by forced marches to Surat, agreeably to the requifition of the Prefidency of Bombay.— This Government, in their difpatches to the Supreme Council, after ftating the defeat of their army, have the effrontery to fay, " that they did not think themfelves obligated by the conditions of the fubfequent treaty, but that, having intentions to enter into another, they had tranfmitted directions to General Goddard accordingly."

Mr. Haftings expreffed his approbation of the tenor of this difpatch, and, declaring " that the treaty, being made by perfons unauthorifed to fubfcribe to fuch conditions, was invalid, propofed that General Goddard be commiffioned to negotiate at the Court of Poonah for the renewal of the treaty

treaty of Poorunder—and that the Prefidency of Bombay be required to prepare for fervice, whether offenfive or defenfive."

Mr. Francis entered in the council-book his reafons for diffenting from the Governor General, in a minute replete with good fenfe and found policy. He admitted " the probability, that peace might be obtained on the terms of the treaty of Poorunder, provided this Government be itfelf in earneft in purfuit of its prefent object, and fuffered not itfelf to be entangled in the defperate fchemes of thofe who now conftitute the Government of Bombay. The re-eftablifhment of peace on the Malabar coaft, I deem," faid this wife and faithful counfellor, " to be effential, not merely to the profperity of the India Company, but to their exiftence. Let a war upon that coaft be conducted how it may, the difference between conqueft and defeat, in my judgment, is little more than the delay or acceleration of the ruin of all our refources. The annexed account fhews that, during the laft five years, they have received little lefs than 116 lacks of current rupees directly out of the revenues of Bengal. Yet their bond-debt accumulated daily, and now amounts to 38 lacks. By the month of October, the Prefident Hornby fays, their finances will be utterly exhaufted—in the interval they will want a fupply of 30 lacks. Of this fum the Prefident propofes poſes to borrow 20 lacks, but doubts the poſſibility of raiſing ſo large a ſum;—and if it could be borrowed, he ſays, they have no funds to pay even the intereſt. We ſhould do well to conſider how long we can maintain a war on ſuch a footing, before we engage in it. I will not ſuppoſe the caſe of new miſcarriages. Let it be admitted, that ſucceſs and conqueſt are as certain as the moſt ſanguine expectation can imagine, it does not follow that the objects to be obtained by them are ſuch as we ought to aim at in our preſent circumſtances, or that victory will pay its own expences. By extending our territorial poſſeſſions, we create irreconcileable enmity in the minds of thoſe powers whom we immediately rob of their property. We fill every other Indian State with jealouſy and alarm, and the territory we acquire comes waſted and depopulated into our hands. The nation now perhaps looks to Bengal as its laſt and greateſt external reſource. But if this demand upon us from home were not ſo preſſing, and ſo likely to increaſe as I think it is, it is time for us to conſider, whether there be in Great Britain a fundamental force equal to the tenure of unbounded acquiſition at this diſtance from the ſeat of empire; or whether we are not arrived at a point at which common prudence dictates to us to fix once for all the limits of our dominion. If my judgment were to prevail, it should be our object to CONTRACT them." To the whole of this most judicious and weighty minute of Mr. Francis, the Governor General was pleased to declare, in very laconic terms, " that, from his anxiety to avoid controversy, he should decline any reply."

A letter was then read by the Governor, in answer to the dispatches from Bombay, which, though strongly objected to by Mr. Francis and Mr. Wheeler, received the sanction of Mr. Barwell, and of Sir Eyre Coote, who had now taken his place at the Board as Commander in Chief of the Company's forces. In this letter, which is written in a style of such artful and studied confusion as to be in many parts really unintelligible, the Governor, in name of himself and Council, acquaints the Presidency of Bombay, in terms which have at least the merit of being plain and explicit, " that the Government of Bengal refuses to ratify even the smallest tittle of the treaty or convention of Worgaum; that General Goddard was invested with full powers to conclude a pacification with the Court of Poonah, on the terms prescribed in his instructions; and that, if the Mahratta ministers shall reject those proposals, and the Company be reduced to the necessity of defending its rights by an open war, a latitude of action is left to General Goddard to avail himself of the situation which fortune shall present to him. With respect to Moodajee

jee Boofla, it is confeffed, that little hope is at this time entertained of his concurrence; but if, beyond expectation, the Rajah fhall difcover a willingnefs to accept of the propofed alliance, inftructions for that purpofe are given to General Goddard. This negotiation is left," to adopt the ftrange and perplexed phrafeology of this letter, " to the fole management of General Goddard, in the authority of thofe inftructions, until the period of their fufpenfion by the refufal or fuch hefitation of Moodajee Boofla as he fhall deem fufficient to warrant his declaring the negotiation fufpended. The future renewal of this negotiation we referve to be determined by our exprefs orders, but without revoking the credentials and inftructions already granted to General Goddard refpecting it." It would be hard indeed if the Governor, in the event of any finifter cataftrophe, could not, under the impenetrable veil of fuch myfterious ambiguity of direction, fcreen himfelf from any difagreeable refponfibility.

Mr. Haftings, in order to enforce the general fyftem of policy contained in this letter, moreover declared to the Council, " that he never would fuffer the object to be loft, for which the detachment now commanded by General Goddard was firft appointed." This paffed in the month of June 1779; and by a letter from General Goddard, dated October following, the Governor and Council are informed, as they had every reason to expect, " that the Peishwa's Minister had, in plain and positive terms, declared to him that his master would not accede to the proposals made by General Goddard, or conclude peace with the English, unless Ragonaut Row, who had escaped, was delivered up to him, and Salsette surrendered to the Mahratta Government; that, in consequence of this declaration, General Goddard had broken off the negotiation, and prepared for war." As was predicted by Mr. Francis, the whole Mahratta race, including the RAJAH of BERAR, together with Hyder Ally Khan, and the Nizam or Subah of the Decan, in the highest degree exasperated and inflamed at the treachery of the English Government, now entered into an alliance, in conjunction with the French, to expel the English nation from India;—a combination of powers truly formidable, and which eventually shook the British empire in the East to its centre.

In the progress of the war, thus wantonly provoked, the Government of Bengal soon found itself reduced to the extremest necessity for money to defray the enormous expence of its complex and extended operations. " Rolling his baleful eyes around," the Governor General at length fixed them on the territory of Benares, a province depending on the Vizieriate of Oude, highly cultivated and populous, and the capital city of which,

situated

situated on the Ganges, has for ages been regarded by the Hindoos as a place of peculiar and indelible sanctity, as the seat and centre of their science, their laws, their philosophy and religion. The late Rajah of Benares, Bulwant Sing, during the wars between the Vizier and the Company, had zealously attached himself to the English interest; and the Court of Directors, in their letter of May 26, 1768, acknowledge " the signal services he had rendered them; and they express their hope, that the attention paid to those who have espoused their interests in this war will *restore* their reputation in Hindostan, and that the Indian Powers will be convinced that no breach of treaty will ever have their sanction."

Two years after this Bulwant Sing died, leaving the succession to his son, Cheyt Sing; and the Council of Calcutta, Mr. Cartier being then President, interposed their influence and authority at the Court of Lucknow, in order to procure from the Vizier just and reasonable terms of settlement. It was finally agreed, that the Rajah should pay to the Vizier a *peshcush*, or fine, equivalent to about 200,000l. and that an annual advance of 30,000l. should be made to the stated tribute. A solemn deed of confirmation was then passed by the Vizier, and the Rajah was invested with the government, amid the loud acclamations of a numerous and happy people.

In the year 1773, at the immediate instance of

Mr. Haſtings, this grant was anew confirmed and ratified by the Vizier, with the additional and expreſs proviſion, that no increaſe of tribute ſhall ever hereafter be demanded; and that the government of Benares ſhall deſcend, on the terms of this agreement, to the heirs of the preſent Rajah.

The Governor General, knowing the enmity which had long ſubſiſted between the Vizier and the late Rajah, declared himſelf " to be well convinced that the Rajah's inheritance, and perhaps his life, are no longer ſafe than while he enjoys the Company's protection, which is his due by the ties of juſtice and the obligations of public faith." In the following year, 1774, the Governor General and Council obtained the aſſignment of the ſovereignty paramount of the province of Benares by treaty with the Nabob Vizier of Oude, " without any encroachment," to adopt the words of the act of Council, " on the juſt rights of the Rajah, or the engagements actually ſubſiſting with him." And at the expreſs recommendation of Mr. Haſtings, by a new grant, farther privileges were conferred upon the Rajah—viz. the ſovereignty of the mint, and the rights of criminal juſtice in the laſt reſort —the Governor, in the record of this tranſaction in the council-book, making uſe of theſe remarkable words: " The Rajah of Benares, from the ſituation of his country, which is a frontier to the provinces of Oude and Bahar, may be made a ſer-

viceable

viceable ALLY to the Company; but, to infure his attachment, his intereft muft be connected with it, which cannot be better effected than *by freeing him totally from the remains of his prefent vaſſalage, under the guarantee and protection of the Company*; and, at the fame time, guarding him againſt any apprehenſions from this Government, by thus PLEDGING its FAITH, that no encroachment ſhall ever be made on his rights by the Company." Such were, at this period, the good-will and even generoſity of Mr. Haſtings, that he propoſed to receive the tribute of the Rajah, amounting to 260,000l. per annum, punctually and cheerfully paid in monthly aſſeſſments—not at Benares, but at Patna, the neareſt provincial ſtation, " left the preſence of a Reſident ſhould in any manner fruſtrate the intention of rendering the Rajah INDEPENDENT—eventually reducing him," as Mr. Haſtings's extreme ſolicitude apprehended, " to the mean and depraved ſtate of a mere Zemindar *."

In this ſtate things remained till, in the year 1777,

---

* It may be tranſiently remarked, without making any invidious application, as the time and occaſion do not coincide with theſe conceſſions and indulgencies of the new Governor, that amongſt the preſents privately received by Mr. Haſtings, and which he originally meant, as he acknowledges, for ever to conceal, but which circumſtances afterwards induced him to diſcloſe, was the ſum of 23,000l. or two lacks of rupees, from the Rajah Cheyt Sing.

the Rajah had the misfortune to give great and mortal offence to the Governor General—an offence, however unintentional, for which his final and utter ruin only could atone. In order to comprehend the nature of his delinquency, it is neceſſary to obſerve, that in the courſe of the preceding year, 1776, Mr. Haſtings, whether actuated by motives of paſſion, caprice, or temporary diſcontent, had, in his private and confidential correſpondence, authoriſed Mr. Maclean, his Agent in England, to ſignify to the Court of Directors his deſire to reſign his office, and to requeſt their nomination of a ſucceſſor to the vacancy which would be thereby occaſioned in the Supreme Council. The Court, after appointing a committee to examine into the powers veſted in Mr. Maclean, unanimouſly reſolved to accept the ſaid reſignation, and named Mr. Wheeler to fill the vacancy occaſioned by the ſame. A regular notification of this acceptance was immediately tranſmitted to India, and the diſpatches were read in Council, June 19, 1777. Mr. Haſtings obſerving a profound ſilence on the ſubject of theſe diſpatches, General Clavering addreſſed a letter to him on the following day, containing a formal requiſition to the Governor General to ſurrender the keys of Fort William and of the Company's treaſury. But Mr. Haſtings, affecting ſurpriſe and indignation, peremptorily refuſed to comply with
this

this demand—denying that his office was vacant, afferting that Mr. Maclean had exceeded his powers, and declaring his refolution to maintain his authority by every legal means. General Clavering, on the contrary, conceiving the office to be irrevocably vacated, and that he himfelf had legally fucceeded to the government, iffued fummonfes to the other members of the Council, Mr. Barwell and Mr. Francis, and in the prefence of Mr. Francis took the oaths as Governor General. On the other hand Mr. Haftings, fupported by Mr. Barwell, iffued directions to the Commandant of the garrifon of Fort William, to the Provincial Councils, and to the Officers on the different military ftations, enjoining them, at their peril, to obey no orders but fuch as fhould be figned by him or a majority of his Council. Sir John Clavering, perceiving that Mr. Haftings was determined rather to rifque a civil war than to refign the government, propofed a reference to the Supreme Court of Judicature; to which Mr. Haftings, confiding in the *known integrity* of Sir Elijah Impey, readily confenting, a decifion was given in favor of Mr. Haftings.

But this judicial confirmation of his authority by no means fatisfied the haughty and revengeful fpirit of the Governor. Omitting, therefore, to fummon Sir John Clavering and Mr. Francis to the next meeting of Council; the Governor, fupported by the faithful Barwell, entered in the

the council-book a formal refolve, importing, " that General Clavering having USURPED the Prefidency of Bengal, had thereby relinquifhed and vacated the office of Senior Counfellor and Commander in Chief of the Company's Forces— and that, for the prefervation of the legality of their proceedings, the faid General Clavering be not in future fummoned or admitted as a Member of the Council." This refolve was notified to Sir John Clavering, and iffued in general orders to the officers civil and military of the three provinces. At the enfuing meeting of Council, Mr. Francis moved the reverfal of thefe proceedings; but Mr. Haftings declared his determination to adhere to them, faying, " that they were not the precipitate effects of an inftant and paffionate impulfe; but the fruits of long and *temperate deliberation*, and of the ftricteft fenfe of public duty." The Chief Juftice Impey having his reafons for declining to fupport the Governor in this exercife of his PUBLIC DUTY, Mr. Haftings thought proper to move a fubfequent refolution in Council, conformably to the advice of the Judges, " That all parties be replaced in the fame fituation in which they ftood before the receipt of the laft advices from England."

Thus terminated this extraordinary bufinefs: but, moft unfortunately for the Rajah Cheyt Sing, on the firft intelligence of General Clavering's advancement to the government, he had, with officious complaifance, deputed a *vakeel*, or ambaffador, to congratulate the new Governor on his acceffion. This, Mr. Haftings, in his fubfequent juftification, urges as a prefumptive proof of the Rajah's difaffection to the Englifh Government; and the affront thus offered to him appears to have rankled in his proud and malignant mind, till he found a fit opportunity for gratifying his dire revenge. Confcious of his unlimited and uncontrollable power, the Governor propofed in Council, July 9th, 1778, Sir John Clavering being now deceafed, " That the Rajah of Benares fhould *confent* to the eftablifhment of three battalions of fepoys, to be raifed and maintained at his own expence;" and notwithftanding the alarm of the Rajah at the firft intimation of this defign, and the vigorous oppofition of Mr. Francis and Mr. Wheeler, the refolve was carried into effect by the cafting vote of the Governor. The fum of five lacks of rupees, which was fuppofed to be equivalent to the expence of raifing the three battalions, was demanded of the Rajah to be paid in fpecie within five days; and in cafe of non-compliance, the Refident Fowke was peremptorily enjoined to refrain from all further intercourfe with him. The affrighted Rajah paid the money without delay or hefitation. But the fame demand being renewed the following year, he ventured to remind the Governor in a moft refpectful spectful letter, " that he was encouraged to believe the former demand would not be drawn into precedent. I am therefore hopeful," said he, "you will be kindly pleased to excuse me the five lacks now demanded, and that nothing may be demanded of me beyond the amount expressed in the *pottab*." In reply to this submissive application, the Governor repeated his demand, that the Rajah should, without evasion or delay, pay the five lacks of rupees—in case of his refusal, informing him that measures would be taken to oblige him to a compliance. The third year the same demand being made, the Rajah again entreated a remission, but without effect; and as a punishment for his *continued contumacy*, the Governor General, of his own authority, imposed upon him an additional fine or mulct of 10,000l. These outrages failing to produce the effect intended on the mild and timid temper of the Rajah, a sudden demand was made, in addition to the tribute and subsidy, to provide a body of 2000 cavalry for the service of the Company. It was in vain that the Rajah protested he had no more than 1300 horse in his service; 500 of which, and 500 burkundasses or match-lockmen, should be ready to march to whatever place they should be sent. Mr. Hastings deigned no answer whatever to this representation, but declared, "that he was determined to convert the faults of the Rajah into a public benefit—that he would exact the

the sum of 500,000l. as a punishment for his breach of engagements and other acts of misconduct—and that if the Rajah should refuse the demand, he would deprive him of his government."

Mr. Barwell and Mr. Francis having by this time returned to England, and Mr. Wheeler only remaining in Council, the sole power and responsibility of Government centred in the person of Mr. Hastings. For the purpose of executing more effectually these preconcerted designs, the Governor determined upon a journey to Benares; previous to which he vested in himself, by a formal act, the entire powers of the Supreme Council. At the eve of his departure, however, he condescended to inform Mr. Wheeler, "that the offences of the Rajah required punishment: and as his wealth was great, and the Company's exigencies pressing, it was a measure of policy and justice to exact from him a large pecuniary mulct for their relief."

On the entrance of the Governor General into the province, he was met by the Rajah in person with a magnificent attendance. Nevertheless, to shew his confidence in the justice of the Governor, he entered alone the pinnace in which the Governor had proceeded up the Ganges, and, in a lowly and suppliant manner, putting his turban in his lap, entreated his favor. He was, however, repulsed with great arrogance; and on the arrival of the Governor at Benares, he received an injunction from

from Mr. Haftings not to enter his prefence without his permiffion.

On the fucceeding day, the Governor fent articles of accufation in writing to the Rajah, importing, 1. That he had endeavored to excite diforders in the Government on which he depended. 2. That he had fuffered with impunity the perpetration of robberies and murders, even in the ftreets of Benares, to the great and public fcandal of the Englifh name. 3. That he had delayed the payment of the fums required of him for the Company's fervice: and, 4. That he had not complied with the demand of cavalry—all of which amounted, as the Governor afferted, to a direct charge of difaffection and *infidelity* to the Government on which the Rajah depended—And to thefe articles of impeachment he demanded an immediate anfwer. On the evening of the fame day, the Rajah fent in his defence, denying, in the moft pofitive manner, the truth of the aforefaid articles. " My enemies," faid he, " with a view to my ruin, have made falfe reprefentations to you. Now that, *happily for me*, you have yourfelf arrived at this place, you will be able to afcertain all the circumftances: 1. relative to the horfe; 2. to my people going to Calcutta; 3. the dates of the receipts of the particular fums above mentioned. I have never fwerved in the fmalleft degree from my duty to you. It remains with you to decide on all thefe matters. I am in every

every thing your flave. What is juft I have reprefented to you—May your profperity increafe!" At this reply the Governor expreffed great wrath, declaring it to be lefs a vindication of the Rajah than a recrimination on him; and that it was couched in terms of defiance, manifefting a dangerous fpirit of independency.

In confequence of the Rajah's offenfive and audacious conduct, Mr. Haftings conceived himfelf obliged to adopt fome decifive plan—and an order was therefore immediately iffued to put the Rajah under an arreft in his own palace. To this indignity the Rajah, fhocked as he appeared to be, fubmitted with the moft paffive humility: " He hoped," he faid, " that the Governor would allow him a fubfiftence in confideration of his father's fervices—but as for his zemindary, his forts and his treafures, he was ready to lay them at his feet, and his life if required." Being at once dejected with the ignominy, and difmayed with the danger of his fituation, furrounded by a guard of fepoys with their fwords drawn, he wrote to the Governor—" Whatever be your pleafure, do it with your own hands. I am your flave. What occafion can there be for a guard? It depends on you alone to take away, or not to take away, the country out of my hands."

The higheft alarm and aftonifhment being excited in the city of Benares, by this arreft of the Rajah,

Rajah, great numbers of people assembled round the palace, nor could the earnest and repeated entreaties of their Prince restrain them from acts of violence: and believing the person of the Rajah, who was much beloved by his subjects, to be exposed to extreme hazard, they at length broke through the enclosure, and falling suddenly upon the guard of sepoys and English officers, nearly the whole were cut to pieces. In the tumult the Rajah made his escape over the walls of his palace by means of a cord formed of turbans tied together; and, crossing the Ganges in a boat, fled to a place of refuge, whence he directed a suppliant letter to Mr. Hastings, to which the Governor affirmed " he did not think it becoming him to reply." On the contrary, leaving Benares with precipitation, he ordered the Rajah's troops to be every where attacked, as if the Rajah had been in avowed and open rebellion. So inconsiderable, notwithstanding, was the force by which he was attended, that the Governor acknowledged the fate of the British empire in India to be exposed, by these daring, or, to speak more properly, these rash and frantic measures, to the most imminent danger; for the fate of the empire he supposed, at this critical moment, to be closely connected with that of his own person. " Mean as its substance may be, its accidental qualities," says the Governor General, " were equivalent to those which, like the characters of a talisman in the Arabian

bian mythology, formed the eſſence of the State itſelf." By a confeſſion humiliating in proportion to its truth he declares, " that EVERY STATE *around would have* RISEN IN ARMS *againſt the* ENGLISH; *and* EVERY SUBJECT *of their own dominion would, according to their ſeveral abilities, have become an* ENEMY." Theſe few lines contain perhaps the bittereſt ſatire ever written upon any government, or upon any ſyſtem of deſpotiſm and oppreſſion that has impudently aſſumed the name.

The troops in the province of Benares being, however, quickly re-inforced, the territories of the Rajah were completely reduced. The Rajah having himſelf made his eſcape to the camp of the Mahrattas, orders were given by Mr. Haſtings to ſeize upon the fortreſs of Bidjegur, the reſidence of the Rannee Pauna, mother of Cheyt Sing, repreſented as a woman ſingularly amiable and virtuous, and againſt whom no delinquency was even pretended. The treaſures of the Rannee being very conſiderable, ſhe was deſirous to capitulate upon conditions, in order to ſave ſomething from the wreck of her fortunes. But Mr. Haſtings wrote to the commander, Major Popham, " I think every demand the Rannee has made to you, except that of ſafety and reſpect for her perſon, unreaſonable.—I apprehend that ſhe will contrive to *defraud* the captors of a conſiderable part of the booty, by being ſuffered to retire without

VOL. III. K examina-

examination. But this is your confideration, and not mine. As to making any conditions with her for a provifion, I will never confent to it."—In a fecond letter he fays, " If fhe delays the furrender beyond the term of twenty-four hours, it is my pofitive injunction that you put a ftop to the negotiation, *and on no account renew it*—Nor will I grant her ANY CONDITIONS WHATEVER; but leave her expofed to thofe dangers fhe has chofen to rifque, rather than truft to the CLEMENCY and GENEROSITY of *our* Government."

The caftle being accordingly furrendered within the time fpecified, the articles of the capitulation, by which an allowance of 15 per cent. was referved to the Rannee, were neverthelefs fhamefully and outrageoufly broken, the perfon of the Rannee and her attendants grofsly infulted, and their effects plundered. Notwithftanding the efforts and reprefentations of Major Popham the commander, a man of humanity and honor, no redrefs was obtained from the Governor, who, now wholly intent upon the vindication of his conduct, evidently refulting from the moft obdurate pride and fteadfaft hate, had caufed a great number of affidavits and depofitions, aiming to prove the exiftence of a confpiracy againft the Englifh Government, to be taken by Sir Elijah Impey, who *happened* at this time, in the courfe of *an excurfion for the benefit of his health*, to be fortunately refident at Benares.

In

In his subsequent famous narrative of this transaction to the Court of Directors, Mr. Hastings hesitated not to assert, " that the Rajah of Benares had no claim to the title or privileges of a Prince—that the deeds which passed between him and the Board upon the transfer of the zemindary in 1775 were not to be understood to bear the quality and force of a treaty between equal States—that the payments to be made by him were not a tribute, but a rent—that, being nothing more than a *common Zemindar*, he owed a personal allegiance and *an implicit and unreserved obedience* to the authority of the Company, at the forfeiture of his zemindary, and even of his life and property*." Conceiving it

---

* Perhaps the records of history do not exhibit a position more enormously extravagant, than that the Sovereign of a province in the interior parts of Hindostan, exercising the powers of government over a happy and consenting people, should owe *implicit and unreserved obedience* to a company of traders inhabiting a *barbarous island* on the other side of the globe. In vindication of the arbitrary and excessive fine of 500,000l. imposed by Mr. Hastings on the Rajah, the Governor, in his MINUTES OF DEFENCE, pretends, " that, notwithstanding the privileges guarantied to the Rajah, the *right of fine* was expressly reserved to the Company:"—and he affirms this right to be woven into the texture of the Mogul Government. If so, it is evident that all stipulations for the payment of a specific tribute are trifling and ridiculous. But his authorities most egregiously fail him. 1. He tells us that the Vizier Sujah ul Dowla levied a fine on the death of the father for the investiture of the son.—True: but the agreement was, in this case, on both sides optional—the zemindary or principality

it possible, nevertheless, that these extraordinary positions might stagger the faith of some perverse or sceptical persons, he thought proper to subjoin an argument which could not fail to operate in his favor, viz. " That, if he *had* acted with an unwarrantable rigor, and even INJUSTICE, towards Cheyt Sing; yet, first, if he did believe that extraordinary means were necessary, and those exerted with a strong hand, to preserve the Company's interests from sinking under the accumulated weight that oppressed them—or, 2dly, if he saw a political necessity for curbing the overgrown power of a great member of their dominion, and to make it contribute to the relief of their pressing exigences— that his error would be excusable, as prompted by an *excess of zeal* for the Company's interest operating with too strong a bias upon his judgment."

After the deposition of the Rajah Cheyt Sing, Mr. Hastings, in virtue of the commission with

not being hereditary in the family of Bulwant Sing till so declared, by the subsequent treaty of 1773. 2. He alleges, that when the right of the Mint was transferred to the Rajah, it was articled, that the proper weight and standard should be preserved by the Rajah, under pain of forfeiting the Mint, and being *liable to any penalty* the Board might think proper to impose. But in this, as in the former instance, the Rajah voluntarily accepted the grant with the condition annexed. Yet from these premises Mr. Hastings preposterously infers, that the enormous fine arbitrarily imposed by him was " consonant to the engagements between the Company and the Rajah."

which

which he had invested himself, exercised an authority over the province of Benares nothing less than despotic. Setting aside all former agreements, although evidently made with the Rajahs not in their personal but political capacity, he increased the tribute, or stated rent-charge, from 260,000 to 400,000l. per annum. Having bestowed the government on a youth called Mehip Narrain, a descendant by the mother from the Rajah Bulwant Sing; he, in addition to the tribute, imposed such heavy and grievous duties on merchandize, as threatened the absolute annihilation of their commerce; charging moreover pensions on the revenues of the province, and sending large bodies of troops into the territory of Benares, to be maintained by the oppressed and impoverished inhabitants.

The father of the new Rajah, Durbitzee Sing, who was appointed guardian and administrator to his son, was by Mr. Hastings in a short time deposed from his office, on a vague and general charge of mal-administration and DEFICIENCY in his PAYMENTS, and thrown into prison. His property being confiscated, and his person endangered, he in a short time died, overwhelmed with distress and ruin.

"When a new system was to be formed with the successor of Cheyt Sing," says Mr. Hastings, "I saw no objection to making the Company's interests

interests my *first principle of action*. The easy accumulation of too much wealth had been Cheyt Sing's ruin. It had buoyed him up with extravagant and ill-founded notions of independency, which I much wished to discourage in the future Rajah. Some part, therefore, of the superabundant produce of the country I turned into the coffers of the Sovereign, i. e. the Company, by an augmentation of the tribute."

Here the grand object of the British Government in India, as administered by Mr. Hastings, is openly and undisguisedly avowed—*The filling the Company's coffers with money*, was by him held to be the *first principle of action*. Happy would it indeed have been for the inhabitants of Hindostan, if even this abominable and infamous principle had been pursued by rational and politic means, such as would have secured, unimpaired, the *sources of prosperity*, though for the mere purpose of subsequent plunder and emolument.

On the deposition of Durbitzee Sing from the regency, a man of obscure origin, one Jagher Deo Sheo, was exalted to this dangerous pre-eminence. This new minister, warned by the fate of his predecessor, extorted the tribute money and other duties imposed by the Governor, with the most rigorous severity. The trade and cultivation of the province having in a short time declined in an incredible degree, the Resident at

Benares

Benares declared to the Board at Calcutta, that the collection of the revenue was become very difficult. But of this fact the Governor General himself gave the most decisive attestation. Passing through the province of Benares, in his progress to Lucknow, in the spring of 1784, he declares, in a letter addressed to the Council at Calcutta, " that he was *fatigued* with the clamors of the discontented inhabitants. Though the drought of the preceding summer might contribute to heighten the distress, the Governor acknowledges there is reason to believe that the cause existed principally in a defective, if not corrupt and oppressive administration. The avowed principle, says he, on which the present Administration acts, is, that the whole sum fixed for the revenue of the province *must* be collected, and that the deficiency arising in places where the crops have failed, must be supplied from the resources of others where the industry of the cultivators has been more successfully exerted.

" In the management of the customs, the exorbitant rates exacted by an arbitrary valuation of the goods, the practice of exacting duties twice on the same goods, first from the seller, and afterwards from the buyer, and the vexatious disputes and delays drawn on the merchants by these oppressions, were loudly complained of. Under such circumstances, we are not to wonder if the merchants

chants of foreign countries are difcouraged from reforting to Benares.

"One evil I muft mention, becaufe it has been verified by my own obfervation, and is of that kind which reflects an UNMERITED REPROACH on our general and national character.— When I was at Buxar, the Refident, at my defire, enjoined the Naib to appoint creditable people to every town through which our route lay, to *perfuade and encourage* the inhabitants to remain in their houfes, promifing to give them guards, as I approached, for their protection.— But, to my great difappointment, I found every place through which I paffed ABANDONED. I am forry to add, that from Buxar to the oppofite boundary, I have feen NOTHING but TRACES of COMPLETE DEVASTATION in EVERY VILLAGE,— I cannot help remarking, that, except the city of Benares, the province is in effect without a government. The adminiftration of the province is mifconducted, and the people oppreffed; trade difcouraged, and the revenue in danger of a rapid decline from the violent appropriation of its means."

Such is the picture, drawn by the hand of the mafter artift, of the bleffed effects of Britifh Government in India!—In order to remedy thefe evils, the Governor propofed to eject the new adminiftrator from his office; which was foon afterwards

terwards accordingly done, and a temporary administration for the government of the province substituted, without however making any provision for a reduction of taxes, or a remiffion of tribute. The oppreffion of Jagher Deo Sheo being doubtlefs, in the eyes of the Governor, a crime of much lefs magnitude than the impunctuality of his predeceffor Durbitzee Sing, he efcaped with a fimple difmiffion, without incurring the penalties of fine, imprifonment, and death.

If the conduct of Mr. Haftings in relation to the province of Benares fhould be deemed liable to ferious exception, it is to be feared that an examination of his fyftem of policy refpecting the vizieriate of Oude, a far more extenfive fcene of operation, will tend but little to redeem his character. It muft fuffice, for this is not a profeffed hiftory of the adminiftration of Mr. Haftings, lightly to touch upon a few leading points of this too fertile topic.

The terms of the treaty concluded in the year 1765 with the Vizier Sujah ul Dowla, by the late Lord Clive, left that great and powerful province in a confiderable meafure dependent upon the Company. From this fatal period the decay and defolation of the Vizieriate commenced. For to come into contact with the Englifh Government, feemed univerfally and inftantly to produce a fort of political paralyfis. The annual revenue, which

was

was eftimated at more than three millions, had funk in the year 1779 to lefs than one million and a half. The Vizier had contracted to maintain at his own expence a brigade of the Company's troops in his fervice, for fo long time as he might deem them neceffary for the defence of his country. But the Court of Directors, in their letter to the Governor and Council of the 15th of December 1775, exprefsly fay, " If you intend to exert your influence, firft to induce the Vizier to acquiefce in your propofal, and afterwards to compel him to keep the troops in his pay during your pleafure, your intents are unjuft, and a correfpondent conduct would reflect great difhonor on the Company." But Mr. Haftings had long learnt to hold the orders of his fuperiors in contempt, and to fet their authority at defiance. The Nabob Afoph ul Dowla, who had fucceeded his father in the Vizieriate, February 1775, making very earneft fupplication to be relieved from this burden, which the reduced ftate of his revenue rendered him utterly unable to fupport; Mr. Haftings without hefitation declared " the relief defired to be totally inadmiffible;"—farther affirming, " that the *tone* in which the demands of the Nabob were afferted, gave caufe for the moft alarming fufpicions;" though it is difficult to conceive how language more fubmiffive and humble could have been adopted.

" During

"During three years (fays the Nabob) the expence occafioned by the troops in brigade, and others commanded by European officers, has much diftreffed the fupport of my houfehold, infomuch that the allowances made to the feraglio and children of the deceafed Nabob have been reduced to one fourth of what it had been. The attendants and fervants of my court have received no pay for two years paft, and applications from my father's private creditors are daily preffing upon me. All thefe difficulties I have for three years ftruggled through, and found this confolation therein, that it was complying with the pleafure of the Honorable Company, and in the hope that the Supreme Council would make enquiry, from impartial perfons, into my diftreffed fituation : but I am now FORCED to a reprefentation. From the great increafe of expence, the revenues were neceffarily farmed out at a high rate, and deficiencies followed yearly. The country and cultivation is ABANDONED; and as to the European troops, the Nabob declares that they brought nothing but confufion into the affairs of his government, and were entirely their own mafters."

Far from being moved by thefe reprefentations, the Governor General declared, in his inftructions tranfmitted to the Refident Purling at the Court of Lucknow, " that the Nabob ftands engaged to our Government to maintain the Englifh

lish armies formed for the protection of his dominions, and that it was OUR part, and not HIS, to judge and determine in what manner and at what time these shall be reduced and withdrawn." And in a minute of confultation on this fubject, at the Council Board, Mr. Haftings afferted "that the arrangement of meafures between the Britifh Government and the native powers of India muft, in cafe of difagreement about the neceffity thereof, be decided by the STRONGEST."

This being his avowed fyftem of policy, it can excite no wonder that the government and country of Oude fhould proceed, with rapid and accelerated progrefs, to the extremity of political diftrefs and ruin. Mr. Haftings himfelf, towards the clofe of his adminiftration, thus, in a minute of Council, expreffes his fenfe of the fituation of the Vizier:—"Our alliance has proved the extinction of his fovereignty, and the impoverifhment of his country and revenue."

In the year 1781, a commiffion of delegation having been executed at Calcutta, invefting Mr. Haftings with the entire powers of the Supreme Council, the Governor General refolved to vifit the province in perfon. At a meeting which took place at Chunar, on the confines of Benares, a fecret treaty was concluded by the Governor with the Vizier, containing feveral articles of an extraordinary nature; and it has been faid, that

no

no treaty ever contained fo much treachery in fo finall a compafs. By this time the claims upon the Nabob, on various grounds and pretences, arofe to the enormous fum of 2,785,000 l. fterling, which was confiderably more than two years nett produce of the Nabob's revenues. In order to liquidate this debt, Mr. Haftings urged the Nabob, and an article to this effect was inferted in the treaty of Chunar, to a general refumption of the jaghires, or government affignments upon land, throughout the province, to the amount of many hundred thoufand pounds annual rent, including the provifions made by the former Nabob-Viziers for their Princes of the blood, and the antient friends and dependents of their family. The eftates thus confifcated were re-let on rack rents and at the fame time mortgaged to rich bankers of Benares, to fupply the immediate wants of the Englifh Government.

A GIFT from the Vizier of 100,000 l. was alfo at this period accepted by Mr. Haftings; which being, as he confeffed, a fum of too great magnitude to be concealed, he, after fome deliberation, thought proper to apprize the Court of Directors of this violation of *their* commands, and of his *own oath*. But he neverthelefs had the prefumption to exprefs his hope " that, in confideration of his long and faithful fervices, and the fums he had expended from his private fortune

upon

upon their account, they would permit him to apply this donation to his own ufe."

The confufion and diftrefs confequent on the late violent expedient of refumption, and other devices of extortion, it is impoffible in adequate terms to defcribe. The whole fabric of civil government feemed to totter, and verge upon annihilation and anarchy. The regular authority of the magiftracy, and the adminiftration of juftice, totally ceafed; and no power was vifible but that of the farmers of the revenue, attended by bodies of troops to enforce the collections. The country was declared by one of the Nabob's minifters to be " a fpeaking picture of famine and woe." " From the total want of police," fays the Refident Briftow, " hardly a day efcapes but I am informed of fome tragical event, whereof the bare recital is fhocking to humanity:" and he confeffes that his feelings are fenfibly hurt, and his compaffion ftrongly excited, by the difgraceful and miferable ftate of poverty to which the brothers of the Nabob are reduced. From three of thefe princes, Mirza Ali, Mirza Hyder, and Mirza Sief, the Refident received an affecting reprefentation, or memorial, in which they fay, " Our fituation is not fit to be told—For two years we have not received an hubba on account of our *tuncaw* (affignment on the revenue). It is furprifing, having fuch a friend as you, our fituation is arrived at that pafs that we fhould be in diftrefs for bread and clothing—YET we are the sons of Sujah ul Dowla!" But the heart of Mr. Haftings never in any inftance counteracted the defigns of his head, and the wretched inhabitants of Oude were deftined to fee yet greater abominations than thefe.

The mother and wife of the late Nabob kept their court at the city of Fyzabad, where, after the cuftom of the Eaft, they lived in much magnificence, having the charge of educating the numerous offspring of the deceafed Sovereign, and of maintaining a houfehold confifting of 2000 perfons. To fupport this vaft expence, the Nabob had left them a large proportion of his treafures, and had fettled upon them *jaghires* fuitable to their high rank and dignity, and to the importance of the truft committed to them; folemnly and earneftly recommending at the fame time the interefts of his family to the guardian care and protection of the Company, by whom their poffeffions had been fubfequently and authentically guarantied. By the treaty of Chunar, neverthelefs, the prefent Nabob was authorized by Mr. Haftings to feize upon the jaghires, or landed eftates, of thefe illuftrious relatives, and to allow them *penfions* equal to the amount. And this the Governor pretended was conformable to the

Mahom-

Mahommedan law*. The Nabob appearing nevertheless manifestly reluctant to carry this odious project into execution, Mr. Hastings signified his pleasure to *his own* Resident at Lucknow, Mr. Middleton, " that as this measure originated with the English, and was intended for their benefit, the execution was to be FORCED upon him,"—although the express words of the treaty of Chunar were merely, " that the Nabob be *permitted* to resume such jaghires as he may think necessary."

* Soon after the decease of Sujah ul Dowla, a dispute arose between Asoph ul Dowla his successor, and the Begums his relations, respecting the proportion of treasure which legally appertained to them; and the Board of Calcutta, taking cognizance of this matter, unanimously decided (Sir John Clavering, Colonel Monson, and Mr. Francis, then sitting at the Board) that by the Mahommedan law the Princesses were entitled only to the property of their husbands within the zenana or seraglio where they resided. The Begums cheerfully acquiesced in this decision; in consequence of which, a vast sum was refunded by them, and their remaining treasure secured by a formal guarantee, in which Mr. Hastings concurred, though, as he insinuates, without responsibility, " being then an inefficient member of the Board." But for Mr. Hastings to appeal to the KORAN as a sanction for his subsequent enormities, is, to adopt the language of Mr. Sheridan, in his famous speech of February 7, 1787, " as if there were something in the institutions of Mahommed, that made it meritorious for a Christian to be a savage—that rendered it criminal to treat the inhabitants of India with humanity or mercy—that even made it impious in a son not to plunder his mother!"

In

In order to impart some color of justice to this outrage, depositions the most futile and ridiculous were, as recently at Benares, extra-judicially made before Sir Elijah Impey, who unexpectedly presented himself in the course of his progress, after leaving Benares, first at Chunar, then at Lucknow. For this magistrate so miserably degraded his character and station, as to become a principal agent in this business. And such was the silent celerity of his movements, that the Chief Justice has been with humorous allusion compared to the Ghost in Hamlet, exclaiming in almost every quarter at the same instant, " SWEAR !" These affidavits, founded on vague and incoherent rumors, were designed to prove, that the Princesses of Oude fomented the insurrection at Benares, and were even engaged in a plot for the dethronement of their own son, and the utter extirpation of the English nation. Very little stress, however, was at this crisis placed by Mr. Hastings on the validity of these proofs, which were evidently calculated to answer a different and distant purpose*.

" Your

---

* Major Marsack, in the course of his examination at the bar of the House of Commons, May 8, 1786, being asked whether there was any reason to believe that the Begums had, in conjunction with other powers, formed a plan for the extirpation of the English? answered, " that such a thing was too absurd to be credited by any person knowing the position of affairs at that time

" Your pleasure," says Mr. Middleton, " respecting the Begums I have learnt from Sir Elijah Impey.—Finding the Nabob wavering in his determination about the resumption of the jaghires, I this day ordered the necessary *perwannahs* for that purpose. But before they were transcribed, I received a message from the Nabob, entreating that I would withhold them till the morning. As it is possible that the Nabob, seeing the business will at all events be done, may make it an act of his own, I have consented to *indulge* him in this request."

The Nabob at length issued his *perwannahs*, but with extreme reluctance, and, to use the language of Mr. Middleton, " after much trifling evasion and puerile excuses ;"—the irresistible effusions, no doubt, of that natural affection which it is so difficult totally to eradicate from the human heart, but which by men hardened in villany is regarded

time in India." He acknowledged " that a universal disaffection prevailed throughout all the provinces of Oude, owing to the measures of our Government, and the unheard-of oppressions of Colonel Hannay, the commander of the English troops; the effects of which appeared in deserted villages and uncultivated tracts of land from one end of the country to the other.—That on Colonel Hannay's departure for Benares, the inhabitants arose in a tumultuous manner; and he professed his belief that all men under their situation and circumstances, who possessed the feelings and spirit of men, would have extirpated us if in their power."

as fond and childish imbecility. "At the same time the Nabob declared," says Mr. Middleton, "both to me and his ministers, that it was an ACT of COMPULSION."

In a subsequent letter Mr. Middleton informs the Governor, that the Vizier, wishing to evade the measure of resumption, suggested to him, that the debt of the Company might be better and more expeditiously liquidated by taking the amount at once from the treasures left by his father. With all the eager rapacity of a bird of prey, which in the act of seizing with out-stretched beak its helpless quarry aims to grasp another victim also in its talons, Mr. Hastings, still insisting upon the resumption of the jaghires, declared his resolution also to seize the treasures; enjoining upon the Agent Middleton, under menaces of a dreadful responsibility, the execution of this barbarous act, in the following peremptory terms:—" You yourself must be personally present. You must not allow any negotiation or forbearance, but must prosecute BOTH SERVICES until the Begums are at the entire mercy of the Nabob." In conformity to this order, the British Resident, at the head of a body of troops, accompanied by the terrified Vizier, marched to Fyzabad, and with little or no resistance stormed first the town and then the castle. The chief officers of the household, the eunuchs Jewar Ali Khan and Bahar Ali Khan, persons of distinguished rank,

rank, who had been in high trust and favor with the late Nabob, were ignominiously thrust into confinement, in order to extort from them the discovery of the treasures and effects committed to their care. In consequence of these severities, the Bhow Begum, i. e. the mother princess, at length consented to the surrender of her treasures, hid in the most secret recesses of the palace, to the amount of the bond debt due from the Nabob to the Company. But avarice is insatiable as the grave. Another demand of 120,000l. was made for the balance pretended to be due *since* the execution of the bond: and to enforce compliance, the two eunuchs were, by order of the Resident Middleton, committed to close custody, put in irons, and kept from all food. To raise this sum, great part of the furniture of the palaces, the jewels and other effects of the Begums, even to the wardrobe, were disposed of by public sale.

Fully apprised of the distressful situation of the Princesses, Mr. Hastings could, nevertheless, write at this period to the Resident Middleton as follows:—" The Nabob having consented to the resumption of the jaghires held by the Begums, and to the confiscation of their treasures, and thereby involved my own name, and the CREDIT of the COMPANY, in a participation of both measures, I have a right to require and insist on the complete

plete execution of them, and I look to you for their execution, declaring that I hold you accountable for it *."

It may easily be imagined, that the pensions allotted to the Begums and other Jagheerdars, in lieu of their jaghires, would be very ill and defectively paid. In the month of March, 1782, the officer on duty at Fyzabad, Major Gilpin, wrote to the Resident :—" The women belonging to the Khord Mohul, or lesser palace, are in want of every necessary of life, and are driven to that desperation, that they threaten to throw themselves from the walls of the zenana." In a subsequent letter it is said, " The women in the zenana assembled last night on the tops of the building, crying in a most lamentable manner for food."—

* Mr. Hastings has indeed in his defence alleged, that he was *ignorant* of many transactions imputed to him respecting this business. But of those which were in any degree material to substantiate the charge of criminality, he could NOT plead ignorance. " If Mr. Middleton did not give him an exact account of the groans that were heaved, the tears that were shed, the weight of the fetters, or the depth of the dungeon, he stated," says Mr. Sheridan (vide his speech June 1788), " every important step that was taken in the progress and winding up of this relentless tragedy." In fact, nothing of moment was done without the express command of Mr. Hastings; for even Mr. Middleton, " a fellow by the hand of Nature marked to do a deed of shame," discovered no symptoms of alacrity in the execution of his direful commission.

And

And in a third letter—" The repeated cries of the women for subsistence have been truly melancholy. They beg most piteously for liberty, that they may earn their daily bread by laborious servitude, or to be released from their misery by immediate death." At length the Company's Resident, Mr. Bristow, ventured, of his own authority, very little to the satisfaction of Mr. Hastings, to order the removal of the troops, and the release of the prisoners Bahar and Jewar Ali Khan, who had now been confined and in irons for near twelve months. "The quivering lips," says the Commander of the troops at Fyzabad, speaking of their enlargement, " and the tears of joy stealing down the poor men's cheeks, was a scene truly affecting."

The distresses of the zenana nevertheless still continued, and the women, breaking by frantic violence the sacred bounds of the palace, exhibited themselves in this state of degradation and despair to the astonished inhabitants of Fyzabad, in the public bazar or market-place of that great and populous city. But after this act of desperation they do not appear to have been permitted to suffer equal extremity.

In a letter from the Bhow Begum to the Resident Bristow, this unfortunate Princess says: " An accusation was framed against me, which I had never conceived even in idea, of rendering assistance

ance to Rajah Cheyt Sing. Having seized my head eunuchs, Jewar Ali Khan and Bahar Ali Khan, they obliged them to sign a bond for sixty lacks of rupees. They were thrown into prison with fetters about their feet, and denied food and water. I, who had never even in my dreams experienced such an oppression, gave up all I had to preserve my honor and dignity.—My sufferings did not terminate here. The disturbances of Colonel Hannay and Mr. Gordon were made a pretence for seizing my jaghire. The state of the matter is this; When Colonel Hannay was by Mr. Hastings ordered to march to Benares, during the troubles of Cheyt Sing, the Colonel, *who had plundered the whole country*, was incapable of proceeding, from the union of thousands of zemindars, who had seized this favorable opportunity. They harassed Mr. Gordon near Junivard, and opposed his march. Mr. Gordon forded the river upon his elephant. In the mean time a letter was received by me from Colonel Hannay, desiring me to escort Mr. Gordon to Fyzabad. As my friendship for the English was always sincere, I readily complied, and sent some companies of Nejeebs to escort Mr. Gordon and all his effects to Fyzabad; where having provided for his entertainment, I effected his junction with Colonel Hannay. The letters of thanks I received from both these gentlemen are still in my possession.

seffion. But is it not extraordinary that, notwithstanding the juftnefs of my caufe, nobody relieves my misfortunes?"

In the letter of Colonel Hannay, referred to by the Begum, that officer, in the oriental phrafeology, fays: " Begum Saib of exalted dignity! Your exalting letter, fraught with grace and benevolence, I had the honor to receive in a fortunate moment. Your faithful fervant repofeth his moft unbounded hopes and expectation upon your Highnefs, that Mr. Gordon may arrive at Fyzabad without apprehenfion or danger." And Mr. Gordon expreffes himfelf in a ftill higher ftrain of refpect and gratitude—" Begum Saib of exalted dignity and generofity! Your gracious letter, in anfwer to the petition of your fervant from Goondah, exalted me. The welfare of your fervant is entirely owing to your favor and benevolence. Continue to exalt and honor me with your gracious letters—May the fun of profperity continually fhine!"

When the intelligence of thefe aftonifhing tranfactions reached the Court of Directors, that affembly, in which an high fenfe of honor and virtue, *occafionally difcoverable*, too unavailingly contended againft the fuggeftions of ambition and intereft, ordered a letter to be written to the Governor and Council, in which they fay, with reference to the iniquitous and enormous plan of
                                                             feizure

seizure and resumption, "We HOPE and TRUST, for the honor of the British nation, that this measure appeared FULLY JUSTIFIED in the eyes of all Hindostan. It no where appears, from the papers *at present* in our possession, that they, the Begums, excited any commotions previous to the imprisonment of Cheyt Sing; and only armed themselves in consequence of that transaction; and it is probable, that such a conduct proceeded from motives of self-defence, under an apprehension that they themselves might likewise be laid under unwarrantable contributions." And the Court expressly ordered an ENQUIRY to be instituted into this matter, and, if the charge proved to be unfounded, that their jaghires should be restored.

If the Directors of the Company really entertained any serious doubt as to the light in which this daring act of atrocity appeared in the view of the inhabitants of Hindostan, it would be instantly decided by the testimony of Major Brown, Mr. Hastings's *own Resident* at the Court of Dehli, who, in a letter addressed to Mr. Bristow, Resident at Oude, informs him, that in a conference he had lately held with Mirza Shuffee Khan, Prime Minister of the Mogul, speaking of the situation of the Begums, that Minister told him, " There is not a man in HINDOSTAN who will attribute the act to the Vizier of Oude, but EVERY ONE

ONE will fix the odium on the English, who might easily, by the influence they so largely exercise, have prevented such unnatural conduct. This step," he said, " must DESTROY ALL CONFIDENCE in the English nation throughout Hindostan, and excite the bitterest resentment in all those who by blood are connected with the House of Sufdar Jung. If," said this generous Mussulman, " the Vizier can so little regard his honor or his duty, as to wish to disgrace his father's mother for a sum of money, let him plunder her of all she has, and send her safe to Dehli or Agra; and, poor as I am, I will furnish subsistence for her, which she shall possess with security, though it cannot be adequate to her rank." As to the ENQUIRY enjoined by the Court of Directors, Mr. Hastings positively refused compliance, alleging " that it was in effect an order for the justification and acquittal of the Begums; and that it would be productive of evils greater than any which exist in the consequences which have already taken place, and which time had almost obliterated. " Let us," said the Governor in his minute of Council, " at least permit them to be judges of their own feelings, and prefer their complaints before we offer to redress them. The MAJESTY of JUSTICE ought to be approached with solicitation, not descend to provoke or invite it." And wrapped in the veil of conscious innocence, he declares with calm

calm and intrepid countenance, "that whatever may happen of the events which he dreads, he had at least this confolation remaining, that, in the annals of the natives of India, HE shall not be remembered amongst their oppreffors."

His general system of policy muft therefore be prefumed in his own opinion right; yet in his difpatch of April 30, 1784, he paffes the fevereft and moft unequivocal cenfure upon it, by recommending to the Court of Directors, "as his laft and ultimate hope, that their wifdom would put a final period to the ruinous and difreputable fyftem of INTERFERENCE, whether avowed or fecret." And he hefitates not to affert, in his fubfequent difpatch of October 1784, a very fhort time before his departure from India, and which may therefore be regarded as a fort of dying confeffion extorted by the refiftlefs force of truth, "that to no other purpofes than thofe of VENGEANCE and CORRUPTION will Agents armed with authority exercife their powers."

The affairs of Oude cannot with propriety be difmiffed, without tranfiently noticing the cafe of the province of Ferruckabad, a territory, like Benares, depending upon the Vizieriate. Ahmed Khan, late Nabob of Ferruckabad, in the war between the Vizier and the Company, had, as well as Bulwant Sing, fhewn a marked and too partial predilection for the Englifh intereft. After

the

the commencement of the fyſtem of peace, alliance, and *ſubſidy*, the tribute due to the Vizier from this province was aſſigned over to the Engliſh in part of payment; and a *Sezawall*, i. e. a ſequeſtrator, appointed by the Vizier, at the inſtance of the Engliſh Government, in order to enforce the collection; which in conſequence of this arrangement was paid, not to the Nabob, but to the Engliſh Reſident at Oude. The effects of this plan ſoon became viſible.

In the month of May 1780, Mr. Haſtings ſtated to the Board at Calcutta the condition of the province in the following terms:—" To the total want of all order, regulation, or authority in this government, it may, among many other obvious cauſes, no doubt be owing, that the country of Ferruckabad is become an almoſt entire waſte, without cultivation or inhabitants; that the capital, which but a very ſhort time ago was diſtinguiſhed as one of the moſt populous and opulent commercial cities in Hindoſtan, at preſent exhibits nothing but ſcenes of the moſt wretched deſolation and miſery—the Nabob himſelf ſcarcely commanding the means of bare ſubſiſtence." On account of the hardſhips and indignities to which the Nabob was ſubjected by the conduct of the Sezawall, and of which he had preferred frequent complaints, Mr. Haſtings propoſed the removal of the ſequeſtrator, and the appointment of an

Engliſh

English Resident in his room, declaring "that a LOCAL INTERFERENCE was indispensably necessary for realizing the Vizier's just demands." But by an article of the treaty of Chunar, in the following year, it was stipulated that the English Resident be recalled. And in excuse of his conduct, Mr. Hastings declared to the Board of Council, "that if the Nabob of Ferruckabad, Muzuffer Jung, *must* endure oppression, and he DARE NOT at this time propose his total relief, it concerns the reputation of our Government to remove *our* participation in it." As to these oppressions, however, he on another occasion unaccountably asserted, that "whether they were well or ill founded, he never had an *opportunity* to ascertain."

The Sezawall being thus reinstated, the country was again subjected to the most shocking ravages, insomuch that Mr. Hastings himself, of his own authority, ordered the collector to be removed, and the territory of Ferruckabad to be left to the sole management of its natural Prince. But of this *singular* act of goodness Mr. Hastings afterwards complained, "that the Resident of the Nabob Muzuffer Jung at Calcutta had the insolence to report that it was PURCHASED." He therefore formally withdrew his protection, and the Sezawall was a third time re-appointed to his former office. "This was attended," to adopt the words of the Governor General, " with an aggravated renewal of the severities formerly exercised;" and the Prince himself, in a letter addressed to Mr. Haftings, says: "The miseries which have fallen upon my country, and the poverty and diftrefs which have been heaped upon me by the re-appointment of the Sezawall, are such that a relation of them would, I am convinced, excite the strongest feelings of compaffion in your breaft; but it is impossible to relate them. On the one side, my country ruined and uncultivated to a degree of desolation which exceeds all description: on the other, my domestic concerns and connections involved in such a state of diftrefs and horror, that even the relations, the children and wives of my father are starving in want of daily bread, and are on the point of flying voluntary exiles from the country, and from each other." This letter, written in February 1783, Mr. Haftings did not lay before the Board till October following, being, as he then afferted, withheld from causes not necessary to mention.

He now, however, thought it once more incumbent upon him to propose the removal of the Sezawall, and the re-appointment of a British Refident at Ferruckabad. But the end and purpose of this appointment were completely fruftrated by a subsequent letter, rendering him liable to dismiffion at the pleafure of the Vizier. And the Refident Willes,

Willes, a man of acknowledged probity, declared, in his letter of 24th April 1785, " that the situation of the country was more diftrefsful than when the Nabob addreffed himfelf for relief in 1783; and that he was forry to fay that his appointment at Ferruckabad was of no ufe. Ferruckabad," fays he, " once the feat of great opulence and trade, is now daily deferted by its inhabitants—its walls mouldering away, without police, without protection. The ruin that has overtaken this country is not to be wondered at, when it is confidered, that there has been no ftate, no ftable government for many years;—no authority fufficiently predominant to eftablifh any regulations for the benefit of the country, whilft each authority has been exerted, as opportunity offered, for temporary purpofes."

Such was the ftate of things in the Vizieriate of Oude and its dependencies, when Mr. Haftings refigned the Government of India in the fpring of the year 1785. " If," exclaimed on a very memorable occafion a juftly celebrated parliamentary orator *, " a ftranger had at this time gone into the kingdom of Oude, ignorant of what had happened fince the death of Sujah Dowla, that man, who with a favage heart had ftill great lines of character, and who, with all his ferocity in war, had with a cultivating hand

* Vide Sheridan's Speech in Weftminfter Hall, June 1788.

preferved

preserved to his country the riches which it derived from benignant skies and a prolific soil—if this stranger, ignorant of all that had happened in the short interval, and observing the wide and general devastation, and all the horrors of the scene—vegetation burnt up and extinguished; villages depopulated and in ruin; temples unroofed and perishing; reservoirs broken down and dry—he would naturally enquire, What war has thus laid waste the fertile fields of this once beautiful and opulent country? What civil dissensions have happened, thus to tear asunder and separate the happy societies that once possessed those villages? What disputed succession? What religious rage has with unholy violence demolished those temples, and disturbed fervent but unobtruding piety in the exercise of its duties? What merciless enemy has thus spread the horrors of fire and sword? What severe visitation of Providence has thus dried up the fountains and taken every vestige of verdure from the earth? Or rather, What monsters have stalked over the country, tainting and poisoning with pestiferous breath what the voracious appetite could not devour?—To such questions what must be the answer? No wars have ravaged these lands and depopulated these villages—no civil discords have been felt—no disputed succession—no religious rage—no merciless enemy—no affliction of Providence, which, while it scourged for the moment,

moment, cut off the fources of refufcitation—no voracious and poifoning monfters—no; all this has been accomplifhed by the friendfhip, generofity, and kindnefs of the Englifh Nation—They have embraced us with their protecting arms, and, lo! THESE are the FRUITS of their ALLIANCE."

Previous, however, to the blifsful æra of the final departure of Mr. Haftings from India, various other incidents of importance took place; to which, in order to complete the picture of his ever-memorable adminiftration, it is now neceffary to advert.—It muft be called to recollection, that, after the conqueft of Rohilcund by the Nabob Vizier Sujah ul Dowla affifted by the arms of Britain, Fyzoola Khan was confirmed in the government of Rampore and its dependencies by the treaty of Lall-dang. Conformably to the provifions of this treaty, Fyzoola Khan was permitted to retain in his fervice 5000 troops, and not a fingle man more. Alfo, with whomfoever the Vizier fhould make war, it was ftipulated, that Fyzoola Khan fhould fend 2 or 3000 men, according to his ability, to join the forces of the Vizier;—and that, if the Vizier fhould march in perfon, Fyzoola Khan fhould himfelf accompany him with his troops. Fyzoola Khan is defcribed by the Refident Middleton as " a man of fenfe, not poffeffed with the paffion of ambition; but, applying himfelf peaceably to the improvement of his country, it increased greatly in riches and revenue." But peace and prosperity seemed, in the view of Mr. Haftings, to constitute the most unpardonable species of delinquency: and it has been remarked of him, that his favorite and habitual maxim of policy was, *"that where there is treasure there is treason."*

In the years 1777 and 1778, being greatly alarmed at the resumption of a number of jaghires by the young Vizier, and the general oppression prevailing in the government of Oude, Fyzoola Khan made repeated and earnest applications to the Company for a renewal of his treaty with the Vizier—originally attested by Colonel Champion—under the guarantee of the Company, as the only power in which he had confidence, and to which he could look up for protection. This was at length granted with the concurrence of the Vizier, to whom, as well as to the Company, presents were made on the occasion; "such as became the gratitude of one party to offer, and the dignity of the other to receive."

On the breaking out of the war between England and France, Fyzoola Khan voluntarily offered to maintain 2000 cavalry for the service of the Company; for which Mr. Haftings, in the name of the Supreme Council, returned him the warmest thanks, and acknowledged his claim on the generosity no less than the justice of the British Government. But, in the course of the following year, Mr. Haftings

tings suggested to the Vizier to make a requisition of 5000 cavalry from the Rajah of Rampore; although, according to the most rigid construction of the treaty, he was bound to contribute this quota only when the Vizier took the field in person. He represented therefore, in respectful terms, " his inability to comply with this demand—that the whole force allowed him was only 5000 men, of whom 3000 were infantry—the aid of whom was necessary for the concerns of his jaghire." On this Mr. Hastings passed a resolve in Council, himself and Mr. Wheeler being the only remaining members, importing, " that the Nabob Fyzoola Khan had evaded the performance of the treaty with the late Vizier Sujah ul Dowla, to which the *Honorable Company* were guarantees, as to the troops which he is obliged to furnish on the condition by which he holds the jaghire granted to him." And in a letter to the Vizier Mr. Hastings says, " Demand *immediate delivery* of 3000 cavalry;" and if he should evade or refuse compliance, he advises to make a formal protest against him for breach of treaty.

It being already ascertained that Fyzoola Khan had but 2000 cavalry in his service, the Court of Directors, in their subsequent dispatch, hesitated not to declare, " that the said demand carried with it the appearance of a determination to create a pretext for depriving him of his jaghire entirely, or to leave him at the mercy of the Vizier." This demand, however, being peremptorily made, Fyzoola Khan offered, in addition to his 2000 cavalry, a body of 1000 foot, with one year's pay in advance, and regular funds for their payment in future. But the Agent, Johnſon, deputed on this buſineſs, informed him that his orders were, not to receive any palliation, but a negative or affirmative. In conſequence of this refuſal of an impracticable demand, the Vizier propoſed to Mr. Haſtings " to reſume the grant, and to leave Fyzoola Khan to join his other faithleſs brethren who were ſent acroſs the Ganges."

By the third article of the treaty of Chunar, permiſſion was accordingly given to the Vizier, " when time ſhall ſuit, to reſume the ſaid grant,"—although, in the Council minute juſtificatory of this act, the conduct of Fyzoola Khan is expreſsly ſaid " not to amount to an abſolute breach of treaty, but to be uncandid, evaſive, and unfriendly." The time, however, not being as yet judged *ſuitable*, an intimation was given to the Nabob, that, in lieu of his military ſervices and other claims of the Vizier and Company, a commutation in money, conſiſting of a tribute and fines, would be more acceptable—the former being fixed at 20, the latter at 30 lacks. The Nabob, in reply, declared, through his vakeel at Lucknow, " that it clearly appears to be intended to deprive him of his country; as the high demand now made it would be impoſſible

for

for him to comply with. To a chief thus deprived the *Honorable Company* had been accustomed to grant some allowance. This he expected from the Governor's bounty; but if he should be disappointed, he would set off upon a pilgrimage to Mecca and Medina, and renounce the cares of the world. He directs his vakeel to ascertain whether the English intended to deprive him of his country; for, if they do, he is ready to resign it upon receiving an order from the Resident."

The real views of the Governor in this instance extended, however, no farther than the extortion of money; and his adamantine heart being also, perhaps, a little softened by the extreme humility of this declaration, an agreement was at length made to free the Nabob from all obligations of military service, in consideration of the annual tribute of 15 lacks, which Mr. Hastings confessed "to be an ample equivalent for the precarious claims of the Vizier." And being now in the humor to make extraordinary concessions, the Governor farther declared, " that the rumors which had been spread of the Nabob's hostile designs against the Vizier were totally groundless—and if he had been *inclined*, he had not the *means* to make himself formidable. On the contrary, being in the decline of life, and possessing a very fertile and prosperous jaghire, it is more natural to suppose that Fyzoola Khan wishes to spend the remainder of his days in quietness, than

than that he is preparing to embark in active and offensive scenes, which must end in his own destruction." This is the more remarkable, as Mr. Haſtings, in reply to ſome ſevere animadverſions of the Court of Directors on his conduct reſpecting Fyzoola Khan, had held a language totally contrary. The Directors having expreſſed their wiſhes to be conſidered rather as the guardians of the honor and property of the native powers, than as the inſtruments of their oppreſſion ;" Mr. Haſtings concluded his vindication of the whole of theſe tyrannical proceedings in the following inſolent words: " Such are the meaſures which we ſhall ever wiſh to obſerve towards our allies or dependents on the frontiers."

It muſt not be wholly omitted, though the vaſt field of inveſtigation and diſcuſſion to which it leads can, in the *proſpectus* of general hiſtory, be viewed only in remote and obſcure viſion, " that on the departure of Mr. Francis from India early in 1781, Mr. Haſtings, upon whom the entire powers of government devolved, immediately diſſolved the Provincial Councils, and eſtabliſhed a COMMITTEE of REVENUE, with powers in the higheſt degree deſpotic. The general renewal of leaſes coming under the conſideration of this Board, they determined, " that as to the period of the leaſes, it appeared beſt to the Committee to limit them to one year." In this reſpect the Committee

tee of Revenue were lefs lenient than the preceding famous Committee of Circuit. And they acted in direct contradiction to the former opinion of Mr. Haftings, folemnly declared, " that the farmer, i. e. the Government leffee, who holds his farm for one year only, having no intereft in the next, takes what he can with the hand of rigor—he will be tempted to exceed the bounds of right, and to augment his income by irregular exactions, and by racking the tenants, for which pretences will not be wanting where the farms pafs annually from one hand to another. On the contrary, from long leafes, the farmer acquires a permanent intereft in his lands—he will, for his own fake, lay out money in affifting his tenants, in improving lands already cultivated, and in clearing and cultivating wafte lands."—All the evils fo clearly forefeen, and fo little regarded by Mr. Haftings, added to thofe arifing from the vileft and groffeft corruption and peculation, took place under this fyftem; the chief adminiftrator and manager of which was one Govind Sing, a wretch loaded, as Mr. Haftings himfelf acknowledged, with reproaches; and of whom it ftands upon record, " that there was fcarcely a family of rank in the three provinces whom he had not fome time or another diftreffed and afflicted—fcarce a zemindary that he had not difmembered and plundered."

During the long administration of Mr. Hastings, various momentous incidents occurred in the subordinate governments or departments of government in India; but of these a cursory mention must suffice. Mahomed Ali Khan, Nabob of Arcot, had, by means too obvious to need explanation, acquired an unbounded influence over the counsels of the Government of Madras. Supported by the aid and authority of that Presidency, under the express sanction of the Governor and Council of Bengal, the Nabob, on frivolous pretences, declared war against the Rajah of Tanjore, a neighboring prince and antient ally of the Company; and, seizing his dominions, annexed them to his own territory. The Court of Directors, highly indignant at this unjust and violent usurpation, determined upon the restoration of the Rajah: and for this purpose Lord Pigot, a nobleman who had formerly been employed in the Indian service, and whose character, both in a civil and military capacity, stood deservedly high, was appointed to the government with positive orders to that effect. His Lordship arrived at Madras the latter end of the year 1775; and notwithstanding all the opposition and the temptation thrown in his way, he accomplished the grand object of his appointment, in the re-instatement of the Rajah. Disputes running extremely high in the Council in consequence of this measure, the Governor, in the autumn of 1776, suspended two of the members

bers from their functions, by a doubtful and dangerous aſſumption of authority. But ample revenge was ſoon after taken by the remaining malcontents, in the arreſt and impriſonment of his lordſhip, who ſurvived this daring outrage but a very ſhort time.

In the ſeſſion of Parliament which began November 1778, Admiral Pigot, brother to Lord Pigot, brought this affair in all its circumſtances before the Houſe of Commons; and after ſtating, in a ſeries of reſolutions, the principal facts relative to this cataſtrophe, he concluded with moving an addreſs to his Majeſty, " humbly praying that George Stratton, Eſq. and the other members of the Council of Madras, be proſecuted for ordering their Governor and Commander in Chief to be arreſted, and confined under a military force—they being returned to England, and now within the juriſdiction of his Majeſty's Courts of Weſtminſter Hall."

Notwithſtanding the labored juſtification of Mr. Stratton, who was a Member of the Houſe, theſe reſolutions were unanimouſly carried. Theſe gentlemen, being in the ſequel tried and convicted in the Court of King's Bench, were, to the amazement of the public, ſentenced only to pay a trifling fine—and the laws which they had ſet at defiance in India, ſeemed to be put in execution againſt them only to excite their contempt in England.

In

In the last session of 1781, of which the history has been in part related, the affairs of India again attracted the attention of Parliament, in consequence of a petition presented to the House of Commons from the Governor and Council at Calcutta, a second from the British settlers, and a third from the native inhabitants of Bengal, against the Supreme Court of Judicature established by the Regulating Act of 1773. The two former were drawn up in a very masterly style, and demonstrated, in a striking manner, the temerity and folly of those who could attempt to ingraft the laws and juridical maxims of England upon the antient usages and immemorial institutions of Hindostan. The petition of the natives is remarkable for its pathos and simplicity—" When," say the petitioners, " the ordinances of this Court of Judicature were issued, as they were all contrary to the customs, modes, usages, and institutions of this country, they occasioned terror in us; and day by day, as the powers of this Court became more established, our ruin, uneasiness, dishonor, and discredit, have accumulated. We are now driven to the last extremity. Several who possessed means and ability have banished themselves from the country; but we do not all of us possess the means of flight, nor have we power to abide the oppression of this Court. If, which God forbid! this our petition should not be accepted, giving ourselves up with resignation

resignation to our fate, we will sit down in expectation of death. After this, LET the soil of the country remain, and the Court of Justice—LET the Court of Justice remain upon the earth, or the earth cover it!"

On a motion by General Smith for referring these petitions to a Committee, Mr. Boughton Rous took occasion to contrast the established policy of antient Rome with that adopted by England: " In all subjection of territory contiguous to her own," said this able speaker, " Rome gave her own laws, if the people wished to receive them; or she allured them by immunities and honorable distinctions. Thus she assimilated all the petty states of Italy to her laws and manners, till the whole peninsula became one nation.—But in her distant conquests she pursued a very different policy. In these she was satisfied to hold the supreme government, to possess the revenues and military powers, leaving the inhabitants to conduct their internal police by their own native magistrates and laws; avoiding any insult to the religion or prejudices of the vanquished. Much better would it be for Britain to imitate, in this respect, the conduct of the antient Romans, than to persist in rash and injudicious attempts to impose the laws of England upon the natives of India."

Many of the judicial decisions of the Supreme Court, as stated to the House, also wore the aspect

pect of the most flagrant violence and injustice*: and a general conviction seemed to be momentarily excited, of the radical absurdity and

erro-

---

* Of these perhaps the most remarkable was the decision given by the Chief Justice in the famous PATNA CAUSE. It had been the practice of the Provincial Courts established under the English Government, to refer questions of Mahomedan Law to the Cawzee and Muftees—antient and known judicial officers under the former government. A cause of great importance respecting a disputed property, referred, in the accustomed manner, by the Council of Patna to the Cawzee Sadhi and two Muftees his assessors, being decided by them in a mode which approved itself to the public judgment as highly equitable and satisfactory, an *action of trespass* was nevertheless brought in the Supreme Court against the Cawzee and Muftees by the losing party. The action being admitted to lie, the Cawzee was arrested by warrant of the Chief Justice, to the consternation and astonishment of the inhabitants, in the public streets of Patna, when returning to his habitation from the exercise of the duties of his office. The Sheriff having the execution of the writ was directed not to admit the Cawzee or his assessors to bail under the enormous sum of 400,000 rupees: and had it not been for the interposition of the Provincial Council, the defendants must have been dragged to Calcutta, at the distance of 500 miles, and have languished in prison till their doom was determined. "The seizure of the Cawzee in this disgraceful manner," say the Provincial Council of Patna in their letter to the Supreme Council of Calcutta, "coming from the execution of his office, has struck a general terror into the inhabitants of this city; we thought it therefore expedient, for the honor of Government and the preservation of its authority, to offer the bail required for the enlargement of one of its first officers.—How can we expect," say they, "the other

officers

erroneousness of the present system. Nevertheless, the weight of regal influence, ever jealous and abhorrent of reform in every shape; the natural partiality

officers of these courts to carry any orders of consequence into execution, till they are assured of safety and protection in the discharge of their duty?"

The circumstances of cruelty and atrocity attending this business are fully detailed in the second article of impeachment exhibited against Sir Elijah Impey, in the House of Commons, December 12, 1787, by Sir Gilbert Elliot. In the sequel, the decision of the Cawzee was, upon grounds the most scandalously frivolous and futile, reversed by the Supreme Court; and the Cawzee and Muftees condemned to pay damages and costs to the amount of 300,000 rupees, which was in effect a sentence of perpetual imprisonment. The Cawzee Sadhi, being aged and infirm, in a short time funk under the weight of this persecution; the other defendants remaining in prison upwards of two years, till they were set at liberty by express orders from England, commanding not only their release, but the restoration of the Muftees to the offices they had before occupied with fair and unsullied characters.

As a specimen of the evidence on which the Chief Justice's sentence of reversal was founded, a small part of the examination of one Cojah Zekereah may be cited: Sir Elijah Impey declaring, from the bench, the testimony of this man to be consistent and unimpeached. It was adduced to prove and establish the authenticity of various signatures professing to witness a certain devise or deed of conveyance, styled, in the technical language of the Mahomedan Courts, the *Hebenamah*, on the validity of which the merits of the whole cause absolutely depended.

Q. Who wrote the writing which is round the seals?

A. What is wrote about my own seal and that of Ghyrut

Beg

tiality of the Minister to his own original plans, and the pressure of affairs still more urgent, prevented the adoption of any great or decisive measures of relief. From the contracted genius and

Beg in the Hebenamah, I remember writing myself; but the other three I do not remember writing. I am sure that above the seal of Mazum Beg is not mine—that around Ullah is not my writing.

Q. You must know your hand-writing—answer, Is it your hand-writing, YES or NO?

A. It is not.—It is not in my *memory* that it is. I do not *remember* it, if it is my hand-writing.—IT MAY BE SO.

Q. You must know your hand-writing—you need not look at it so frequently.

A. If it *is*, it may be I do not *recollect* it. If it may be, it may be I do not *recollect* it. IT IS CERTAINLY MY HAND-WRITING.

Q. Now you have sworn it is your hand-writing, and that it is not, which is true? One or the other of them must be true.

A. IT IS MY HAND-WRITING.

Q. You did not see Mahomed Iwaz write Ullah; therefore, why did you write *under it*?

A. I remember that when Ghyrut Beg affixed his seal, as he could not write, the deceased, Shawbaz Beg Khan, desired me to write over it; and having procured Iwaz to write in my absence Ullah, he desired me to write Ullah.

Q. You have said, I think, that you never saw the Hebenamah after your own seal was put to it, and till after the death of Shawbaz Beg Khan; and that when you did put your seal to it, the other seals were not put to it, nor the signature Ullah: How came you now then to say, that, after the seal of Ghyrut Beg was put to it, and the signature Ullah, that Shawbaz Beg Khan desired you to write upon the Hebenamah?

A. It

and policy of the exifting Adminiftration, nothing great, decifive, or comprehenfively beneficial, could indeed be expected. A bill was, however, introduced and paffed, explanatory of the powers of the Supreme Court of Judicature, and in fome points

A. It is true, that when he defired me to put my feal to it, there was no other feal than his. But about the fame time, or a day after, when the other witneffes witneffed it, I was by, and he defired me to witnefs it. I was *always* prefent with Shawbaz Beg Khan.

Q. Were you by when Mahomed Iwaz wrote the word Ullah?

A. I was not prefent then. When Imayet Ullah Beg and Ghyrut Beg put their feals to it, I was prefent.

Q. Why—if you did write under, the word Ullah, as you now fay you did—why did you not immediately fay that you did write under it?

A. I was in doubt about my own hand-writing; and, having fworn, I was cautious in acknowledging it.

Q. What did you mean by faying that you never faw the paper after you had put your feal to it till after the death of Shawbaz Beg Khan, if Shawbaz Beg Khan did in fact produce it to you to write upon it at any time after you had put your feal to it?

A. It is not a contradiction. After all the feals were put to it, after that time, I meant to fay, I never faw it till after the death of Shawbaz Beg Khan.

Q. Is all the writing over the feals of your hand-writing?

A. The LAST is not my hand-writing.

Q. Look to it, and be fure.

A. This *is* alfo my hand-writing.

Q. Why did you fay it was not your hand-writing when it is?

A. I did not *remember* writing it: but on feeing it is the fame flow of the pen, I acknowledge it to be my hand-writing.

limiting

limiting and restraining its jurisdiction, which had been extended, by the arbitrary encroachments of the Chief Justice, far beyond the real and obvious intent of the Regulating Act.

At this period the war in India had become very general; a most formidable combination of the Country Powers in opposition to the English had taken place, which, assisted by the fleets and armies of France, seemed to menace the very existence of the empire of Britain in India. Hyder Ali, the antient and inveterate enemy of the Company, in the month of July 1780 broke into the Carnatic with a vast army, and committed the most dreadful ravages. On the 10th of September he attacked and surrounded a considerable detached corps under Colonel Baillie, which were entirely cut to pieces or made prisoners. He then attacked and made himself master of Arcot; and scarcely did the Government at Madras believe itself to be in safety, when Sir Eyre Coote arrived to take the command of the Company's forces on the coast of Coromandel, and Hyder was in repeated engagements foiled and defeated by this fortunate and gallant veteran.

Various naval encounters also took place between the French and English fleets, commanded by M. Suffrein and Admiral Sir Edward Hughes, with equal skill, courage and success. The naval force of both nations was gradually increased, in the

the progress of the war, to a degree far beyond what had been known at any former period in India, amounting at the last, on the part of the British, to eighteen ships of the line of battle. But the proportion continuing nearly the same, the mutual accessions of strength served only to increase the number of human victims: and the successive battles being obstinately and even heroically contested, the bloodshed in this unavailing contest was uncommonly great.

To enter into the detail of such transactions can answer no valuable purpose, except it be to exhibit the miseries of war in their genuine colors, divested of that fascination which accompanies the idea of victory, though attended perhaps to the victors themselves with no solid advantage, to the vanquished with all the horrors of distress and ruin. Doubtless, in every region of the world wisdom and humanity exist more than sufficient, could they be brought into action, to remedy these fatal and inexpressible follies; but it is melancholy to reflect how small a portion of either falls to the lot of the generality of those by whom the affairs of the world are conducted; and how remote, and on a transient survey almost hopeless, is the prospect of any essential amelioration in the system of human policy*.

A Secret

---

* "Voici," says the celebrated Monarch of Prussia, "l'erreur de la plupart des Princes," i. e. of the men styled in the vocabulary

A Secret Committee having been appointed, in the year 1781, to enquire into the causes of the Mahratta war, and that in the Carnatic; a very able report was brought up early in the session of 1782, by the Lord Advocate of Scotland, Mr. Dundas, Chairman of the Committee, in which the general system of policy pursued by the Governor

of human folly, Most Serene, Most Gracious, and Most Sacred Sovereigns! "Ils croient que Dieu a creé exprès et par une attention toute particulière pour leur grandeur, leur félicité, et leur orgueil, cette multitude d'hommes dont le salut leur est commis ; et que leurs sujets ne sont destinés qu'à être les instrumens et les ministres de leurs passions déréglées. Dès que le principe dont on part est faux, les conséquences ne peuvent être que vicieuses à l'infini ! et de là ce désir ardent de tout envahir, de là la dureté des impôts dont le peuple est chargé, de là la paresse des princes, leur orgueil, leur injustice, leur inhumanité, leur tyrannie, et tous les vices qui dégradent la nature humaine. Si les princes se défaisoient de ces idées erronées, et qu'ils voulussent remonter jusqu'au but de leur institution, ils verroient que ce rang dont ils sont si jaloux, que leur élévation n'est que L'OUVRAGE DES PEUPLES.—Ce principe ainsi établi, il faudroit qu'ils sentissent que la vraie gloire de princes ne consiste point à opprimer leurs voisins, point à augmenter le nombre de leurs esclaves, mais à remplir les devoirs de leurs charges, et à répondre en tout à l'intention de ceux qui les ont revêtus de leur pouvoir, *et de qui ils* TIENNENT *la* GRANDEUR SUPRÊME*." Such is the ingenuous and noble confession of the Royal Historian and Philosopher, and such the language which at Berlin is applauded as the effusion of a magnanimous and enlightened patriotism, and in London stigmatized, and perhaps punished, as the result of disaffection to the Government, if not amounting to actual sedition and conspiracy.

* OEUVRES de FREDERIC III. tome iv.

General Hastings was reprobated in terms of extreme severity. Mr. Dundas in the course of his speech said, " that the Governor had no right whatever to fancy he was an Alexander or an Aurengzebe, and to prefer frantic military exploits to the improvement of the trade and commerce of the country."

Sir Thomas Rumbold also, who had recently relinquished the government of Madras, was criminated as guilty of gross peculation, embezzlement, and oppression. General Smith, in moving that the report of the Secret Committee be referred to a Committee of the House, took notice that Sir Elijah Impey, his Majesty's Chief Justice in India, had so far degraded his character and office, as to accept of a place under the Company, contrary to the solemn engagements under which he held his appointment*. An Address was in consequence presented to the King, to beseech his Majesty to recall Sir Elijah Impey from India to answer for his conduct. A bill was likewise brought in by the Lord Advocate, Mr. Dundas,

---

* The place thus accepted by Sir Elijah Impey was that of Judge of a Court of Appeal, established at Calcutta under the appellation of the Court of Sudder Dewannee Adawlet, whose jurisdiction extended over the inferior provincial courts of Mofussell Dewannee Adawlet. To this office, held at the pleasure of the Governor and Council, with a salary of 8000l. per annum, Sir Elijah Impey was advanced a few months previous to his memorable expedition to Benares and Oude.

for inflicting certain pains and penalties on Sir Thomas Rumbold, for high crimes and misdemeanors. This bill, which at first excited very great expectation and attention, and which was continued from seffion to seffion in a manner wholly unprecedented, was at laſt ſuffered to ſink into neglect and oblivion.

On the 28th of May 1782, the Houſe of Commons paſſed a ſeries of Reſolutions, in the moſt deciſive terms condemnatory of the whole ſyſtem of Indian politics. The laſt Reſolution imported, " That Warren Haſtings, Eſq. Governor General in Bengal, and William Hornby, Eſq. Preſident of the Council at Bombay, having in ſundry inſtances acted in a manner repugnant to the honor and policy of this nation, and thereby brought great calamities on India, and enormous expences on the Eaſt India Company, it is the duty of the Directors of the ſaid Company to purſue all legal and effectual means for the removal of the ſaid Governor General and Preſident from their ſaid offices, and to recall them to Great Britain." But this Reſolution, though confirmed by the Court of Directors*, the Proprietary refuſed to ratify:

---

* The Resolution of the Court of Directors, paſſed October 1782, was expreſſed in the following terms :—" Resolved, that it is the opinion of this Court, that a ſteady perſeverance in the ſyſtem of conduct ſo frequently enjoined by the Court

of

ratify: and the House of Commons, with the characteristic indecision and inconstancy of a popular assembly, took no subsequent measures to enforce it.

The war in India was still carried on with various success. The valuable settlements of Negapatnam on the Coromandel coast, and Trinquemale in the island of Ceylon, belonging to the Dutch, were captured by the English. On the other hand, Colonel Braithwaite, with a detachment of the Company's troops, was totally routed on the banks of the Coleroon by Tippoo Saib, son of Hyder Ali, assisted by a body of French troops; after which Cuddalore surrendered to the victors.

The operations of the war on the Malabar coast were conducted by General Goddard with a great display of military skill and spirit. Invading the province of Guzzerat, in the year 1780, he reduced the city of Amedabad, its capital; and on the second of April he stormed the camp of the Mahrattas, commanded by Madajee Scindia, whom he totally defeated. Entering into a treaty with the Rana of Gohud, Major Popham, by or-

---

of Directors, cannot be expected from those servants whose ideas of extension of dominion, either by negotiation or conquest, have led them to depart from orders so often enforced; and THEREFORE, that it is expedient to remove Warren Hastings, Esq. from the office of Governor General of Bengal."

der of the General, attacked and carried, in the course of the summer, the strong fortress of Gualior, which was garrisoned by the Mahrattas, though within the territory of the Rana.

Early in 1781 General Goddard sat down before Basseen; and after reducing this important place, he desisted from farther active operations, in consequence of the succors he was under a necessity to send to Sir Eyre Coote. In the province of Malva, Colonel Carnac surprised, April 30, the camp of the enemy, and Madajee Scindia was a second time totally routed. After this the Mahratta Chieftain made secret overtures for a separate peace; and a cessation of hostilities between England and the Mahratta States took place in the month of October 1781. The definitive articles of peace were signed in May following, at Salberg, by Mr. Anderson on the part of the Company, and by Scindia, General and Plenipotentiary, on the part of the Peishwa. By this treaty Basseen, and the other recent acquisitions in the Guzzerat, were restored to the Mahrattas, the island of Salsette only of the late conquests remaining to the English; for, at the *request* of Madajee Scindia, the English consented also to relinquish their claim to the city of Baroach and the contiguous districts. Ragonaut Row was for ever abandoned, and compelled to quit the territories of the Company; and their ally, the Rana of Gohud, who

who appears indeed without scruple to have opposed duplicity to duplicity, was, under pretext of "leaving him to settle his own affairs," virtually delivered up to the mercy of his enemies.— But the most extraordinary article of the treaty was that whereby the Peishwa engages that Hyder Ali Khan shall be made to relinquish, within six months, all such territories belonging to the Company or their allies as he shall have taken possession of since the 9th of the month Ramzan. The fact was, that not only a treaty of peace, but of the strictest alliance and friendship, was now formed by the Governor General Hastings with the Mahratta Court; and a secret project was believed to be already in contemplation for the partition of Hyder's dominions. And thus, notwithstanding the ill success of his former schemes of conquest, no sooner was this "daring pilot" of the State, who "sought the storms" and invoked the tempests, obliged to relinquish one vast and hazardous plan of aggrandizement, than he entered with equal eagerness into another. The Nizam of the Decan and the Rajah of Berar were also parties in this accommodation, for their accession to which they received large pecuniary gratifications.

This pacification with the Mahrattas induced the Presidency of Bengal to risque a bold attempt on the dominions of Hyder Ali on the Malabar side,

side. The kingdoms of Canara and Mysore, both under subjection to that prince, stretch along the western coast of Hindostan, nearly in the latitude of Arcot. The chief city of the former is Bednore, a name changed by its present possessor to Hydernagore. A considerable force, already landed in the kingdom of Mysore, had relieved the city of Tellicherri, a post or factory on that coast belonging to the English, and reduced the neighboring town of Calicut. It was with difficulty, nevertheless, that the English kept their footing in this country, when General Matthews arrived from Bombay with very large reinforcements, and immediately laid siege to the important fortress of Onore, which was carried by storm on the 5th of January 1783. The carnage on this occasion is said to have been terrible; and the indiscriminate seizure of treasure, public and private, there deposited, exhibited, in the most odious light, the rapacity and avarice of the Commander.

At this period the hopes of the English were raised to the highest pitch by the death of Hyder Ali, a name ever memorable in the annals of India. He was succeeded by his son Tippoo Saib, who had already given proofs of valor and ability not unworthy his descent.

From Onore General Matthews proceeded through *the Ghauts*, or the passes of the mountains, to Hydernagore, which surrendered to him without

out refiftance. Here, as at Onore, the General was accufed of combining the meannefs of fraud with the ferocity of violence: and Colonel Macleod, fecond in command, and feveral other officers, retired in difguft from the army. After this Annampore, Carwa, and Mangalore, were fucceffively fubdued; the former by ftorm, with circumftances of fingular barbarity: four hundred beautiful women perifhed in the general maffacre, under the brutal licentioufnefs of the foldiery.

In the mean time Tippoo prepared for the relief of Myfore and Canara; and, leaving a ftrong force to guard his conquefts in the Carnatic, he marched his army acrofs the peninfula with unexpected and unexampled expedition, and arrived in the vicinity of Hydernagore in the month of April 1783. By a feries of excellent military manœuvres he made himfelf mafter of the Ghauts in the rear of General Matthews, by which means all communication with the fea was entirely cut off. The force of General Matthews being now centred in Hydernagore, this city was invefted by Tippoo with a vaft army, computed at 150,000 men, covering the hills on every fide as far as the eye could reach. The Englifh, reduced to extremity, were foon obliged to furrender on capitulation, by the terms of which the public treafure was reftored to the Sultan; but not a rupee being found in the fortrefs, General Matthews was

was charged by the conqueror with grofs collufion and a direct infraction of the treaty; and being conducted in chains to Seringapatam, the capital of Myfore, he was thrown into a dungeon, and, with the greater part of his officers, perifhed miferably in confinement under various devices of torture.

Notwithftanding the departure of Tippoo from the Carnatic, the Prefidency of Madras had ftill to cope with fuperior force. Although the utmoft exertions of Sir Eyre Coote had not been wanting, no decifive advantage had been gained in the laft campaign with Hyder; and the ill ftate of health of this able commander obliged him to refign the army into the hands of General Stuart, and to retire at the conclufion of the year 1783 to Bengal. Early in the enfuing fpring, believing himfelf fomewhat recovered, he returned to Madras in order to refume his command; but two days only after his arrival, he expired in an advanced age, having acquired in more than thirty years military fervice in India a reputation, the luftre of which could be deemed fcarcely inferior to that of his predeceffor, Lord Clive. The important fettlement of Trinquemale was retaken by M. Suffrein in the courfe of the laft fummer, and a very large reinforcement of French troops landed in the Carnatic under M. de Buffi. Notwithftanding all oppofition, General Stuart invefted vested Cuddalore, and made confiderable progrefs in the fiege, when an exprefs arrived with the intelligence of a treaty of peace having been concluded between the Belligerent Powers, on which an immediate ceffation of hoftilities took place.

After the conqueft of Hydernagore, and the recapture of the inland country by Tippoo, he laid fiege to Mangalore, the principal place yet remaining in the hands of the Englifh. An obftinate refiftance was made by the garrifon; but a practicable breach being at length effected, a general affault was in contemplation, when news arrived of the pacification which had taken place in Europe; and the French troops and engineers in his fervice informed him, that they muft immediately withdraw their affiftance. Tippoo, after much paffionate expoftulation, therefore affented to an armiftice, in a few days after which event Colonel Macleod arrived with powerful reinforcements from Bombay. A negotiation was immediately commenced for a definitive peace. This was accelerated by a declaration which the Sultan received from the Peifhwa of the Mahrattas, that if Tippoo did not confent to an immediate evacuation of the Carnatic, he would unite with the Englifh againft him.

During the continuance of the truce and the negotiation, the *Bibby*, or Princefs of Cannanore, a diftrict depending on the kingdom of Canara,
having

having seized some boats with sepoys belonging to the garrison of Mangalore, accidentally forced by stress of weather on her coast, Colonel Macleod attacked and stormed the fortress of Cannanore, making the Princess herself prisoner. Although loud complaints were made by Tippoo of this violation of the armistice, it does not appear much to have retarded the negotiation, the articles of peace being signed March 11th, 1784, on the terms of mutual restitution, and a renunciation on the part of the Sultan of his claim to the sovereignty of the Carnatic. This claim, there is every reason to believe, would never have been enforced, or perhaps advanced, if the rash and violent conduct of the English Government respecting the Mahrattas had not encouraged and incited the attempt. To this purpose Mr. Whitehill, President of Madras, in his exculpatory minute of November 1780, says, " The offensive line of conduct adopted against the Mahrattas threw them, i. e. the Governor and Council of Bengal, into a scene of action so extensive and so full of difficulty, that neither their forces nor their revenues were capable of bearing them through with any possibility of success. Had the experience of former times been called in to their aid, they would have seen that Aurengzebe, one of the most formidable monarchs that ever sat upon the throne of Dehli, was, after a twenty years

years struggle, with all the power and riches of Hindoftan, obliged to abandon a fimilar attempt. The truth is, the Mahratta war has been the real fource of all the mifchief that hath befallen the Carnatic. Had peace exifted in that quarter with the Englifh, Hyder Ali Khan would never have ventured from his own dominions.—He faw the extremity to which we were reduced, and feized the occafion to diftrefs us where he knew we were moft vulnerable."

But the conduct of Mr. Haftings, fubfequent to the reftoration of peace in India, is perhaps the moft extraordinary, certainly the moft myfterious part of his dark and inextricable policy. The peace concluded with the Mahrattas, it has been already remarked, was followed by an alliance of the moft ftrict and confidential kind. And from that period it feemed to be the great and favorite object of the Englifh Governor General, to confirm and aggrandize the power of that State, which he had ever before affected to confider as moft formidable and adverfe to the Englifh interefts; and whom he had even ftyled " the NATURAL ENEMIES of the Company."

In the month of March 1783, Mr. Haftings difpatched, by no authentic act, but as his own fecret agent, Major Browne to the Court of Dehli, in order to make propofals to the Emperor, Shah Allum,

Allum, to enter into engagements with the Company and the Mahratta Government, for the accomplishment of certain defigns in favor of the Emperor, but of a very hoftile nature to feveral powers of the continent then in amity with the Company. And Major Browne was commiffioned to offer to the Mogul, to provide for the entire expence of any troops the Emperor might require; which propofal was accepted with every fymptom of eagernefs and fatisfaction. And the negotiation being fufficiently advanced, Mr. Haftings openly brought forward a propofition in Council, October 5, 1783, to affift the Mogul with a military force: and at a fubfequent meeting of the Board, he laid before them a letter from Major Browne, dated Dehli, December 30, 1783, containing, amidft much mifcellaneous matter, the following extraordinary paffages:—" The bufinefs of affifting the SHAH can and muft now go on, if we wifh to be fecure in India, and regarded as a nation. We have offered, the Shah has accepted the offer of affiftance.——We have annexed conditions, the Shah has approved of them."

The project thus unexpectedly and forcibly obtruded on the Board by Mr. Haftings, was, however, very ill received by his colleagues, Mr. Wheeler and Mr. Stables, who ftrongly remonftrated againft involving the Company in new wars

wars and dangerous foreign connections. But Mr. Hastings was not a man to be discouraged by trivial obstacles.

Early in the following year, 1784, Mr. Hastings made a progress to the city of Lucknow, and there had an interview with the Prince Mirza Jehander Shah, eldest son of the Mogul, and who, as the Governor General in his public letter says, " had long held the principal part in the administration of the King his father." From Mr. Hastings's account of this interview, which he represents as wholly unexpected and fortuitous, the Prince having left the Court of Dehli without even the knowledge of the Emperor, it appears that urgent solicitations were made by the heir of the Mogul Empire to the English Governor, for aid and assistance to raise the KING, his father, from that state of degradation and insignificance into which he had fallen: intimating his readiness even to go in person to England, to represent the distresses of the Emperor of Hindostan, in the hope of obtaining relief. Mr. Hastings in reply informed the Prince, " that the English nation, just emerged from a state of universal warfare, required repose, and would be alarmed at any movement of which it could not immediately see the issue or the progress, but which might eventually create new hostilities; that as to himself, he could not engage, *if he chose it*, in a business of this nature,
without

without the concurrence of his colleagues in office, who he believed would be averse to it; that he would, however, represent his situation to the joint members of his own Government, and wait their determination. In the mean time he advised him to make advances to Madajee Scindia, as the effective head of the Mahratta State, and who was in intimate union and sworn connection with the English."

In his subsequent dispatches to the Council at Calcutta, Mr. Hastings requests to be invested with discretionary powers of acting in relation to the Court of Dehli, under a vague promise of " not *proceeding* against their sense." The Council, in reply, not only refused to grant any such powers, but exhorted him " most sedulously and cautiously to avoid, in his correspondence with the different potentates of India, whatever might commit, or be strained into an *interpretation* of committing, the Company as to their army or treasure—observing, that the Company's orders are positive against their interference in the objects of dispute between the *Country Powers*." But this injunction the sophistical subtlety of Mr. Hastings was at no loss how to evade; for, in his letter of June 1784, to the Court of Directors, he says, " The faction which now surrounds the THRONE, is widely different from the idea which your commands are intended to convey by the expressions to which
you

you have generally applied them, of 'Country Powers,' to which that of permanency is a necessary adjunct, and which may be more properly compared to a splendid bubble, which the slightest breath of opposition may dissipate, with every trace of its existence—That if the Mogul's authority is suffered to receive its final extinction, it is impossible to foresee what power may arise out of its ruins, or what events may be linked in the same chain of revolution with it.—Your interests *may* suffer by it; your reputation certainly *will*, as his right to our assistance has been constantly acknowledged; more especially as, by the movements which the influence of our Government by too near an approach has excited, it has unfortunately become the efficient instrument of a great portion of the King's present distresses and dangers."

According to this most curious logic, the Company's orders, not to interpose in the disputes of "the Country Powers," were not violated by entering into a war for the re-establishment of the authority of the Mogul; *because*, the Imperial Crown of Hindostan being reduced to a "splendid bubble," the Emperor could not now be reckoned amongst the Country Powers. But either recollecting or forgetting himself, he immediately offers another argument directly the reverse of the former, viz. " that the authority of the Mogul, even in its prefent ftate, was fo confiderable that, if it was fuffered to be annihilated, great danger might arife to the Company's interefts, from the power which fhould be eftablifhed on its ruins:" And laftly he urges, " that the Englifh Company are bound in equity and juftice to affift in raifing the throne of the Mogul to its former ftate of exaltation, becaufe they have been the efficient inftrument of its prefent diftrefs and degradation:" alluding no doubt to the deprivation of his tribute and the feizure of his demefne; in lieu of which they were now bound *in honor* to enable him to feize upon the property of others; and his Imperial Majefty would, no doubt, deem himfelf bound in return to reward his honorable allies, the Company, with a reafonable fhare of the plunder.

On the firft advice of the flight of the Prince from Dehli, Mr. Haftings wrote to the Mahratta Chief, Madajee Scindia, to apprize him of this event, and profeffing *himfelf unprepared*, to afk his advice how to act in this emergency: and certain confidential agents from the Mahratta Chief, repairing to Lucknow, held frequent and fecret conferences with the Governor, the purport of which was never communicated to the Board at Calcutta.

The whole of this tiffue of cabals and intrigues terminated, however, very unexpectedly, in the
fudden

sudden invasion of the Emperor's territories by the Mahrattas, who made themselves masters of Dehli; and the Emperor, being a second time prisoner in their hands, was obliged to declare the Head of the Mahratta State to be Vicegerent of the Mogul Empire; in which capacity great and indefinite claims of superiority were advanced on the part of the Peishwa, and a specific claim set up to the tribute due to the Emperor from Bengal.

Far from being alarmed at this addition to the Mahratta power, Mr. Hastings declared, " that such was the attachment of Scindia to the English, that, while he lives, every accession of territory obtained by him will be an advantage to this Government." Upon which it has been authoritatively remarked, " That if this were true respecting the personal disposition of Scindia, yet does it not lessen the criminality of establishing a power, which must survive the man to whom a power more than personal was given *."

What is perhaps the most extraordinary circumstance in these extraordinary transactions, Mr. Hastings, embracing the opportunity when the Mahrattas were assembled in great force upon the frontiers of the Vizieriate of Oude, entered into an AGREEMENT with the Vizier, after seven years

* Vide Articles of Impeachment exhibited against Warren Hastings, Esq.

useless retention of them at a ruinous expence, to withdraw a very great proportion of the British troops in this moment of danger from the province; asserting, in contradiction to the whole tenor of his conduct and former declarations, " that this government has not any right to force defence with its maintenance upon the Nabob." The Council refusing in present circumstances to ratify this *agreement*, Mr. Hastings moved, in his minute of December 4, 1784, " that if, contrary to his opinion, the said troops should not be reduced, they should be employed under the Prince Mirza Jehander Shah (now notoriously under the absolute control of the Mahrattas) to assist in carrying on a war against the nation called the SEIKS, the antient enemies of the Mahratta State; a warlike people, possessing an extensive territory to the north-west of India, on the confines of Tartary. I feel," says he, " the sense of an obligation imposed upon me, by the supposition I have made, to state a mode of rendering the detachment of use in its prescribed station, and of affording the appearance of a cause for its detention."

Mr. Hastings indeed admitted, that there was no *present danger* to the Company's possessions from this remote and almost unknown people; but he declared, " that their military and enthusiastic spirit, the hardiness of their natural constitution, the dangers which *might* arise from them in some future

ture time, if they *should ever happen* to be united under one head, were reasons in favor of this war; and he predicted great danger from them, at no very distant period, if they be permitted to grow into maturity without interruption. Acknowledging that the urgent solicitations of the Prince had their weight with him, he professed nevertheless that a stronger impulse, arising from the hope of blasting the growth of a generation whose strength *might* become fatal to our own, pleaded in his mind for supporting his wishes."

The Council, unable to explore the dark and unfathomable abyss of the Governor's politics, and astonished, doubtless, at an inconsistency so gross and flagrant as that of warring against a power *lest it should become formidable*, in favor of a power *already formidable*, negatived the proposition, and the peace of India was for this time happily preserved.

The Governor, perceiving his influence in the Council lost, knowing his reputation at home to be greatly in the wane, and fearing most probably a disgraceful dismission, now thought it expedient to RESIGN the GOVERNMENT. On his arrival in England he was, after a long previous investigation of his numerous delinquencies, most deservedly IMPEACHED at the Bar of the House of Lords, by the Commons of Great Britain, of HIGH CRIMES

CRIMES and MISDEMEANORS in the execution of his office.

The political character of Mr. Hastings, on a cool and impartial review of his conduct, so forcibly impresses itself upon the mind, that it can derive little aid from any adventitious illustration. Daring in the conception, and ardent in the prosecution of his designs; fertile in resources, and relying with confidence and even with pride on the strength of his own genius, his character acquired a certain stamp of dignity and superiority from the inflexibility of his temper, and the apparent force of his own conviction respecting the rectitude and propriety of his measures: to which must be added, that in his public dispatches he possessed the dangerous art of giving plausibility to the most absurd and pernicious measures by artful and imposing glosses, branching out sometimes into studied ambiguities, sometimes into bold assumptions, under a perpetual external show of ingenuousness, liberality, and candor.

The numerous individuals returning in rapid succession from India, whom Mr. Hastings had engaged in his interest by various obligations, contributed also to enhance his reputation, by the high eulogiums which they almost universally bestowed upon his conduct; and in which, dazzled by the brilliant exterior of the Governor's administration,

niftration, and unequal to the clear comprehenfion of an extenfive and complex fyftem, they were probably for the moft part very fincere. The truth however is, that this man, for thirteen years the fcourge of the Eaft, and whom ignorance and folly have prepofteroufly ranked with the SULLYS and the CHATHAMS of the Weft, has never been, and never can become, the theme of difcerning and rational panegyric. Not to fpeak of his total and flagrant difregard of the fole legitimate end and object of government, the happinefs of the governed, his conduct will be found, in almoft all its parts, and in the choice and profecution of his own purpofes, abfurd, perplexed, capricious and inconfequent. His courfe was one perpetual deviation from the ftraight and luminous path of political and moral rectitude; and his general reputation was fupported merely by his habitual vigor of mind and perfonal courage, which were in him intimately blended, and feemed to rife on fome occafions even to the femblance of magnanimity. His exertions in the laft war for the prefervation of the Carnatic, which he had fo wantonly and rafhly endangered, were generally and juftly fpoken of as highly meritorious; but even in this moft fplendid and boafted part of his political conduct, he could challenge only the praife of a madman, who fires a houfe and then labors strenuously to extinguish the flames.

The administration of Mr. Hastings has been truly said, in the glowing expressions of eloquence *, " to exhibit a medley of meanness and outrage, of duplicity and depredation, of prodigality and oppression, of the most callous cruelty contrasted with the hollow affectation of liberality and good faith. The sordid system of commercial policy, to which all the arrangements and regulations of the Company are ultimately to be traced, was under his government carried to its utmost extent.—Thus have nations been extirpated for a sum of money, whole tracts of country laid waste to furnish an investment, princes expelled for the balance of an account, and a bloody sceptre wielded in one hand, in order to replenish the empty purse of mercantile mendicancy displayed in the other."

The concessions of Mr. Hastings himself are indeed occasionally very large and ample; for his views seldom seem to have extended beyond the precise object which he wished at the moment to compass. The ruinous effects of British perfidy and British barbarity in India, are very strongly and distinctly stated in his letters, dispatches, and

* Vide Sheridan's speech on the Begum charge, in the 14th article of impeachment.

minutes

minutes of Council. In his minute of September 29, 1783, he says, "By a sacred and undeviating observance of every principle of public faith, the British dominion might have by this time acquired the means of its extension, through a virtual submission to its authority, to every region of Hindostan and Decan.—But the Powers of India ALL dread the connection.—The subjection of Bengal, the usurpations in the Carnatic, the licentious violations of the treaty with the Nizam, the effects of our connections with the Vizier, stand as TERRIBLE PRECEDENTS against us." Yet as to himself, the *primum mobile* of the whole system, he declares in his famous Minutes of Defence, "that he had the conscious satisfaction to see all his measures terminate in their designed objects; that his political conduct was invariably regulated by truth, justice, and good faith; and that he resigned his charge in a state of established peace and security, with all the sources of its abundance unimpaired, and even improved." To reconcile these apparent incongruities, we are required, therefore, by a species of faith which can work miracles, to believe that there existed in India crimes without a criminal, oppressions without an oppressor, and tyranny without a tyrant *. In fine,

* If it be possible yet to entertain any shadow of doubt respecting the effects of the general policy adopted by the English Govern-

fine, when we confider with ferious attention the origin and progrefs of the British Government in India, the friendfhip and generofity with which the Englifh nation was received and permitted to form eftablifhments in that country, the black and bafe ingratitude with which thofe obligations were requited, and the unexampled, unprovoked, and unatoned exceffes which have been perpetrated on the princes and inhabitants of Hindoftan, is it the weaknefs of fuperftition merely, to tremble at the fecret apprehenfion that fome mighty vengeance is yet in ftore for this king-

Government in India, it muft affuredly vanifh, when we hear the decifion of Lord Cornwallis, the noble fucceffor of Mr. Haftings, who, in his difpatch of Auguft 2, 1789, fays, " Independent of all other confiderations, I can affure you that it will be of the utmoft importance for promoting the folid interefts of the Company, that the principal land-holders and traders in the interior parts of the country fhould be RESTORED to fuch circumftances as to enable them to fupport their families with *decency*. —I am forry to be *obliged* to fay, that agriculture and internal commerce have for many years been gradually declining; and that at prefent, excepting the clafs of Shroffs and Banians, who refide almoft entirely in great towns, the inhabitants of thefe provinces were advancing haftily to a general ftate of poverty and wretchednefs. In this defcription I muft even include ALMOST EVERY ZEMINDAR in the Company's territories."—And in his minute of Council, dated September 18, 1789, his Lordfhip afferts, and the affertion is furely enough to ftrike us with amazement and horror, " That ONE THIRD of the Company's territory is now a JUNGLE inhabited by WILD BEASTS.".

dom;

dom; and to apply to BRITAIN the sublime and terrible prophetic denunciations originally uttered against the proud, corrupt, and tyrannic states of antiquity? "THUS saith the LORD GOD—Behold I am against thee—I will stretch out mine hand against thee, and I will make thee most desolate. I will lay thy cities waste, and thou shalt be desolate, and thou shalt know that I am the LORD.— Because thou hast had a perpetual hatred, and hast shed the blood of this people by the force of the sword; because thou hast said, These nations and these countries shall be mine, and we will possess them; therefore, as I live, saith the LORD GOD, I will even do according to thine anger, and according to thine envy, which thou hast used out of thine hatred against them—and thou shalt know that I am the LORD, and that I have heard all thy blasphemies which thou hast spoken, saying, They are laid desolate, they are given us to consume.—I have heard them; therefore, when the whole earth rejoiceth, I will make THEE desolate, and they shall know that I am the LORD."

We are now to revert from this long but necessary and important digression, to the regular narrative of events in England.

On the 18th of July 1781, the session was closed by a speech, in which his Majesty observed, "that the great efforts made by the nation, to surmount the difficulties of the present arduous and

and complicated war, must convince the world that the antient spirit of the British nation was not abated or diminished; and he was resolved to accept of no terms or conditions of peace, than such as might consist with the honor and dignity of his crown, and the permanent interests and security of his people."

The military history of the present year was marked, in its commencement, by a spirited though abortive attempt on the part of the French, to capture the island of Jersey by a *coup-de-main*.— Early on the 16th of January 1781, a landing was effected by the Baron de Rullecourt, at the head of about 800 men, at the Bank du Violet; and to the astonishment of the inhabitants, when the day began to dawn, the market-place of St. Helier was found occupied by French troops. The Governor's house being entirely surrounded, he was compelled to surrender himself prisoner, and was so far intimidated as even to sign articles of capitulation. But when Elizabeth-Castle was summoned, Captain Aylward, the commander, far from paying the least regard to the acts of the Governor in his present state of durance, fired upon the French and obliged them to retreat; and Major Pierson, a young and gallant officer, second in command, having assembled the regular troops and militia of the island on the heights near the town, attacked the enemy with the greatest

reso-

resolution and vigor. Baron Rullecourt being at the commencement of the action mortally wounded, the French troops in lefs than half an hour laid down their arms, and furrendered themfelves prifoners of war. Unfortunately almoft the laft fhot fired previous to the furrender proved fatal to Major Pierfon, in whofe conduct, during the whole of this tranfaction, difcretion and valor had been equally confpicuous.

Early intelligence of the rupture with Holland having been tranfmitted to the Weft Indies, Admiral Rodney and Gen. Vaughan appeared, February 1781, with a very confiderable naval and military force before the ifland of St. Euftatia, that famous depofit of wealth and mart of traffic. So little apprehenfive were the inhabitants of this event, that it was with difficulty they were brought to give credit to the fummons. Being totally deftitute of the means of refiftance, they were compelled to furrender at difcretion. But fo far were the Britifh commanders from imitating the noble example of lenity and policy fet by the Marquis de Bouillé, that, with a rigor unknown and unheard-of amongft civilized nations, the immenfe property found on the ifland was declared to be confifcated, on pretence of the affiftance afforded by the inhabitants to the Americans; as if the inhabitants of Euftatia were amenable to the laws of Great Britain. The ftores and merchandize, eftimated at

three

three millions sterling, were publicly sold for about one fourth of their real value; and the world saw with astonishment British naval and military officers, of the highest rank and reputation, degraded by a kind of harlequin metamorphosis into salesmen and auctioneers. A prodigious number of trading vessels lying in the harbour also became the property of the victors, with two men of war, one of which was a flag-ship commanded by Admiral Count Byland.

Nearly at the same time the Dutch settlements of Demerary, Berbicia and Issequibo, on the Southern Main, also submitted without resistance to the arms of his Britannic Majesty. Here, however, the same indiscriminate confiscation of private property did not take place. But the proceedings at St. Eustatia excited universal consternation; and a memorial was presented to Admiral Rodney and General Vaughan, by the hands of Mr. Glanville, his Majesty's Solicitor General for St. Christopher's, strongly representing, " that if by the fate of war the British West India islands should fall into the hands of an enraged enemy, the conduct at St. Eustatia would be a pretext for them to retaliate; that the conquerors of all civilized countries had avoided the invasion of private property; that the generosity of the enemy had been very conspicuous; and even in the case of Grenada, which had been taken by storm, the rights

rights of individuals had been held sacred; that Euſtatia was a free port, and the rich and various commodities found there were ſo far from being the ſole property of the Dutch, that a great proportion of them belonged to Britiſh ſubjects; and that, previous to the declaration of war, the trade to Euſtatia was ſtrictly legal, and the officers of his Majeſty's cuſtoms cleared out veſſels from all the ports of Great Britain and Ireland for this iſland. And not merely the legality, but the propriety of this trade, was confirmed by the conduct of his Majeſty's naval officers in thoſe ſeas; for if the King's enemies were ſupplied by the trade of his ſubjects through Euſtatia, they were likewiſe ſupplied, through the ſame channel, by the ſale of the prizes captured by his Majeſty's ſhips of war."—The Admiral haughtily replied to Mr. Glanville, "that he had no LEISURE to peruſe the memorial; but that the iſland of Euſtatia was Dutch, every thing in it was Dutch, every thing was under the protection of the Dutch flag, and as Dutch it ſhould be treated."

While the Britiſh arms were thus ignobly employed, the French fleet under Court de Graſſe, after a partial engagement with Admiral Hood, who in the abſence of Sir George Rodney commanded the Engliſh fleet, ſteered its courſe to the iſland of Tobago, on which M. de Bouillé, with a conſiderable land force, made an immediate deſcent.

scent.. Admiral Rodney, on receiving intelligence of this attack, detached a squadron for the relief of the island, which finding the French in great force was obliged to return; and the Admiral, accompanied by General Vaughan, now sailed in person with the whole fleet for Tobago, off the coast of which he arrived the 4th of June, but had the mortification to learn that the island had surrendered on the second.

At the latter end of the year the island of Eustatia was lost in a manner not less disgraceful than that by which it had been gained. M. de Bouillé, receiving certain intelligence of the habitual negligence of the garrison, landed by night about four hundred troops, part of a much larger force which the tempestuousness of the weather had separated, in a cove at the back of the island. This spirited officer, confiding in his fortune, advanced with his troops, as soon as day-light appeared, to the citadel, which they immediately stormed, and carried with little difficulty; and the surprise being very complete, near seven hundred men, with Colonel Cockbourne their commander, were, by a most humiliating necessity, constrained to surrender themselves prisoners of war. The generosity of M. de Bouillé was on this occasion, as on every other, no less conspicuous than his gallantry, forming a contrast with the conduct of the late captors, very flattering to the feelings

of

of his countrymen. Restitution, so far as circumstances would permit, was immediately made to those unfortunate individuals who had been stripped and plundered of their property; and a declaration published, that the forces of his Most Christian Majesty defended the island only till relieved by the troops of their High Mightinesses.

On the continent of America, the war in the central colonies, though conducted by the opposing Commanders in Chief, seemed to languish, and affords scarcely any incident worthy of historic regard. Early in the present year it happened that the whole Pennsylvania line in the continental army, from causes of dissatisfaction not well ascertained, at once revolted; and, collecting the artillery, stores, &c. belonging to them, moved in an entire body out of the camp. General Clinton, anxious to improve to the utmost this seeming advantage, immediately passed over to Staten Island with a large body of forces, and dispatched messengers to the revolters with almost unlimited offers of pay, pardon, and protection. These propositions were not only rejected with disdain, but the messengers were actually delivered up by them to Congress; and having obtained a promise of the redress of grievances, they soon returned to their duty.

An expedition under the conduct of General Arnold and General Philips was soon after this undertaken into Virginia, where they signalized themselves by laying waste the country, and did much damage to the Americans by the destruction of an immense quantity of provisions, merchandize, and stores depofited in different parts; and a permanent station was established at Portsmouth in order to co-operate with Lord Cornwallis, whose transactions to the southward were still carried on with spirit and success. A plan having been formed between the French and American Commanders, Count Rochambeau and General Washington, to invest the post occupied by General Arnold, a warm engagement took place in the month of March between Admiral Arbuthnot and a French squadron under M. Destouches, at the entrance of the Chesapeak, in which the former obtained the advantage, and was left master of the navigation of the bay: and in his dispatches to the Admiralty, the Naval Commander writes, " The Count Rochambeau must feek another opportunity of vifiting Virginia—the plan of the REBEL campaign is entirely difconcerted." But the event of the campaign ill correfponded with the confidence of this prediction.

At the conclufion of the year 1780, General Gates, whose recent difafters had obliterated the memory of his former fucceffes, was superfeded in his command by General Green; a man who, in military talents, appears to have been inferior to no officer employed in the fervice of the American

States

States during this war. Early in the month of January 1781, Lord Cornwallis began his march to North Carolina, General Green retiring at his approach beyond the Pedee, having previoufly detached Colonel Morgan at the head of the light troops to the weftward of the Wateree, to penetrate into South Carolina and watch the motions of the Englifh at Wynnefborough and Camden. Lord Cornwallis, not choofing to leave fo confiderable a corps in his rear, ordered Colonel Tarleton at the head of a fuperior force, and who had been hitherto uniformly fuccefsful in all his enterprifes, to drive Morgan from his ftation.

On the 17th of January the Americans were difcovered pofted at a place called the Cowpens, near an open wood, and drawn up in two lines; the firft of which confifted of militia only, the fecond of continental infantry and Virginia riflemen; and a chofen body of cavalry was pofted as a *corps de referve* at fome diftance in the rear. Colonel Tarleton led on the attack with his ufual impetuofity; and the American militia, as Colonel Morgan had forefeen, gave way on all quarters. The Britifh then advanced, fecure of victory, to the attack of the fecond line; and the continentals, after an obftinate conflict, retreated towards the cavalry. In the mean time the militia had formed again, agreeably to their previous orders, on the right of the continentals; and the American *corps de reserve*, perceiving the British troops disordered in the pursuit, now came forward to the attack—the militia and continentals at the same time vigorously charging with fixed bayonets. Nothing could exceed the astonishment of the British troops at these unexpected charges. The advanced corps immediately fell back, and communicated a general confusion and panic, which all the efforts of Colonel Tarleton could not remedy. Such was the precipitate flight of the cavalry, that the officers, in attempting to rally their men, were overborne and carried away with the torrent; and the greatest part of the infantry, perceiving themselves abandoned, threw down their arms and begged for quarter. The cannon, colors, and baggage waggons, with more than 700 prisoners, fell into the hands of the victors. Colonel Morgan received, as he well deserved, the thanks of the Congress accompanied with a gold medal for this important victory, which left his antagonist destitute of all consolation, excepting that arising from the consciousness of his own gallant personal exertions; and Colonel Tarleton might exclaim in the language of Francis I. after the fatal defeat of Pavia, " All is lost except our honor !"

Instead of being overwhelmed with their repeated disasters, the Americans seemed to rise with fresh courage from each misfortune. The affair of Cowpens, which so soon followed the defeat of
Major

Major Ferguſon, might have ſufficed to deter an officer leſs enterpriſing than Lord Cornwallis from proſecuting his bold and hazardous projects. His Lordſhip, who in his public diſpatches ſtyled the defeat of Tarleton an unexpected and ſevere blow, in the hope of recovering the priſoners captured at the Cowpens, and intercepting the victorious Americans, immediately marched with the greater part of his army by rapid movements in purſuit of Colonel Morgan. That officer had croſſed the Catawba a few hours only before the arrival of Lord Cornwallis on its ſouthern banks, where, by heavy rains, he was detained two or three days.

On the 1ſt of February, however, the paſſage was found practicable; but Colonel Morgan had by this time croſſed the Yadkin, and effected his junction with General Green, who, on the 5th, wrote confidentially to a military correſpondent, General Huger, that he was preparing to receive the enemy's attack. "It is," ſays he, " not improbable, from Lord Cornwallis's puſhing diſpoſition and the contempt he has for our army, that he may precipitate himſelf into ſome capital misfortune." At length the whole American army, after croſſing the Dan into Virginia, ſuddenly returned into the province of North Carolina; and with powerful reinforcements took (March 14) a ſtrong poſition near Guildford Court-Houſe. At day-break, on the 5th, Lord Cornwallis advanced to the attack of the Americans, who were formed in three lines ready to receive him. Through the misbehavior of the North Carolina militia, who were posted in front, the British troops soon forced their way to the second line composed of Virginians, who made a much better defence, and, when at length thrown into disorder, effected a good retreat. The continental troops, who formed the third line, were last engaged; and here the contest was long and severe, but the British ultimately carried their point by superiority of numbers and discipline. The Maryland brigade being broke, an attempt was made to turn the flank of the Americans, and to surround the continental troops; on which General Green drew off the army, and left the field of battle, with the artillery consisting of four field pieces, to the enemy. The Americans retired in good order, and took post behind a river three miles only from the scene of action.

This was a victory very different from that of Camden, and dearly purchased on the part of the English by the loss of about 600 veteran troops. Instead of pursuing his advantage, his Lordship found himself under the necessity, in order to procure the requisite supplies for his army, to direct his march towards Wilmington, situated near the mouth

mouth of Cape-Fear river, a post already occupied by a detachment of British troops, where he arrived on the 7th of April.

General Green, perceiving Lord Cornwallis reduced to a state of reluctant inaction, immediately, by a bold and decisive manœuvre, directed his march to the southward, and unexpectedly attacked the important post of Camden. This was gallantly maintained by Lord Rawdon; but the surrounding stations of Fort-Motte, Orangeburg, Congarees, and Augusta, being successively forced, his Lordship was compelled to evacuate Camden, and retire to the south of the Santee. General Green then laid close siege to the town or township of Ninety-six, which was considered as commanding the whole of the back country; and on the approach of Lord Rawdon, who had recently received great reinforcements from England, attempted to storm the garrison; but was repulsed with loss, and retired with his army behind the Saluda. Being advised by divers of his officers, on this misfortune, to retreat back to Virginia, he replied with true military enthusiasm, " I will recover the country, or die in the attempt." Thus, in situations where feeble minds droop and languish, the ardor of genius burns with redoubled lustre. No sooner was the British army divided and weakened by the several detachments necessary to occupy their former posts, than General Green again crossed

crossed the Saluda in force. Lord Rawdon, surprised and unprepared for action, retired to Orangeburg; and the important post of Ninety-six, so gallantly defended by Colonel Cruger, was now evacuated. The garrison joining Lord Rawdon, with other troops drawn from the advanced posts, General Green took a strong position on the high hills of Santee, whence he detached different parties to intercept the convoys and beat up the quarters of the English between Orangeburg and Charlestown.

The British, now under the command of Colonel Stuart, having advanced to the point of junction between the Wateree and Congaree, in order to cover the country to the south and south-east of those rivers, General Green passed the Congaree with a view to inclose the Brititish army in its present insulated situation, or compel them to retreat towards Charlestown. Colonel Stuart immediately fell back forty miles, to a place called Eutaw Springs, where he took an advantageous position, his right extending to the Eutaw, and his left to a rising ground which was occupied by a *corps de reserve*. General Green, with the American army, advanced, September 8, 1781, to the attack with the greatest resolution. The Virginian and Maryland continentals charged the left wing of the British with trailed arms through a heavy cannonade and shower of musquetry, and bore down all before them. The American cavalry, at the same time,

turned

turned the left flank of the British, and attacked them in the rear. The whole army gave way in great confusion; but in their retreat, gaining an open field, they were, with much address, rallied by Colonel Stuart, and formed again under protection of an effective and well-directed fire from a large and moated house which served them in the stead of a redoubt; and from whence the Americans, after repeated efforts, were not able to dislodge them. And the right wing of the British pressing on the left flank of the Americans, General Green thought proper to order a retreat, leaving four pieces of artillery in the hands of the British, two of which had been taken by the Americans in the early part of the engagement. The English were in no condition to pursue, and General Green carried off with him all his wounded and several hundred prisoners also. About five-hundred men were killed and wounded on the part of the British, by the account of Colonel Stuart, in this well-contested battle, in which the officers on each side fought hand to hand, and sword to sword. The loss of the Americans in all these respects was much inferior; but as Colonel Stuart was left in possession of the field and several pieces of cannon, he claimed, agreeably to military etiquette, the honor of the victory; but he might well exclaim with the Monarch of Epirus, " Such another victory, and I am undone!"

In

In the evening of the next day, he abandoned the Eutaw and moved towards Charleftown, after deftroying a great part of his ftores; leaving behind him many of his wounded, and about a thoufand ftand of arms. This engagement was decifive of the fate of the war in the fouthern colonies—the Britifh not being able from this time to appear in the open field, and fcarcely could they maintain their pofts in the vicinity of Charlestown and Savannah; and in the courfe of the next year thofe towns were finally evacuated.

Lord Cornwallis, to whofe operations it is now neceffary to revert, on the march of General Green's army to the fouthward, found himfelf reduced to a perplexing dilemma—either to abandon the Carolinas to their fate, or facrifice his hopes of future conquefts, and entirely difappoint the high and fanguine expectations, which he knew to be formed in England, of the refult of the prefent campaign. His pride at length overbalancing his prudence, he determined to profecute his march to Virginia.

The Roanoke, the Meherrin, and the Nottaway rivers were fucceffively croffed by the Britifh army with trifling oppofition, and on the 20th of May his Lordfhip arrived at Peterfburg, where he was joined by the powerful detachment recently conducted thither by Generals Arnold and Philips. The force under his Lordfhip's command was now very

very formidable; and the Marquis de la Fayette, who was at the head of the troops collected for the defence of the province, was compelled to keep a guarded distance, and conducted himself with so much judgment, that no confiderable advantage could be obtained againſt him. From Peterſburg Lord Cornwallis advanced to James River, which he croſſed at Weſt Town; and thence marching through Hanover County, croſſed the South Anna or Pamunky River, whence, by a rapid movement, Colonel Tarleton had nearly ſurpriſed the Aſſembly of Virginia now ſitting at Charlotte-ville.

Various expeditions were undertaken to different parts of the province with uniform ſucceſs; and Lord Cornwallis, by a well-concerted manœuvre, having taken a poſition between the American army and its grand *depôt* of ſtores at Albemarle Court-Houſe, could not avoid exulting in his ſuperiority. Knowing that the Marquis de la Fayette was on his march to prevent that important capture, and believing that he could not make his approach but with great diſadvantage and hazard, he in an unguarded moment exclaimed, " The boy cannot eſcape me!" But the Marquis had the addreſs to extricate himſelf from this difficulty, by opening in the night a nearer and long diſuſed road to the Court-Houſe: and the next day, to the ſurpriſe of Lord Cornwallis,

he

he had taken a pofition which effectually covered it from attack.

Lord Cornwallis, finding his plan fruftrated, proceeded to Williamſburg, the capital of the province, which he took poffeffion of, June 26th, without oppofition. Here he received advices from Sir Henry Clinton, which informed him that the Commander in Chief, conceiving New York to be in danger from the united forces of the French and Americans, defired the troops under General Arnold, which he had detached to Virginia, to be returned. This was the beginning of difafters. With this requifition Lord Cornwallis was compelled, however reluctantly, to comply. Knowing that his adverfary had been lately reinforced by a ftrong body of troops under General Wayne, he did not think his prefent force adequate to maintain his ftation at Williamſburg; he therefore determined to crofs James River to Portfmouth.

From falfe intelligence General Wayne arrived with the van of the American army on the banks of the river, in expectation of attacking the rear of the Britifh, unfortunately before any part of the army had paffed. Perceiving his miftake, he deemed it the beft policy to charge boldly, though his corps did not amount to more than eight hundred men. After fuftaining a very unequal conflict for fome time with great refolution, Wayne
ordered

ordered a rapid retreat; and Lord Cornwallis, amazed at the circumstances of this attack, and suspecting that it must be meant to draw him into an ambuscade, forbade all pursuit; and thus the courage of Wayne, as it often happens, availed more to his safety than if he had acted with the most timid and scrupulous caution. In the night Lord Cornwallis passed over to Portsmouth, where he purposed to establish his head-quarters; but, on farther deliberation, removed to York-town, as the more eligible situation.

Hitherto the plan of the campaign on the part of General Washington had wavered in uncertainty. He had long and seriously meditated an attack upon New York, and General Clinton had good reason to believe that this was finally determined upon at an interview between the American General and Count Rochambeau, which took place in May; and in consequence of this project, great preparations were made in the vicinity of New York, indicatory of an approaching siege. But the arrival of considerable reinforcements from England, and the recall of so large a body of troops from Virginia, led General Washington, in his dispatch of July 30th, to observe, " that from this change of circumstances, they should probably entirely change their plan of operations."

At length a letter from Count de Grasse, stating that his destination was unalterably fixed to the

the Chefapeak, left no alternative; and a joint anfwer was immediately fent by the American and French Generals, that they would lofe no time in removing the army to the fouth of the Delawar, there to meet the Admiral. All the appearances of an attack upon New York were, however, ftill carefully kept up, till at length, on the 24th of Auguft, the allied army fuddenly decamped, paffed the North River, and by rapid marches proceeded to Philadelphia, were they arrived on the 30th; the fleet of Count de Graffe, confifting of twenty-four fhips of the line, entering nearly at the fame time the bay of Chefapeak.

So ftrongly impreffed was the mind of the Britifh Commander in Chief with the notion of an attack upon New York, that he for a long time conceived the fouthern march of the American army to be only a feint. But at length, finding that the van of the American army had actually paffed the Delawar, and receiving authentic intelligence that the fleet of Count de Graffe was deftined to the Chefapeak, he communicated, as he tells us, his SUSPICIONS to Lord Cornwallis, at the fame time affuring his Lordfhip, " that he would either reinforce him by every poffible means in his power, or make the beft diverfion he could in his favor."

Doubtlefs, in this critical fituation, the moft unlimited difcretion ought to have been vefted in Lord

Lord Cornwallis, confidering the extreme uncertainty of affording him timely and effectual fuccor, either to have retreated to Carolina, or to have attacked the enemy previous to the arrival of the combined army. " But being affured," to ufe the words of Lord Cornwallis, " that every poffible means would be tried by the navy and army for his relief, he did not think himfelf *at liberty* to attempt either, though he had fo unfavorable an opinion of the poft he occupied, that nothing but thefe affurances would have induced him to attempt its defence."

It is evident that the leading ideas of the two Britifh Generals did not coincide; and it may be remarked, that from the moment Lord Cornwallis began to act in fubordination to orders fent him from New York, he ceafed to be fuccefsful— So effential is it that the fupreme command fhould refide in the centre of action. The Commander in Chief was at this period no more than the Governor of a diftant garrifon; but had Sir Henry Clinton joined Lord Cornwallis in perfon at his entrance into Virginia, or had the fupreme command been then transferred to Lord Cornwallis, the campaign, fo far as we are authorifed to draw a conclufion from concurring probabilities, would not have terminated fo difaftroufly.

On the 5th of September the Englifh fleet, confifting of nineteen fhips of the line, under Admiral

ral Graves, appeared off the Capes of Virginia; and Count de Graffe, expecting a reinforcement from Rhode Ifland, ftood out to fea for their protection. A warm engagement enfued, in which the Englifh appear *not* to have obtained the advantage; and the Count de Graffe, being joined by the fquadron of M. Barras, was left undifputed mafter of the Chefapeak. Relief was from this time wholly impracticable; and Lord Cornwallis withdrew within his works, making every preparation for a vigorous defence. The military talents of this Commander, though of no mean rate, were neverthelefs unequal to fo novel and perilous an exigency.

On the 17th of September the fagacity of General Green pronounced, in writing to his military friend and correfpondent, Baron Steuben, " Nothing can fave Lord Cornwallis but a rapid retreat through North Carolina to Charleftown." But his Lordfhip ftill lingered, and ftill indulged eager and fruitlefs hopes of fuccor. York-town being fituated nearly at the extremity of a narrow peninfula, inclofed between York River to the north and James River to the fouth, it was invefted with great cafe and advantage by an enemy who commanded the navigation of the two rivers.

On the 14th of October the befiegers, notwithftanding the well-directed and inceffant fire of the enemy, had advanced far in their fecond parallel.

Being

Being greatly incommoded in their approaches by two redoubts at the distance of two hundred yards from the British lines, it was determined to attack them at the same time by different detachments of French and Americans. Actuated by the spirit of emulation, they carried both redoubts sword in hand with resistless impetuosity. On marching to the assault, the general exclamation was, "Remember New London!" a place on the coast of Connecticut, which the regenade Arnold, in one of his predatory expeditions, had recently taken and destroyed, putting the troops which defended it to the sword. On the submission, nevertheless, of the British stationed in the two redoubts, their lives were spared: and when the Americans were afterwards interrogated why they did not carry their previous resolve into execution, they replied, "they could not tell how to put men to death while begging on their knees for quarter." By this time the batteries of the besiegers were covered with one hundred pieces of heavy ordnance; and the British works, enfiladed in almost every part, and nearly demolished, could scarcely mount a single gun. In this extremity no other resource remained than to endeavor to transport the garrison across York River to Gloucester Point, opposite to York Town, where works had been also erected, and were still occupied by part of the British army. But this intention being totally frustrated by a violent storm after the embarkation had actually commenced, Lord Cornwallis was reduced to the hard and terrible necessity of proposing terms of capitulation, which were granted only on condition of his Lordship's surrendering himself, and the forces under his command, to the amount of above 7000 men, prisoners of war. The honor of marching out with colors flying, which had been refused to General Lincoln on his giving up Charlestown, was now refused to Lord Cornwallis; and General Lincoln was appointed to receive the submission of the army of York Town, precisely in the same way his own had been conducted eighteen months before.

Such was the final issue of the eager hopes and sanguine expectations excited by the first brilliant successes of this noble and gallant commander. The joy of the Americans on the capture of a second royal army was unbounded. In a circuitous march of 1100 miles, from Charlestown to Williamsburg, every place through which they passed experienced the effects of their rapacity: and instead of endeavoring to conciliate the minds of the inhabitants by acts of lenity, they alienated even those who were most friendly, by their relentless and systematic severity. Yet was Lord Cornwallis, as an individual, generous, disinterested, and humane; but the favorite and avowed maxim of the British Government at this time, a maxim

from

from which the military commanders seem not to have thought themselves at liberty to depart, was, "that the extreme of rigor, by making the war intolerable, and resistance hopeless, was *in effect* the greatest mercy, and the mode of all others to be adopted, therefore, by the *parental affection of Britain* for reclaiming his Majesty's *deluded subjects* of America." A marble column, with a suitable inscription and trophies, was ordered by the Congress to be erected at York Town, in commemoration of this glorious and decisive event; and a solemn thanksgiving to Almighty God was appointed throughout all the States of the Union, "for the signal successes with which he had vouchsafed to bless the armies of America, combating in defence of their rights and liberties."

The remaining miscellaneous transactions of the year must now be succinctly noticed.

Early in the spring Governor Johnstone, late one of the Commissioners to America, was invested with a naval command, and with a considerable squadron was detached on an expedition to the Cape of Good Hope. The Court of Versailles, knowing the present inability of the States General to protect their foreign dominions, sent a superior squadron under M. Suffrein to counteract the designs of the English; and coming up with them at Port Praya, in the island of St. Jago, the French Admiral scrupled not to violate the neutrality of the

Portugueze flag, by attacking the squadron of Commodore Johnstone while it lay dispersed and scattered, unsuspicious of danger, in the harbor. Happily the French, rather by extraordinary efforts of valor on the part of the British seamen, than of skill on that of their Commander, were beaten off; but immediately proceeding to the Cape, they effectually secured that important settlement from any hostile attempt. Commodore Johnstone, on his subsequent and tardy arrival, was obliged to content himself with the capture of several Dutch East Indiamen in Saldanha Bay; and those of his ships which were destined for the East Indies prosecuting their voyage thither, the Commodore returned home with his prizes, from his inglorious though lucrative expedition.

In the course of the summer an engagement took place off the Dogger Bank, between an English squadron commanded by Admiral Hyde Parker, and a Dutch squadron of equal force under Admiral Zoutman, who had under convoy the Baltic trade bound to the Texel. On perceiving the English fleet bearing down, the Dutch Admiral, who was to leeward, lay-to, and the English were suffered to approach within half musquet shot without firing a gun, when a dreadful cannonade commenced, which was kept up without interruption for three hours and forty minutes; and the action then ceased only because the ships on both sides, fides, from the damages they had respectively sustained, were no longer found manageable. The Dutch, after some time, bore away with their convoy for the Texel, which they reached with great difficulty, one of their largest ships sinking before they could make the harbor.

Admiral Parker, who had unavailingly applied to the Admiralty for a reinforcement, returned in great discontent and in a shattered condition to the Nore, where he received the signal honor of a visit from his Majesty on board his own ship, and was offered *knighthood* as the reward of his valor. But his haughty refusal shewed how little he was flattered by these petty and puerile distinctions.

The Dutch on their part bestowed rewards more liberal and solid on the officers and sailors of their fleet, and Admiral Zoutman was received at Amsterdam with great applause and acclamation: and the event of this remarkable action shewed, that the Dutch seamen were still possessed of that determined courage which had distinguished them in the days of De Ruyter and Van Tromp.

About this time the Emperor, now resident in the Netherlands, issued a placart, by which Ostend was declared to be a free port; and in the month of October he acceded in form to the armed neutrality, as the Kings of Prussia and Portugal had also previously done.

Notwithstanding the great concessions made by the Parliament of Great Britain to the people of Ireland, that country, finding its own strength, remained in a state far short of satisfaction; for it had still much to ask, or rather to demand. . The army on the Irish establishment had been hitherto invariably governed and directed by the sole prerogative of the Monarch; but as the spirit of liberty and independence increased, a Mutiny Bill, on the model of the English, had been recently introduced into the Irish Parliament, and passed into a perpetual law. But a measure originally highly popular was now the subject of loud complaint; and it was affirmed, not without reason, that liberty could never be secured on just and constitutional grounds, so long as the Monarch was irrevocably invested with the unlimited power of the sword; that in England the Mutiny Bill was passed only from year to year, and in the very preamble of it, standing armies without consent of Parliament are declared illegal; the troops themselves, the law that regulated, and the power that commands them, are by this bill limited to one year. Thus was the army of England rendered a parliamentary army, and the constitutional ascendency of the subject over the soldier preserved.

In numerous county and provincial meetings the supremacy of the British Parliament was in formal

formal resolves positively denied, and the absolute independence of Ireland on the British Legislature boldly asserted. The unconstitutional powers of the Irish Privy Council, where, agreeably to the famous law of Poyning, all laws must originate, were reprobated, a Habeas Corpus Act loudly called for, the abolition of all superfluous places and pensions insisted upon. The zeal and activity of the military associations sufficiently evinced their determination to enforce their claims by a mode of application which was in no danger of being disregarded.

Such was the state of things when the second session of the present Parliament commenced at Westminster, on the 27th of November 1781. In the speech from the throne his Majesty observed, " that the war was still unhappily prolonged, and that, to his great concern, the events of it had been very unfortunate to his army in Virginia, having ended in the total loss of his forces in that province. But he could not consent to sacrifice, either to his own desire of peace or to the temporary ease and relief of his subjects, those essential rights and permanent interests upon which the strength and security of this country must ever principally depend." His Majesty declared, " that he retained a firm confidence in the protection of Divine Providence, and A PERFECT CONVICTION of the JUSTICE of his CAUSE;"—

and he concluded by calling " for the concurrence and support of Parliament, and a VIGOROUS, ANIMATED, and UNITED EXERTION of the FACULTIES and RESOURCES of his PEOPLE." Upon the whole, this speech was plainly indicatory of a fixed and resolute determination to prosecute a war, of which it might well be supposed, that " fools as gross as ignorance made drunk" might by this time have seen the hopelessness and the absurdity.

The Monarch had now swayed the sceptre of these kingdoms more than twenty years, and, in the course of a long and variegated series of events, his character both personal and political was completely matured and developed.

If we wish to

to reverſe the medal, a view of the private life and domeſtic habits of the King will indeed diſcover a life paſſed without any remarkable deviation from the rules of propriety and decorum, and much leſs any direct violation of the higher and more ſerious obligations of morality and religion. But the virtues of the man, were they ſuch as to entitle him to the honors of papal canonization, unfortunately afford to the public a moſt inadequate and wretched compenſation for the errors and imperfections of the monarch.

The ſpeech from the throne underwent, as may well be imagined, the ſevereſt animadverſion.— Mr. Fox ſaid he had expected, and he knew it had been expected by many others, to hear on this occaſion his Majeſty declare from the throne, that he had been deceived and impoſed upon by miſinformation and miſrepreſentation; that, in conſequence of his deluſion, the Parliament had been deluded, but that now the deception was at an end; and requeſting of his Parliament to deviſe the moſt ſpeedy and efficacious means of putting an end to the public calamities: inſtead of which, they had heard a ſpeech breathing little elſe than vengeance, miſery, and blood. Thoſe who *were ignorant of the perſonal character of the Sovereign*, and who imagined this ſpeech to originate with him, might be led to ſuppoſe that he was an unfeeling deſpot, rejoicing in the horrid ſacrifice of the

the liberty and lives of his subjects, who, when all hope of victory was vanished, still thirsted for revenge. The Ministers who advised this speech he affirmed to be a CURSE to the country, over the affairs of which they had too long been suffered to preside. From that unrivalled pre-eminence which we so lately possessed, they had made us the object of ridicule and scorn to the surrounding nations. "But," said he, "the time will surely come when an oppressed and irritated people will firmly call for SIGNAL PUNISHMENT on those whose counsels have brought the Nation so near to the brink of destruction. An indignant Nation will surely in the end compel them to make some faint atonement, for the magnitude of their offences, on a PUBLIC SCAFFOLD." He concluded with moving, "That of the Address proposed the whole be omitted excepting the first paragraph, and the following words inserted:—'And we will without delay apply ourselves with united hearts to propose and digest such counsels as may in this crisis excite the efforts, point the arms, and, by a total change of system, command the confidence of all his Majesty's subjects."

This amendment was vigorously supported by Mr. Pitt, who declared, "That the duty he owed his Sovereign and his Country compelled him to exert every effort to prevent the House from precipitately voting an Address, which pledged them

to

to the support of that fatal system which had led this country, step by step, to the most calamitous and disgraceful situation to which a once flourishing and glorious empire could be reduced.—Was it becoming the Parliament of a free people to echo back the words which a Minister, long practised in the arts of delusion, had dared to put into the Royal mouth? He implored the House not to vote for an Address fraught with treachery and falsehood, which could not have been framed by any who felt for the honor of the King, the dignity of Parliament, or the interest of the Nation."

An amendment of the same import was moved in the Upper House by the Earl of Shelburne, and supported by the Duke of Richmond, who declared " the misfortunes of this country to be owing to that wretched system of government which had been early adopted in the reign of his present Majesty, and to the influence of that INTERIOR CABINET which (he said) had been the ruin of this country;" and he recalled to the recollection of the House the memorable declaration of the late Earl of Chatham, " that he was duped and deceived, and that he had not been ten days in the Cabinet before he felt the ground rotten under his feet."

In both Houses, however, the Addresses were carried by great majorities, and a most melancholy

and

and alarming profpect prefented itfelf to the Nation, of a fatal perfeverance in a war which, from an involuntary and irrefiftible conviction univerfally impreffed, was now regarded as defperate, and paffionately deprecated as tending to certain and remedilefs ruin.

In a very few days, a motion being made by Sir Grey Cooper for the Houfe to refolve itfelf into a Committee of fupply, a vehement debate arofe. Mr. Fox, in the courfe of a moft animated fpeech, afked " if Minifters would give any fatisfactory affurance to the Houfe, that the military forces which fhould hereafter be fent acrofs the Atlantic, would be employed more fuccefsfully or honorably than thofe which had already been fent thither? Did the American Secretary wifh to difpatch a third army to America, that General Wafhington might a third time receive them as prifoners of war? Did he wifh that more Britifh troops fhould be devoted to flaughter, captivity and difgrace? Notwithftanding the defeat and difhonor which had attended the meafures of Adminiftration, they had yet difcovered no figns of humiliation or penitence. Inftead of acknowledging that they turned their eyes with inquietude and fhame upon the criminal expenditure of fruitlefs millions, they did not blufh to move for an increafe of grants, that they might profecute, till ruin fhould have flopped their infamous careet,

hofti-

hostilities which were the result of barbarous ambition, of implacable malevolence, of a detestation of liberty, of a contempt for every principle of justice, equity, and honor."

The Ministers were so vigorously pushed in this debate, and seemed so utterly incapable of defending themselves or their measures, that it was probably a welcome surprise to them, to find in their favor, on the division, 172 voices to 77.

It being understood that preparations were making for another embarkation of troops from Ireland to America, a very important motion was on the 12th of December made by Sir James Lowther, "That it be resolved by the House, that the war carried on against the Colonies and Plantations of North America had been ineffectual to the purposes for which it was undertaken; and that it was also the opinion of this House, that all farther attempts to reduce the Americans to obedience by force, must be injurious to this country, by weakening her powers to resist her antient and confederated enemies." In support of this motion, which was indeed the plain dictate of common sense, the mover observed, "that the late speech from the throne had given a just alarm to the Nation—it had shewn them that the Ministers were determined to persevere in the American war—that more blood and more money were to be lavished in this fatal contest; the men invested

vested with the powers of government derived no advantage from experience—the surrender of one army only gave them spirit to risque a second, and the surrender of the second only instigated them to venture a third. There was no end of loss nor of madness. The unexampled ignorance and misconduct of the Ministry were now visible to all the world. It was therefore become the indispensable duty of that House to come to some solemn resolution, in order to mark and define their idea of the American war, and to convince their constituents that they were awake to the real situation of the country."

The motion was seconded by Mr. Powys, member for Northamptonshire, who acknowledged, " that a variety of pretexts insidiously advanced by the Ministers, and too credulously received by the majority of that House, had seduced them, from one session to another, to move with fatal steps along the path to national destruction. The war with the Colonies was the idol of his Majesty's Ministers; they had bowed before it themselves, and had made the Nation bow. The conduct which at the commencement of hostilities might be denominated firmness, had now degenerated into obstinacy; an obstinacy which called upon all honest and independent men to desert the present Administration, unless a change of measures were adopted. That men who were

indebted

indebted to war for their emoluments, power, and influence, should persevere in such iniquitous and selfish measures, was not extraordinary; but it was a just cause for wonder that they should be supported by individuals of independent principles and independent fortunes. The insidious pretence of revenue was grown too stale for imposition. The American war had been a war of delusion from beginning to end. Every promise had been broken, every assertion had been falsified, every object relinquished. It was now a war of this sort, then a war of that sort; now a war of revenue, then a war of supremacy; now a war of coercion, and then a war of friendship and affection for America: but it was time to put an end to these chicaneries. Whatever might be the nature of the war, no prospect of success in it remained. He therefore not only gave the motion his full concurrence, but he should feel the highest pleasure if it received the general approbation of the House."

This speech bore a very ominous aspect with relation to the Ministers; for, Mr. Powys being himself a principal leader of the independent interest, or *country gentlemen*, in the House, there was reason to apprehend the speedy and general defection of that high and haughty class of Members: and a mere ministerial majority of placemen and pensioners, it is superfluous to say, affords only a rotten and treacherous support, whenever

ever a furmife prevails that fupport is really wanted.

In the courfe of the debate General Burgoyne acknowledged " that he was now convinced the *principle* of the American war was wrong, though he had not been of that opinion when he engaged in the fervice. Paffion and prejudice and intereft were now no more, and reafon and obfervation had led him to a very different conclufion: and he now faw that the American war was only one part of a fyftem levelled againft the conftitution of this country, and the general rights of mankind."

Notwithftanding the utmoft oppofition of the Minifter, the numbers, on dividing the Houfe, appeared to be 179 in favor of the motion, againft 220 who oppofed it. This was a majority in which the Miniftry had little reafon to exult. It afrefh excited the moft fanguine hopes of the public, who, with the exception of the high Tory and Prerogative faction, were now perfectly unanimous in their reprobation of the war and its authors.

On the 14th of December, two days only after the motion of Sir James Lowther, the army eftimates were laid before the Houfe by the Secretary at War, from which it appeared that the whole military force required for the year 1782, including the provincial corps ferving in America, amounted to to 195,000 men. One hundred thousand seamen and marines had been already voted by the House. It was however stated by Lord George Germaine, "that the Ministry were of opinion, considering the present situation of affairs, and the misfortunes of the war, that it would not be right to continue any longer the plan on which it had hitherto been conducted; and that a fresh army would not be sent to supply the place of that captured at York Town. It was intended only to preserve such posts in America, as might facilitate and co-operate with the enterprises of our fleets."

In the debate which ensued, Sir George Saville particularly distinguished himself. "At length, then," said this firm and faithful patriot, "we are given to understand that a change is to be made in the MODE of conducting the American war. The Ministers do not intend to prosecute it in the same manner as before.—Why? Because they could not if they would. But it appeared that they were determined to prosecute it with all the feeble efforts of which they were yet capable. Being detained in the country by ill health, he had not heard the King's speech on its first delivery; but when it reached him in his retirement, he had read it with HORROR, announcing as it did the continuance of the present war in its most destructive form. As to the Address of that House, in answer to the Speech, it was a mere echo

echo without meaning, a futile and empty sound. So servile was the dependence of that House on the Executive Power, and so little solicitous were they to conceal their dependence, that if the King's Speech had contained the line, ' What beauties does Flora disclose!' he doubted not but the Address would have filled up the couplet by repeating, ' How sweet are her smiles upon Tweed!' The Ministers had lost the two hands of the empire in the prosecution of this frantic and ineffectual war; by a continuance of it they would risque the head. Such a conduct resembled, if it did not indicate, the violence of infanity. Could the House so far forget their dignity, and relinquish their understanding, as not to resist this madness? Would they intrust lunatics with the management of the public purse? Would they place the sword within their hands, and bid them use it at their DISCRETION?"

General Conway declared himself " anxious for a recall of our fleets and armies from America. Of two evils he would choose the least, and submit to the independence of America, rather than persist in the prosecution of so pernicious and ruinous a war. As to the idea now suggested of a war of posts, what garrisons, he asked, would be able to maintain them, when it was well known that even Sir Henry Clinton, at New York, did not consider himself as secure?"

Mr.

Mr. Fox remarked, " that four years ago, after the disaster of Saratoga, the Noble Lord at the head of affairs had amused the House with the same language. Then the plan of future hostilities was to be differently modified, and the war conducted on a smaller and more contracted scale. On this contracted scale, however, we had lost another great army, besides suffering other grievous defeats and irretrievable calamities."

Mr. Pitt reprobated with the utmost force of language, " as a species of obstinacy bordering upon madness, the idea of any further prosecution of the American war with our fleets opposed by a superior force, and our armies in captivity. He appealed to the whole House, whether every description of men did not detest and execrate the American war, and whether it were uncharitable to implore the Almighty to shower down his vengeance on the men who were the authors of their country's ruin?"

The impression made by the successive speeches of the principal leaders of Opposition in this debate, was too great to be concealed; but the estimates, as originally moved, were at length voted by a considerable majority.

Nearly at this time a petition was presented by the City of London to the King, in which the calamities resulting from the war are stated in terms peculiarly impressive and eloquent. In conclusion they say, " We beseech your Majesty no longer to continue in a delusion from which the Nation has awakened, and that your Majesty will be graciously pleased to relinquish entirely and for ever the plan of reducing our brethren in America by force. And we do further humbly implore your Majesty, that your Majesty will be graciously pleased to dismiss from your presence and councils all the advisers, *both public and secret*, of the measures we lament, as a pledge to the world of your Majesty's fixed determination to abandon a system incompatible with the interest of the Crown and the happiness of your People."

Soon after the recess of Parliament, Mr. Fox renewed his former motion of censure against the First Lord of the Admiralty; and such strength had the Opposition now acquired, that in a House of near four hundred Members, it was rejected by a majority of only twenty-two. The unpopularity of the American Secretary was so great and manifest, that he now thought it expedient, seeing parliamentary censures likely to become again in fashion, to resign the seals of that department, and for his *eminent services* he was by his Majesty raised to the dignity of the Peerage. But before the Great Seal was affixed to the patent, the Marquis of Carmarthen moved in the House of Peers, " that it was highly derogatory to the honor of that House, that any person laboring under the sentence of a court martial, styled in the public orders issued by his late Majesty ' a censure much worse

worse than death,' and adjudged unfit to serve his Majesty in any military capacity, should be recommended to the Crown as a proper person to fit in that House."

The motion was evaded by the question of adjournment; but Lord George Germaine having actually taken his seat in the House under the title of Lord Viscount Sackville, the Marquis of Carmarthen renewed his attack, and urged, " that the House of Peers being a court of honor, it behoved them to preserve that honor uncontaminated, and to mark in the most forcible manner their disapprobation of the introduction of a person into that assembly who was stigmatized in the orderly books of every regiment in the service."

Lord Abingdon, who seconded the motion, styled the admission of Lord George Germaine to a peerage " an insufferable indignity to that House, and an outrageous insult to the public.— What, (said his Lordship) has that person done to merit honors superior to his fellow-citizens? His only claim to promotion was, that he had undone his country by executing the plan of that accursed invisible, though efficient Cabinet, from whom, as he received his orders, so he had obtained his reward."

Lord Sackville, in his own vindication, denied the justice of the sentence passed upon him, and affirmed " that he considered his restoration to the Council Board, at a very early period of the present

sent reign, as amounting to a virtual repeal of that iniquitous verdict."

The Duke of Richmond strongly defended the motion, and said " that he himself was present at the battle of Minden, and was summoned on the trial of Lord George Germaine; and had his deposition been called for, he could have proved that the time lost when the Noble Viscount delayed to advance, under pretence of receiving contradictory orders, was not less than *one hour and a half*; that the cavalry were a mile and a quarter only from the scene of action; and it was certainly in his Lordship's power, therefore, to have rendered the victory, important as it was, far more brilliant and decisive; and he had little reason to complain of the severity of the sentence passed upon him."

Lord Southampton also, who, as Aid-de-camp to Prince Ferdinand on that memorable day, delivered the message of his Serene Highness to his Lordship, vindicated the equity of the sentence.

The motion was likewise powerfully supported by the Earl of Shelburne, the Marquis of Rockingham, and other distinguished Peers.

On the division, nevertheless, it was rejected by a majority of ninety-three to twenty-eight voices: but to the inexpressible chagrin of Lord Sackville, a protest was entered on the Journals of the House, declaring the promotion of his Lordship

to

to be "a measure fatal to the interests of the Crown, insulting to the memory of the late Sovereign, and highly derogatory to the dignity of that House."

Mr. Fox, on the 20th of February 1782, again brought forward his motion of censure, somewhat varied, on Lord Sandwich, which was negatived by a majority of nineteen voices only, in a House consisting of 453 Members; but to the astonishment of the nation, the Noble Lord still daringly kept possession of his office, although 217 Members of the House of Commons had pronounced him "guilty of a shameful mismanagement of the naval affairs of Great Britain." The Opposition appearing every day to gain strength in the House of Commons, the downfall of the Ministry began at length to be confidently predicted.

On the 22d of February, General Conway moved "for an Address to the King, earnestly imploring his Majesty, that he would be graciously pleased to listen to the humble prayer and advice of his faithful Commons, that the war on the continent of North America might no longer be pursued, for the impracticable purpose of reducing that country to obedience by force." This was opposed in a long speech by Mr. Welbore Ellis, the new Secretary for the American Department, who declared, "that it was now in contemplation to contract the scale of the war, and to prosecute hostilities

hostilities by such means as were very dissimilar from the past. That *unhappy faction* in America which still continued its resistance to the government of this kingdom, though *less numerous than the party of the royalists*, could only be rooted out by pushing the war with vigor against France. In order to obtain peace with America we must vanquish the French; and as, in the late war, America had been said to be conquered in Germany, so in this, America must be conquered in France. In present circumstances, the Administration were conscious of the necessity of drawing into a narrow compass the operations of the American war, a change of circumstances demanding a correspondent change of measures." That this miserable mixture of falsehood and folly should fail to make impression upon the House, cannot be deemed wonderful; and the Ministry themselves seemed to despair of their cause, when they committed the defence of it to so contemptible an advocate;—whom Mr. Burke, in reply, overwhelmed with the supercilious and poignant disdain of his ridicule. " This war," Mr. Burke said, " had been most amazingly fertile in the growth of new statesmen; the Right Honorable Gentleman was indeed an old Member, but a young Secretary. " Having however studied at the feet of Gamaliel, he had entered into full possession of all the parliamentary qualifications, by which his predecessor

predecessor had been so conspicuously distinguished;—the same attachments, the same antipathies, the same extravagant delusion, the same wild phantoms of the brain, marked the Right Honorable Gentleman as the true ministerial heir and residuary legatee of the Noble Viscount. And notwithstanding the metamorphosis he had recently undergone, he was so truly the same thing in the same place, that justly might it be said of him, '*alter et idem nascitur*.' Being of the caterpillar species, he had remained the destined time within the soft and silken folds of a lucrative employment, till having burst his ligaments he fluttered forth the butterfly Minister of the day." On the division, however, the Ministry had still a *majority*, but a fearful majority of ONE voice only! the numbers being 192 for, and 193 against the motion; so that the pyramidal edifice of ministerial power seemed now, by a marvellous and magical inversion, to rest upon its apex.

Mr. Fox immediately gave notice, that in a few days the question would be revived under another form. Accordingly, on the 27th of February, General Conway moved, "That it is the opinion of this House, that a farther prosecution of offensive war against America would, under present circumstances, be the means of weakening the efforts of this country against her European enemies, and tend to increase the mutual enmity so fatal

fatal to the interests both of Great Britain and America." The General spoke with indignation of the objection urged against the last motion, that it was an unconstitutional interference in matters pertaining to the executive power. He said, it had been ever the custom of that House to interpose its advice whenever it thought proper, in all matters of peace and war, as their journals incontrovertibly proved.

In order to evade an immediate determination upon the question, the Attorney-General Wallace moved, " that a bill should be prepared, enabling his Majesty to conclude a truce with America, and to enter into a negotiation on this ground." This proposition was negatived by a majority of 19, the numbers being 234 to 215; and the original motion of General Conway was then carried without a division.

The General next moved an Address to the King, founded on the precise words of the motion. This was agreed to, and it was resolved, that the Address should be presented to his Majesty by the whole House; which was accordingly done on the 1st of March: and his Majesty most graciously replied, " That in pursuance of the advice of the House of Commons, he would assuredly take such measures as should appear to him most conducive to the restoration of harmony between Great Britain and her *revolted* Colonies."

This

This not being deemed by the now glorious majority of the House sufficiently explicit, General Conway on the 4th of March moved another Address to his Majesty, returning him thanks for his gracious assurances, and affirming, " That nothing could so essentially promote the great objects of his Majesty's paternal care, as the measures his faithful Commons had humbly, though earnestly, recommended to his Majesty." This was agreed to NEM. CON. and by a second motion it was resolved, " That the House will consider as enemies to his Majesty and the Country, all those who should advise a prosecution of offensive war on the continent of North America." The glory of General Conway, who had sixteen years before restored peace to the empire by his motion for the repeal of the Stamp Act, was now complete.

The Minister giving notice of his intention to postpone for some days laying before the House the additional taxes, which were to pay the interest of the new loan of thirteen millions and a half, Mr. Burke seized the occasion to observe, " that he had lately been taking a view of the blessed fruits of the Noble Lord's administration; and he had found we were already loaden with ten new taxes, viz. beer, wine, soap, leather, houses, coaches, post-chaises, post-horses, stamps, and servants. It was indeed no wonder that the Minister should be at a loss about new taxes, for what

what fresh burdens could he add to this unhappy Nation? We were already taxed if we rode, or if we walked; if we staid at home, or if we went abroad; if we were masters, or if we were servants. In the course of the Noble Lord's administration, we had expended one hundred millions of money, and sacrificed one hundred thousand lives, and all this without producing in return the least benefit to the nation. On the contrary, the nation had been, in consequence of the wretched misconduct of the Minister, deprived of thirteen colonies, to which might be added the loss of Senegal, Pensacola, Minorca, and some of our best West India Islands."

Notwithstanding the late majorities in the House of Commons, in opposition to the Ministers, they seemed to entertain no thoughts of resigning those offices which they had so long and so undeservedly enjoyed. It was therefore thought necessary to move a direct vote of censure upon them, at the close of a series of Resolutions brought forward by Lord John Cavendish on the eighth of March, importing, as the result of the whole, " that the chief cause of all the national misfortunes is want of foresight and ability in his Majesty's Ministers."

The motion was seconded by Mr. Powys, who remarked, " that the Noble Lord at the head of affairs had declared, that whenever Parliament should withdraw its confidence from him, he
                                                                would

would refign. That period was now come. The confidence of Parliament was withdrawn. It was therefore neceffary that he fhould retire from power; and whenever the happy moment fhould arrive, in which the Noble Lord, to the unfpeakable joy of the nation, fhould really go to his Sovereign to refign his employments, he hoped he would not forget to lay before the King a fair reprefentation of the flourifhing ftate in which he found his Majefty's empire when the government of it was intrufted to his hands; and the ruinous condition in which he was about to leave all that remained of it." After a long debate, the order of the day was moved, and on a divifion was carried by a majority of ten voices, the numbers being 226 to 216.

In a few days a refolution was moved by Sir John Rous, Member for Suffolk, a man once zealoufly attached to the prefent Miniftry, " that the Houfe, taking into confideration the debt incurred and the loffes fuftained in the prefent war, could place no farther confidence in the Minifters who had the direction of public affairs." A vehement debate enfued, in the courfe of which a fpeech was made by Sir James Marriott, Judge of the Court of Admiralty, vindicatory of the Miniftry and of the war, which he afferted was juft in its origin, however unfortunate in its confequences. " And though it had been *pretended*, that the inhabitants

tants of America were not reprefented in Parliament, "the fact, he faid, was certainly otherwife; for the 'grant and charter of the lands of the province of Virginia, with which the fubfequent grants correfponded, were expreffed in the following terms: ' To have and to hold of the King or Queen's Majefty, as part and parcel of the manor of Eaft Greenwich in the county of Kent, *reddendum* a certain rent at our caftle of Eaft Greenwich, &c.' fo that the interefts of America were in truth, by the nature of their tenure, reprefented in Parliament by the Knights of the County of Kent." This aftonifhing *legal* difcovery was received by the Houfe with much lefs gravity than it was communicated by the learned Judge, who feemed not to be at all aware, that no authority of law could give weight to folly, or refpectability to nonfenfe. On the divifion, the numbers were 227 for, and 236 againft the motion. But with fuch a majority victory was defeat.

Four days after this, March 19, the Earl of Surry had propofed to move a Refolution of fimilar import to that of Sir John Rous. But when his Lordfhip was about to rife, Lord North addreffed himfelf to the Speaker, and faid, "that as he underftood the object of the Noble Lord's motion to be the removal of Minifters, he wifhed to prevent the neceflity of giving the Houfe farther trouble, by an explicit declaration, THAT HIS MA-
JESTY

jesty had come to a determination to make an entire change of administration: and he and his colleagues only retained their official situation till other Ministers were appointed to occupy their places. His Lordship thanked the House for the indulgence he had experienced from them in the discharge of his duty, and declared himself ready to answer to his country for his conduct whenever he should be called upon for that purpose." Lord Surry consented, not without reluctance, and by a lenity most pernicious in its consequences, upon this communication, to wave his motion, which, he declared, "was intended to prevent the farther perpetration of those abuses of their trust, to which with impunity, and to the disgrace and detriment of the State, the *late Ministers* had for such a length of time proceeded." Thus was this famous, or, to use a term more characteristically appropriate, this infamous Administration, so long the bane and curse of the British empire, and of the world at large, suddenly and totally dissolved, to the inexpressible joy of all ranks and orders of people. It was however by many feared, that great difficulty would arise in the formation of a new and efficient Administration, on account of the unfortunate division which had long subsisted among the Whigs in opposition to the Court. Of the two parties, that of Lord Rockingham was by far the most numerous

merous and powerful; but, from various caufes eafily and diftinctly afcertainable by attentive obfervers, the other party, of which fince the death of Lord Chatham the Earl of Shelburne was accounted the head, were in lefs disfavor with the King;—and the higheft department of government was upon this occafion exprefsly offered to that Nobleman by his Majefty. For, not to defcend to fubordinate reafons of preference, it is evident that the chief of the inferior party, Lord Shelburne, would, from his comparative weaknefs of connection, have been more immediately and neceffarily dependent than his competitor Lord Rockingham upon the Crown for protection and fupport. But the Noble Lord had the generofity and wifdom to refift the temptation; and the Marquis of Rockingham, to the univerfal fatisfaction of the kingdom, was a fecond time, in a manner the moft honorable and flattering to his character and feelings, placed at the head of the Treafury; under whom Lord John Cavendifh acted as Chancellor of the Exchequer; the Earl of Shelburne and Mr. Fox were nominated Secretaries of State; Lord Camden was appointed Prefident of the Council; the Duke of Grafton reinftated as Lord Privy Seal; Admiral Keppel, now created Lord Keppel, placed at the head of the Admiralty; General Conway, of the Army; the Duke of Richmond, of the Ordnance. The Duke of Portland

land succeeded Lord Carlisle as Lord Lieutenant of Ireland; Mr. Burke was constituted Paymaster of the Forces; and Colonel Barré, Treasurer of the Navy. Lord Thurlow alone, by the unaccountable and unmerited indulgence of the new Ministers, continued in possession of the Great Seal. Whiggism was now once more triumphant. The Tories, though they escaped by a critical resignation the direct censure of the House of Commons, had continued in office till they were reduced to the lowest extremity of shame, humiliation and contempt; and a fair prospect, after a long night of storms and darkness, *seemed* to open, of a bright and brilliant day of national prosperity.

The first act of the new Administration was to signify by a letter from Mr. Fox to M. Simolin, the Russian Ambassador, his Britannic Majesty's willingness to accept the mediation offered by the Empress for a separate accommodation with Holland, on the basis of the treaty of 1674. But this their High Mightinesses thought proper to decline; and considering how much Holland was at this time in the power of his Most Christian Majesty, whose troops were now in actual possession of the settlement of the Cape, and the island of Eustatius, a compliance was scarcely to be expected. On the contrary, Mr. Adams was at this period formally acknowledged and received by the States General, as Minister Plenipotentiary of the United States

States of America. Negotiations for a general peace were however almoft immediately commenced between France and Great Britain, and Mr. Grenville was fent to Paris, invefted with full powers to treat with all the parties at war.

Previous to the change of Adminiftration, Sir Henry Clinton had refigned to Sir Guy Carleton his command in America, which he had held fince the refignation of Sir William Howe in the fpring of 1778, an interval of near four years, in all which time Sir Henry had only taken one town and loft another; and the conqueft of Charleftown, in the general eftimate of fubjugation, was fully counterbalanced by the evacuation of Newport and the other Britifh pofts in Rhode Ifland. Inftructions were now fent to the new Commander and Admiral Digby, to acquaint the Congrefs of the pacific views of the Englifh Court, and of their readinefs to treat on the bafis of American Independence.

Bills formerly introduced, and negatived, were at a very early period after the appointment of the new Minifter, revived by Mr. Crew and Sir Philip Jennings Clerke, for difabling revenue-officers from voting at elections, and excluding contractors from the Houfe of Commons. Thefe now paffed with approbation and applaufe; Mr. Secretary Fox declaring, that not an hour fhould be loft in giving the public the ftrongeft proofs that his Majefty's Minifters were fincerely determined to make fuch reforms as fhould be neceffary, and to enforce that fyftem of government which they had repeatedly called for when not in place. He faid, " his worft fufpicions of the negligence and fcandalous mifmanagement of the late Minifters were now matured into knowledge; that, bad as things had been defcribed, the reprefentation was by no means fo bad as the reality. And he fhould not think that the prefent Minifters acted fairly or honeftly by that Houfe, or by the people at large, if they did not inflitute enquiries which might give the country a true and correct idea of the prefent fituation of affairs."

Thefe bills were vehemently though ineffectually oppofed in the Houfe of Peers by the Lord Chancellor, who feemed to hang as a dead weight on the meafures of the prefent Adminiftration, whofe fentiments could never affimilate with thofe of men of liberal and comprehenfive views, and who now appeared as the avowed and determined enemy of every fpecies of civil or political reform. The attention of Parliament was however foon occupied by affairs of much higher moment.

In the month of November laft, Mr. Grattan, a diftinguifhed Member of the Irifh Parliament, had moved for a limitation of the perpetual Mutiny Bill. This was rejected by a great majority, extremely

tremely to the dissatisfaction of the people of that kingdom.

At a subsequent meeting of the representatives of one hundred and forty-three corps of volunteers assembled at Dungannon, RESOLUTIONS passed, DECLARATORY of the RIGHTS of IRELAND, and in express terms asserting, " that the claim of any body of men, other than the KING, LORDS, and COMMONS of IRELAND, to make laws to bind that kingdom, was unconstitutional and illegal, and a grievance of which it was their decided and unalterable determination to seek the speedy and effectual redress. They knew," they said, " their duty to their Sovereign, and were *disposed* to be *loyal*; but they knew also what they owed to themselves, and were RESOLVED TO BE FREE."

In a very short time after these resolves passed, Mr. Grattan moved the House for an Address to his Majesty, consonant with, and founded upon, the same principles. This motion, after a long and warm debate, was also rejected. But, on the 16th of April 1782, he again moved " a Declaration of Rights, under the form of an Address to the Throne." In his speech on this occasion, he pronounced an animated panegyric on the volunteers, and the late conduct of the Irish nation—" He beheld," he said, " with joy and admiration, her progress from injuries to arms, from arms to liberty.

The Irish volunteers had supported the rights of the Irish Parliament against those temporizing trustees, who would have relinquished them. Allied by liberty still more than by allegiance, Great Britain and Ireland formed a constitutional conderacy. The perpetual annexation of the two Crowns was a powerful bond of union, but Magna Charta was more efficacious still. It would be easy any where to find a King, but to England only can we look for a Constitution. Ireland was planted by Britons, and was entitled to British privileges. It was by charter, and not by conquest, as had been falsely asserted, that the mutual connection of the two countries was originally established. Every true Irishman would say, Liberty with England, if England is so disposed; but at all events LIBERTY. The Irish nation were too high in pride, character, and power, to suffer any other nation to claim a right to make their laws. Was England ready to acknowledge the Independency of America, and would she refuse liberty to Ireland? If she was capable, after enabling his Majesty to repeal the Declaratory Act against America, of wishing to retain that against Ireland, the Irish nation was not capable of submitting to it." Such was the spirit which now pervaded the kingdom, and such the resistless enthusiasm excited by the eloquence of Mr. Grattan, that the Address was voted without a dissentient voice; and being unanimously unanimoufly acceded to by the Peers, was immediately tranfmitted to the King. In this famous Addrefs the two Houfes affirm, "That the Crown of Ireland is an Imperial Crown, infeparably annexed to the Crown of Great Britain, on which connection the intereft and happinefs of both countries effentially depend: but that the kingdom of Ireland was a diftinct kingdom, with a parliament of her own, the fole legiflature thereof. In this right they conceived the very effence of their liberty to exift. It was a right which they, in behalf of all the people of Ireland, claimed as their birth-right, and which they could not yield but with their lives." They declared, "that they confidered the claims of the Parliament of Great Britain, in the Act paffed for better fecuring the dependency of Ireland, to be irreconcileable to the fundamental rights of that nation." They added, " that they had a high veneration for the Britifh character, and the people of Ireland did not defire to fhare the freedom of England without likewife fharing her fate ;—and it was their determination to ftand or fall with the Britifh nation."

Happy indeed was it that a radical change of counfels had taken place in Britain before thefe high and peremptory, though juft and equitable, claims were preferred on the part of Ireland ; for the folly, obftinacy, and pride of the late Minifters would fcarcely have fcrupled to involve the
Empire

Empire in a second civil war, rather than have conceded in points which militated so strongly against what they would undoubtedly have styled "the honor and dignity of the Crown and the essential interests of the People."

Some days previous to the motion of Mr. Grattan, a Royal Message was delivered to the House of Commons by the Secretary of State, "recommending to their most serious consideration the state of affairs in Ireland, in order to such a final adjustment as may give a mutual satisfaction to both kingdoms." And on the 18th of May, Mr. Fox, at the close of a long and able speech, moved for the repeal of the obnoxious act for securing the dependency of Ireland; which he called " a measure of necessity, resulting, however unpleasant it might be to some, from the conduct of the late Ministry, who had awakened the present spirit in Ireland, by refusing their most modest and reasonable requests." With that generosity and openness of sentiment by which this eminent Statesman has been so long and so remarkably distinguished, Mr. Fox observed nevertheless, " that his own decided opinion had always been, that Ireland, being a part of the British empire, was entitled to the full and equal participation of all the benefits and immunities enjoyed in England, and which were consonant to the principles of the British Constitution. His ideas of Ireland corresponded," he said, " exactly

"exactly with his ideas relative to America. He thought it abfurd and unjuft for any country to pretend to legiflate for another without, much lefs againft, their confent and concurrence ;—nor could it at any time fo legiflate to any good purpofe. As to Ireland, he made no fcruple in the moft exprefs and unequivocal terms to declare, that he confidered her prefent claims to be fubftantially juft, and that he felt himfelf inclined to move the refolution which he was about to propofe, in favor of Ireland, as much on the ground of juftice as prudence." This repeal, which paffed both Houfes without oppofition, was confidered in both countries as a virtual renunciation of the claim of legiflating for Ireland. And fo highly gratified were the Irifh Parliament and Nation with the liberality of thefe conceffions, that a vote of the Houfe of Commons in that kingdom paffed unanimoufly for raifing twenty thoufand feamen for the fervice of the Britifh navy.

On the 15th of April another meffage was delivered to the Houfe by Mr. Fox from the King, ftating, "That his Majefty, taking into confideration the fupplies which have been given with fo much liberality, and fupported with fuch uncommon firmnefs and fortitude by his people in the prefent extenfive war, recommended to his faithful Commons the confideration of an effectual plan of œconomy throughout all the branches of the public

public expenditure." An Addrefs of Thanks was then moved for, and immediately agreed to by the Houfe; at the clofe of which it was faid, " That a King of Great Britain cannot have fo perfect or fo honorable a fecurity for every thing which can make a King truly great or truly happy, as in the genuine and natural fupport of an uninfluenced and independent Houfe of Commons." This was language novel and highly pleafing to the refpectable part of the public, who had been fo long naufeated by the fulfome adulation of the Addreffes prefented of late years to the Throne, fo contrary to the fpirit of Freedom, which requires the Reprefentatives of the People to refpect the Majefty of the People, and to ufe language confonant to the high and dignified fituation in which they themfelves are placed.

In confequence of this meffage, Mr. Burke's Reform Bill was a third time brought forward, under far more favorable aufpices than before. By this bill, which now paffed the Houfe with little difficulty, the Board of Trade, and the Board of Works, with the Great Wardrobe, were abolifhed; together with the office of American Secretary of State, now rendered ufelefs by the lofs of the American Colonies;—the offices of Treafurer of the Chamber, Cofferer of the Houfehold, the Lords of Police in Scotland, the Paymafter of the Penfions, the Mafter of the Harriers, the Mafter of the

the Stag-hounds, and Six Clerks of the Board of Green Cloth. Provifion alfo was made to enable his Majefty to *borrow* a fum for the liquidation of a new arrear of three hundred thoufand pounds, by a tax on falaries and penfions; for a debt to this amount had been again contracted by the fhameful prodigality of the late Minifters, notwithftanding the addition of one hundred thoufand pounds per annum, fo recently made to the Civil Lift.

The œconomical abolitions and retrenchments of the Reform Bill met with a violent oppofition in the Upper Houfe, from the Lords Thurlow and Loughborough, but it finally paffed by a great majority. A bill fent up from the Commons, for disfranchifing certain voters of the borough of Cricklade, who had been proved guilty of the moft fhameful and fcandalous acts of bribery, was alfo impeded and embarraffed in all its ftages by the fame Law Lords, with every poffible fubtilty of legal quibble and chicanery. The Duke of Richmond was upon this occafion provoked to charge the Chancellor with indifcriminately oppofing every meafure of regulation and improvement which was laid before the Houfe. And Lord Fortefcue, with the unguarded warmth of ariftocratic difdain, remarked, " that what he had long feared was at length come to pafs;—from the profufion of Lawyers introduced into that Houfe,

it

it was no longer an House of Lords, it was converted into a mere Court of Law, where all the solid and honorable principles of truth and justice were sacrificed to the low and miserable chicanery used in Westminster Hall. That once venerable, dignified, and august assembly now resembled more a meeting of pettifoggers than an House of Parliament. With respect to the Learned Lord on the woolsack, who had now for some years presided in that House, he seemed to be fraught with nothing but contradictions and distinctions and law subtilties. As to himself," Lord Fortescue with a noble pride added, " he had not attended a Minister's levee, till very lately, for these forty years; and the present Ministry he would support no longer than they deserved it. But as they came into office upon the most honorable and laudable of all principles, the approbation of their Sovereign, and the esteem and confidence of the Nation, it filled his breast with indignation when he beheld their measures day after day thwarted and opposed, by men who resembled more a set of Cornish Attornies than Members of that Right Honorable House."

On the 3d of May, after a debate of some length, it was resolved by the House of Commons, " That all the declarations, orders, and resolutions of that House respecting the election of John Wilkes, Esq. be expunged from the Journals of the House, as subversive

versive of the rights of the whole body of electors in the kingdom." Mr. Wilkes, in a public letter addressed to his constituents, "congratulated them on the signal reparation they had now obtained for their violated franchises, and the injuries they had sustained under the former flagitious Administration." But on this point the feelings of the public were no longer in unison with those of Mr. Wilkes. The vote by which those resolutions were rescinded, which had thirteen years before thrown the whole nation into a flame, was scarcely noticed; and the case of the Middlesex Election was now regarded with nearly as much indifference as that of any other elective decision.

In the same month a subject of infinitely higher importance, and of a nature truly and permanently interesting, was brought under the immediate cognizance of the House, in consequence of a motion made by Mr. Pitt for the appointment of a Committee to enquire into the State of the Representation of the People in Parliament. It is remarkable, that notwithstanding the prodigious and glaring inequality of the national system of Representation as now constituted, the idea of a parliamentary reform may be considered in great measure as a novelty in politics. The patriots of elder days, sensible of the dangers arising from the rapid and enormous increase of the regal influence, strongly and repeatedly urged the remedial measures of Triennial Parliaments,

Parliaments, of Civil and Military Reductions, of Place and Pension Bills; but it was a species of merit reserved for the present times to strike at the root of the evil, by an effort to extend and equalize that popular representation, on the purity and integrity of which the national prosperity and welfare so essentially depend.

The evils attending this defective and corrupt state of the representation had at no former period of our history been so flagrantly apparent as in the present reign; and it was with grief and indignation that the intelligent and independent part of the public saw the House of Commons degenerate into an assembly apparently possessing neither will, nor power, nor wisdom, but what they derived from the permission and *fiat* of the Minister, who also frequently appeared himself the sport of some capricious and invisible agent. The affair of the Middlesex Election, otherwise comparatively unimportant, wore in this view a most alarming aspect, as it shewed how far the House would venture to carry their complaisance to the Crown, in opposition to the decided, unanimous, and persevering resistance of the people. " The virtue, spirit, and essence of an House of Commons," says Mr. Burke in his famous political tract published at that period*, "consists in its being the express image of the feelings

---

* Thoughts on the Causes of the present Discontents.

of the Nation. An addressing House of Commons, and a petitioning Nation—an House of Commons full of confidence when the Nation is plunged in despair, who vote thanks when the Nation calls upon them for impeachments, who are eager to grant when the general voice demands account, who in all disputes between the People and Administration presume against the People, who punish their disorders, but refuse to enquire into the provocations to them:—this is an unnatural, a monstrous state of things in this Constitution. Such an assembly is not to any popular purpose an' House of COMMONS."

The obstinate prosecution of the American war, and the contemptuous dismission of the petitions for a reform in the public expenditure, afforded still more recent and striking instances of obsequious and unlimited devotion on the part of the national representatives to the executive power, and their total disregard of the sentiments of their constituents. So struck was the late Earl of Chatham with the obvious and manifold mischiefs arising from the present incongruous system, that he scrupled not to hazard a peremptory prediction, that the *rotten boroughs* would not survive the present century —and that if Parliament did not reform itself from WITHIN, it would be reformed with a VENGEANCE from WITHOUT." Nevertheless it must be acknowledged there were not wanting many wise

and

and excellent perfons, true and firm friends to Liberty, whofe minds forcibly revolted at the novelty and boldnefs of the idea of *new-modelling* the reprefentation of the country. They conceived the actual advantages refulting from the Conftitution, when *rightly adminiftered*, under the prefent form, too great to rifque any experiment, however plaufible in theory, of fuch magnitude as to draw after it confequences which no human fagacity could pretend to trace or fathom.

Totally to annihilate the influence of the Crown in the Houfe of Commons, would give fuch an afcendency to the republican part of the Conftitution, that the prerogative of the Monarch would in a fhort time be reduced to as low an ebb as the authority of a King of Poland or a Doge of Venice; the executive power would lofe its weight and energy, and the State would be torn with the oppofite and equal claims of hoftile and contending factions. To afcertain the precife degree of influence which the Monarch ought to poffefs, was indeed confeffed to be a difficult problem to folve. It is the radical and remedilefs defect of the Britifh form of government, in other refpects fo admirable, that too much depends on the perfonal character of the Sovereign ; and under the reign of a weak, obftinate, and bigoted prince, intoxicated with the pomp and pride of royalty, fuch as imagination can eafily feign, the excellence of that celebrated Conftitution ſtitution may be put to a very ſevere teſt indeed—particularly if, by an accidental concurrence of circumſtances, ſuch a Monarch, thus palpably unfit to govern, ſhould riſe to high and undeſerved popularity.

On the other hand, it may doubtleſs happen that the executive power may poſſeſs juſter and more enlightened views of policy than the nation at large; and a more popular ſyſtem of repreſentation would in ſuch circumſtances be a real and ſerious evil. This was remarkably the caſe in the reigns of King William and King George I. who exerted with very incomplete ſucceſs their utmoſt influence to extend and enlarge the general ſyſtem of Liberty. The grand object of every Conſtitution of Government which aſpires on rational grounds to political perfection is not, as the wild and viſionary ſpeculatiſts of modern times abſurdly ſuppoſe, to carry the will of the majority at all events into effect, but to concentrate the wiſdom, the knowledge, and the virtue of the community; to endow them with influence, and arm them with power. Above all, it excited the alarm of the moderate, the judicious, and truly enlightened, that a great proportion, perhaps a majority, of the advocates for a parliamentary reform maintained the exiſtence of certain abſtract rights independent of utility—which is in truth the baſis both of right and obligation—in conformity to which the people had a clear, original,

ginal, and imprescriptible claim to the privilege of UNIVERSAL SUFFRAGE, without the exercise of which it was pretended that no liberty could exist.

The Duke of Richmond, who had signalized himself as a public and zealous patron of this scheme, expressly says, in his famous Letter to Colonel Sharman, Chairman of the Military Convention at Dungannon, " that all plans of a merely speculative nature, not tending to the effectual recovery of their RIGHTS, neither could nor *ought* to influence the people in their favor." His Grace, in conformity to these sentiments, declares, " that he did not think himself *at liberty* to speculate on the subject, for that every man not laboring under natural or moral disability had an inherent *right of suffrage* paramount to all considerations of civil or political expediency." To this new species of *divine right*, therefore, all the inferior and vulgar considerations of public good, of public order, of peace, happiness, and rational subordination, must bow with reverential awe; but it is evident that this inherent right of suffrage cannot exist alone. It necessarily involves in it a right to command, countermand, and dismiss their representatives at pleasure. If the people have an inherent abstract right to elect, then the exercise of this right must be determined by the same abstract rules of political justice—and an equal number of electors must return an equal number of representatives; in other words, population

lation is the fole bafis of reprefentation—If therefore the metropolis be fuppofed to contain one fixth of the entire population of the kingdom, and the reprefentative body to confift of fix hundred individuals, London might on this abftract metaphyfical hypothefis plead an inherent indefeafible right to fend one hundred Members to Parliament. Other large and populous towns poffeffing a fimilar right to elect in the fame proportion, a combination of local and particular interefts would be formed, totally incompatible with the general interefts of the community. But where fhall we ftop? or how fhall the monarchical or ariftocratical parts of our Conftitution be maintained againft thefe fovereign and indefeafible rights—thefe paramount and tranfcendent claims?

All thefe grofs and dangerous abfurdities, involving in them the moft alarming confequences, proceed from the fatal error of confounding the power of the people with the liberty of the people. To liberty they have a right, fo far as it is promotive of happinefs; and to power fo far, and fo far only, as it is a fecurity to liberty. For, to the blind, capricious, and felf-deftructive will, even of the majority, it is ever lawful—nay more, it is in the higheft degree laudable; it is indeed the pureft and nobleft act of virtue—at the greateft perfonal rifque, to oppofe the dictates of reafon, equity, and juftice. Allowing, however, the full force of thefe general arguments,

arguments, it could not be denied that the influence of the Crown, first systematically employed as an engine of Government by Sir Robert Walpole, had in this reign extended itself far beyond all its antient bounds and limits. Under that justly celebrated Minister also, this influence, however corruptly obtained, was *upon the whole* employed wisely and well; but since the commencement of the NEW SYSTEM OF GOVERNMENT, which was in fact no other than the old Tory system revived and varnished, it had been perverted to the most vile and pernicious purposes. It was no wonder, therefore, that a measure which was regarded as alone adequate to the effectual reduction of this influence should be pursued with zeal and ardor.

Early in the present year it was resolved by the City of London, assembled in Common-Hall, "That the unequal representation of the People, the corrupt state of Parliament, and the perversion thereof from its original institution, had been the principal causes of the unjust war with America, and of every grievance of which the nation complained." Similar resolutions were passed by the County of York, and many other counties and cities; and after so long and bitter an experience of the evils arising from the present defective state of the representation, it would indeed have argued not so much a wise and well-weighed caution, as a reproachful excess of political timidity in the nation to have hesitated fitated in applying the moſt permanent and efficacious remedy. The motion of Mr. Pitt, though eloquently enforced by the mover, and ſupported by Mr. Fox with a great difplay of difcrimination and judgment, was rejected, notwithſtanding its prefent popularity, on a divifion, by a majority of 161 to 141 voices.

Hitherto the new Miniſtry, though compoſed of diſſonant and jarring materials, had conducted public affairs with at leaſt the appearance of perfect and cordial unanimity—the Earl of Shelburne in the Upper Houſe bringing forward the fame motions, and ſupporting them by the fame general arguments as Mr. Fox in the Lower. But an event now took place which was tne fubject of deep and univerfal regret, and the confequences of which cannot be fufficiently deplored, in the death of the Marquis of Rockingham, July 1, 1782, in the meridian of his age, and at the very height of his political reputation—the weight and influence attached to which, combined with the excellence of his private character, and the mild benignity of his manners, formed that power of attraction which held together the whole miniſterial fyſtem; and when this ceafed to operate, diforder, confufion, and mutual repulfion took place. The fplendor of the new conſtellation faded, and " certain ſtars ſhot *madly* from their ſpheres."

To drop all metaphorical and poetical allufion, it

it is neceſſary to ſtate in plain language, that on the very day ſucceeding the deceaſe of the Marquis of Rockingham, the Earl of Shelburne was declared Firſt Lord Commiſſioner of the Treaſury. The acceptance of this high and pre-eminent office, without any previous communication with his colleagues in Adminiſtration, was conſidered by the Rockingham party as equivalent to a declaration of political hoſtility on the part of Lord Shelburne. It was in effect telling his allies, that he conceived his influence in the Cabinet to be ſufficiently ſtrong to enable him to ſtand without their aſſiſtance. It was evidently ſetting up a diſtinct and oppoſite intereſt, depending upon the ſecret aſſurances of royal favor and ſupport. Preciſely the ſame reaſons, which had induced the Earl of Shelburne three months before to decline the offer then made, ſtill exiſted in full force; but he was no longer proof againſt temptation—though the experience of his illuſtrious friend Lord Chatham might have convinced him on how precarious a ground thoſe Miniſters ſtood who depended on courtly promiſes and profeſſions for protection and ſafety.

On this promotion, Mr. Fox reſigned the Seals as Secretary of the Northern Department; Lord John Cavendiſh his office as Chancellor of the Exchequer; the Duke of Portland his Government of Ireland; Lord Althrop, Lord Duncannon, Mr. Frederic Montague, &c. their ſeats at the Boards of of Treafury and Admiralty; and Mr. Burke his poft of Paymafter of the Army. In confequence of thefe refignations and removes, the Seals of the Southern Department were given to the Earl of Grantham; and of the Northern to Mr. Thomas Townfhend, late Secretary at War; Sir George Yonge fucceeded Mr. Townfhend; Colonel Barré was made Paymafter of the Forces; and the Lord Advocate of Scotland, in his room, Treafurer of the Navy. The Earl of Temple, eldeft fon of the late George Grenville, fucceeded the Duke of Portland in the Lord Lieutenancy of Ireland; but the promotion which attracted moft of the public attention was that of Mr. William Pitt, who, at the age of three-and-twenty, was conftituted Chancellor of the Exchequer; an office which had been always fuppofed to require, in order to its proper difcharge, not fo much brilliancy of talents, as long previous ftudy and experience, and confirmed habitudes of diligence and induftry.

It was evident from feveral of the late promotions that a mixture of the *old leaven* was again ominoufly introduced into the prefent *Whig Adminiftration*, to which, notwithftanding the late feceffion, the names of Lord Camden, General Conway, the Dukes of Grafton and Richmond, Lord Keppel, and others, gave great refpectability—*exclufive* of the new Premier himfelf, whofe public conduct had been uniformly confiftent and meritorious, who
had

had never deviated in any inftance from the principles of genuine Whiggifm, whofe political knowledge was extenfive, whofe abilities were unqueftionable, and whofe general rectitude of intention the public had no juft ground to doubt. The only charge brought againft the Minifter, which feemed to make any confiderable impreffion, was that which accufed him of the habitual and fyftematic practice of a certain duplicity and *fineffe*, which entirely precluded all open, ingenuous, and confidential intercourfe.

In a few days fubfequent to his refignation, Mr. Fox ftated in the Houfe of Commons the grounds and reafons of his conduct. He faid, " that political differences of opinion of great importance had taken place in the Cabinet, and that he had withdrawn himfelf from it to prevent that diftraction in the public counfels, which he conceived to be ruinous to the public welfare. He had reafon, he affirmed, to believe that the day was come when the fyftem on which the Adminiftration of Lord Rockingham had been formed was to be abandoned, and a new fyftem was to be fubftituted, or rather the old one revived, with the affiftance of the *old men*, or indeed of any men that could be found.—NOR SHOULD HE WONDER IF IN A SHORT TIME THEY WERE JOINED BY THOSE VERY PERSONS WHOM THAT HOUSE HAD PRECIPITATED FROM THEIR SEATS. He therefore chofe to refign, voluntarily relinquifhing the pomps, the profits, and the patronage of office, as he could no longer continue in place with honor to himfelf, or benefit to the public."

General Conway, in reply, " lamented the defection of the diftinguifhed characters who had recently withdrawn themfelves from office, at a time when their country fo much needed their fupport. He protefted that he knew of no defalcation in the prefent Minifters from thofe principles which they had originally profeffed: nor any diverfities of opinion in the Cabinet, beyond thofe *fhades of difference* which muft always arife amongft men of ftrong and independent minds."

On the following day the Duke of Richmond expreffed in the Houfe of Lords fimilar regret at the late refignations. " So long, and fo long only, as the Noble Lord who now prefided at the Board of Treafury fhould adhere to the principles on which the Adminiftration was originally formed, fo long would he give him his cordial fupport. Whenever thefe principles were abandoned, he would be his moft determined opponent."

The Earl of Shelburne now rofe to declare " his perfect fatisfaction at being fupported upon the terms ftated by the Noble Duke." He faid, " he lamented as much as any man the death of the late Marquis of Rockingham, and the lofs
fuftained

sustained by the Cabinet in the retreat of two persons so remarkably distinguished, one by the splendor of his abilities, the other by the unimpeached integrity of his character. The office he now held, his Lordship affirmed, was within his grasp when the first arrangements were forming, but he had then given way to the Noble Marquis; though he had now accepted the post, as that Nobleman was no more: and this, he believed, was the only reason that the late Right Honorable Secretary had withdrawn himself. But if the Monarch was divested of the power of appointing his own *servants*, he would be reduced to the condition of a King of the Mahrattas, who had nothing of sovereignty but the name. He had been charged, his Lordship said, with inconsistency relative to America: but his opinion still was, as it ever had been, that whenever the Parliament of Great Britain acknowledged that point, the sun of England's glory was set for ever. Other Lords however thought differently, and the question would soon come under the full and impartial discussion of Parliament: but he repeated, that if Parliament conceded that point, he foresaw that England was undone; for that ruin and independence were linked together—the ruin not of England only, but of America."

It was sufficiently evident from this speech, that
more

more than " shades of difference" had existed in the Cabinet previous to the resignation of Mr. Fox. But it excited the utmost astonishment in America, that such language as this should be held in Parliament by the First Minister, after Sir Guy Carleton had been two months before expressly authorized to declare to the Congress, " that his Majesty, in order to remove all obstacles to peace, had commissioned Mr. Grenville to propose the independency of the Thirteen Provinces in the first instance, instead of making it a condition of a general treaty:" and the discordant language held on the different sides of the Atlantic was indignantly cited as a new instance of British artifice and perfidy. As to the *right* of the King to appoint his own Ministers, on which Lord Shelburne laid so great stress, it was entirely remote from the point in question, which regarded merely the wisdom and patriotism of his Lordship's eager acceptance of an offer, which was evidently calculated to destroy all confidence, and to gratify the aspiring views of a favored individual, to the extreme eventual detriment of the public.

Had the Earl of Shelburne acted with openness and candor in the critical circumstances in which he was placed, there is good ground to believe that his highest ambition might have been gratified, a sincere and cordial union of parties formed, and

and a firm, efficient, and patriotic administration ultimately established, uncontaminated with the detestable leaven of TORYISM.

" On the 11th of July 1782, the session terminated, and the speech from the throne contained the welcome declaration, " that nothing could be more repugnant to his Majesty's feelings, than the long continuance of so complicated a war; and that his ardent desire of peace had induced him to take every measure which promised the speediest accomplishment of his wishes."

The military events of the year yet remain to be narrated. The fortress of Gibraltar still continued closely invested by the Spaniards, and the resolute defence of the garrison began to attract the general attention of Europe. Towards the close of the preceding year, 1781, by a most spirited and successful *sortie*, the stupendous works erected by the Spaniards across the isthmus which connects the rock of Gibraltar with the continent, were stormed and almost totally demolished, when, after immense expence and labor, they were arrived at the highest state of perfection. In less than half an hour five batteries, with all the lines of approach, communication and traverse, were in flames—the magazines blowing up one after another, as the conflagration successively reached them—the astonished Spaniards offering no other resist-

resistance, than a distant and ill directed fire from the forts of St. Philip and St. Barbara.

To balance this success, intelligence arrived early in the spring of the new year, that General Murray, Governor of Minorca, had been compelled, after a long and vigorous resistance, to surrender that island to the arms of his Catholic Majesty. Formerly the loss of Minorca had occasioned the downfall of an Administration; but such were the infinitely greater misfortunes and disasters of the present war, that this event made little impression upon the public, and it was scarcely remarked, that no attempt whatever had been made for its relief during a siege of one hundred and seventy-one days.

The island of Nevis, in the West Indies, also about the same time surrendered to the Marquis de Bouillé and the Count de Grasse; by whom the most liberal terms were granted to the inhabitants. Eight thousand troops, with a formidable train of artillery, were then landed on the important island of St. Christopher. Sir Samuel Hood, who now commanded the British fleet in the West Indies, made strenuous efforts for its relief: and, notwithstanding his disparity of force, in three successive encounters with the Count de Grasse he obtained each time the advantage, and at length, by a dextrous manœuvre, gained possession of the enemy's anchorage at Basseterre Road. Admiral Hood then landed a considerable detachment of troops from Antigua under General Prescot; but General Frazer, the commanding officer on the island, who was strongly posted on an intrenched eminence, sent him word, " that as he had taken the trouble to come with troops to his assistance, he should doubtless be glad of the honor of seeing him, but he was in no want of him or his troops." Notwithstanding this idle vaunt, he was obliged to surrender the island on capitulation, after a siege of five weeks, on the 12th of February 1782.

In the same month Demerary and Isequibo were captured by the French : also the island of Montserrat. The loss of the Bahamas quickly followed, being reduced by a considerable force under Don Manuel de Cigagal, Governor of the Havannah, to the obedience of the Crown of Spain.

On the 19th of February Sir George Rodney arrived in the West Indies with a strong reinforcement of ships from England, and resumed the command of the fleet. Mighty preparations were now making both by the French and Spaniards, for the invasion of Jamaica ; and as the combined force of these powerful nations amounted to above sixty sail of the line, had a junction been effected, the island was irrecoverably lost. The first object of the British Admiral was to intercept a great

convoy

convoy of troops, provisions, and stores expected from Europe: but in this he was disappointed; the enemy found means to escape his vigilance, by making the island of Deseada, to the northward, and keeping close in shore under the high land of Guadaloupe and Dominique, and arrived safe at Fort Royal on the 21ft of March. It was the design of Count de Graffe to proceed to Hispaniola, and join the Spanish Admiral, Don Solano, who was waiting his arrival, in order to make, in conjunction, the pre-concerted attack on Jamaica.

On the 8th of April, at day-break, the French fleet left the harbor of Fort Royal; and Admiral Rodney, who had the earliest intelligence of their movements, instantly made the signal for a general chase. Early the next morning he came up with the enemy under Dominique, where the van of the English engaged the rear of the French, but the continued calms prevented a general or close action. In the morning of the 11th a fresh gale sprung up, and the chase was renewed: and towards evening the headmost ships of the van gained so much on one or two of the enemy's ships, damaged in the late action, that the Count de Graffe thought it necessary to bear down for the purpose of protecting them. Sir George Rodney, who had eagerly watched and waited for this opportunity, now manœuvred the fleet with such skill, as to gain the windward of the enemy during the

the night, and entirely to preclude their retreat. At feven in the morning of the 12th, the two fleets, being ranged in lines directly oppofite, engaged with the greateft fury. The French fhips being crowded with men, the carnage was prodigious; but no vifible impreffion was made, or material advantage gained, till about noon, when Sir George Rodney, in the Formidable, followed by his feconds the Namur and the Duke, perceiving an accidental interval which invited the attempt, bore directly with full fail athwart the enemy's line, and fuccefsfully broke through, about three fhips fhort of the centre, where the Count de Graffe commanded in the Ville de Paris. Being quickly fupported by the remainder of his divifion, the Englifh commander wore round clofe upon the enemy, and actually feparated their line, placing the central fhips of the French between two fires. This bold and mafterly manœuvre proved decifive. The French however continued to fight with the utmoft bravery, and the battle lafted till fun-fet. The Cæfar was the firft fhip which ftruck her colors, having loft her captain, and being almoft torn to pieces by the enemy's fire. Soon afterwards, by fome unfortunate accident fhe blew up, and every foul on board perifhed. The Glorieux, the Hector, the Ardent, now followed the example of the Cæfar, and the Diadem went down by a fingle broadfide.

broadside. The Count de Graffe in the Ville de Paris, befet on all fides, ftill held out with heroic bravery, and, though reduced to a wreck, feemed to prefer finking rather than ftrike to any thing under a flag. At length Admiral Hood, in the Barfleur, approached him juft at fun-fet, and poured in a moft deftructive fire, which the Count yet fuftained for fome time, till having three men only left alive and unhurt on the upper deck, he at length ftruck to his gallant antagonift. Night only clofed the action: the fhattered remains of the French fleet crowded all the fail they could make for Cape François, and in the morning they were out of fight. Sir Samuel Hood being detached to purfue the flying enemy, came up with five fail off Porto Rico, and captured the Jafon and Caton fhips of the line, and two frigates, the third with difficulty clearing the Mona paffage.

Unfortunately the fleet was becalmed for three days after the action, and Sir George Rodney did not efcape cenfure for the previous dilatorinefs of his purfuit. Whether more might have been done, if more had been attempted, it is difficult, perhaps impoffible, to determine.—" What *had* been is unknown, what *is* appears;"—and certain it is, that this was one of the moft glorious and decifive naval victories ever obtained by the arms of Britain.

The number of men flain in this action, and
in

in that of the 9th, on the part of the French, is eſtimated at 3000 men, and the wounded were nearly double; ſo that, taking the priſoners on board the captured ſhips alſo into the computation, the French muſt have ſuſtained a loſs of ten or twelve thouſand men.

Their fleet had on board the land forces intended for the Jamaica expedition; and the whole train of artillery, with thirty-ſix cheſts of money deſtined for the uſe and ſubſiſtence of the troops, were found on board the Ville de Paris and the other ſhips now taken.

The deſigns of the Confederated Powers were thus moſt completely fruſtrated, while the loſs of men, including both killed and wounded, on the part of the Britiſh, did not exceed eleven hundred.

For this great victory Sir George Bridges Rodney was created a Peer of Great Britain, by the title of Baron Rodney, of Rodney-Stoke, in the county of Somerſet, and a perpetual annuity of 2000l. annexed to the title. A motion made and over-ruled in the preceding ſeſſion of Parliament, and intended to have been revived by the preſent Miniſtry, for an enquiry into the conduct at St. Euſtatius, was now no more thought of; and the Admiral received, as he well deſerved, the unanimous thanks of both Houſes for his eminent ſervices.

The campaign of the present year was destined to be for ever signalized in the annals of history, by another event not less glorious to the arms of Britain than the victory of Sir George Rodney. The favorite object of Spain, during the whole of this war, was the recovery of the important fortress of Gibraltar; and after the reduction of Minorca, the whole strength of the Spanish monarchy seemed to be directed to this purpose. The Duc de Crillon, conqueror of Minorca, was appointed to conduct the siege, and, from the failure of former plans, it was resolved to adopt an entire new mode of operation.

A project was formed by the Chevalier d'Arçon, and approved by the Spanish Court, to construct a number of floating batteries, on a model which it was imagined would secure them from being either sunk or fired. With this view their keels and bottoms were made of an extraordinary thickness, and their sides defended by a kind of rampart, composed of wood and cork long soaked in water, and including between them a large layer of wet sand. The roof was made of a strong rope-work netting, covered with wet hides, and calculated by its sloping position to prevent the shells and bombs from lodging, and to throw them off into the sea before they could produce any effect. The batteries, ten in number, were made of the hulls of large vessels cut down for the purpose,

pose, and mounted with heavy brass cannon; and by a most ingenious mechanism, a great variety of pipes and canals perforated all the solid workmanship, in such a manner as to convey a continued succession of water to every part of the vessels.

The preparations were enormous in other respects: about 1200 pieces of heavy ordnance had been brought to the spot, to be employed in the different modes of attack; above eighty gun-boats and bomb-ketches were to second the operations of the floating batteries, with a multitude of frigates, sloops and schooners: and the combined fleets of France and Spain, amounting to fifty sail of the line, were to cover and support the attack, while they heightened the terrible grandeur of the scene. The numbers employed by land and sea against the fortress, were estimated at more than 100,000 men.

With this force, and by the fire of three hundred cannon, mortars and howitzers, from the adjacent isthmus, it was intended to attack every part of the British works at one and the same instant. The Count D'Artois and the Duc de Bourbon, the brother and cousin of the French Monarch, and numerous other volunteers of high rank, had repaired to the Spanish camp, in order to witness the inevitable fall of that famous fortress, which had so long bid haughty defiance to the power of Spain.

Early on the morning of the 13th of September, the ten battering ships, commanded by Admiral Don Moreno, came to an anchor in a line parallel to the rock, at the distance of about one thousand or one thousand two hundred yards.—The surrounding hills were covered with people, as though all Spain were assembled to behold the spectacle. The cannonade and bombardment on all sides, from the isthmus to the sea, and the various works of the fortress, were tremendously magnificent. The prodigious and unintermitted showers of red-hot balls, of bombs and carcasses, which filled the air, exhibited a scene perhaps unparalleled in military history. The whole peninsula, like some vast volcano discharging on all sides its burning lava, seemed enveloped in a sheet or torrent of fire. The battering ships for many hours remained to all appearance unaffected; but about two in the afternoon the Admiral's ship was observed to smoke, and soon after that of the Prince of Nassau was observed to be in the same condition. The whole line of attack was now visibly disordered. At length the day having closed, the two first ships appeared to be in flames, and others were beginning to kindle; and signals of distress were universally made. Captain Curtis, who commanded the English marine force in the Bay, to complete the confusion, having advanced to the attack with his gun-boats, and raked the

whole

whole line of batteries with his fire, the Spanish launches, which had been employed in bringing off the men, no longer dared to appear; but were compelled, after feveral had been funk in the attempt, to abandon their ships to the flames, or the mercy of the English.

The diftrefs of the enemy was now wrought up to the higheft pitch of calamity; and the British officers and feamen, feeing all refiftance at an end, now exerted themfelves to the utmoft to fave the vanquifhed foe, and their humanity was, at the clofe of this memorable conflict, no lefs confpicuous than their valour. Captain Curtis, in particular, expofed himfelf to the moft imminent perfonal danger; and his pinnace was almoft in contact with one of the largeft batteries at the moment of explofion. In the end the floating batteries were all confumed; and the lofs of the Spaniards, exclufive of that fuftained by the troops on the ifthmus, was computed at 1500 men, whilft that of the garrifon amounted to lefs than one third of the number.

In the mean time Lord Howe, who commanded the grand fleet, confifting of thirty-four fail of the line, was on his paffage from Portfmouth in order to throw fuccors into the fortrefs. He arrived at Cape St. Vincent the 9th of October, and on the 11th he paffed the Straits, where the combined fleets had for fome time been ftationed in order to intercept him; but a violent tempest drove them upon the Barbary coast, and prevented all possibility of attack. The St. Michael, of 72 guns, having separated from the fleet, ran on shore on the rock of Gibraltar, and was taken possession of by the garrison. After fully executing the purpose of his destination, Lord Howe set sail for England. The enemy making their appearance off Cape St. Vincent, October 20, the British Admiral lay-to in order to receive them; but they kept at so great a distance, that the cannonade, which lasted from about five in the afternoon till ten at night, did little damage; and his Lordship having no pressing reasons for renewing the fight against so superior a force, continued his voyage without farther molestation to Portsmouth. The Governor of Gibraltar, General Elliot, for his gallant and heroic defence of that fortress, was raised to the Peerage by the title of Baron Heathfield, and a pension annexed to the title equal in amount to that granted to Sir George Rodney.

This was the last transaction of importance during the continuance of the war in Europe; and thus the military career of Britain, after her repeated misfortunes, terminated with great splendor and *eclat*. All the belligerent powers were now inclined to listen to overtures of pacification. The independence of America being virtually recognized by England, and a resolution against offensive operations

tions having paſſed the Houſe of Commons, the war with the Colonies was in fact at an end. The original purpoſe of France being accompliſhed, ſhe could have no motive to perſevere in a conteſt, the expence of which was enormous, and the farther ſucceſs uncertain. Spain, after extraordinary exertions, having failed in both her grand objects, the recovery of Gibraltar, and the conqueſt of Jamaica, had little reaſon to flatter herſelf that her future efforts would be more effectual than the paſt; and Holland would have neither the inclination nor ability to continue the war alone.

During the negotiation with France and Spain, protracted chiefly in conſequence of the demand in which Spain for ſome time reſolutely perſiſted of the ceſſion of Gibraltar, proviſional articles of pacification between Great Britain and America were ſigned on the 30th of November 1782, by which the thirteen provinces were declared free and independent ſtates; and by a boundary line very favorable to America, the whole country ſouthward of the lakes on both ſides of the Ohio, and eaſtward of the Miſſiſippi, was ceded to the Colonies, with a full participation of the fiſheries on the Banks of Newfoundland and the Gulph of St. Laurence. In return for which the Congreſs engaged to RECOMMEND to the ſeveral States to provide for the reſtitution of the confiſcated eſtates of the Loyaliſts. But this recommendation eventually proved, as might

might have easily been foreseen, nugatory and useless; and this wretched portion of his Majesty's *deluded subjects* migrated in great numbers to the inhospitable wilds of Nova Scotia, and the barren shores of the Bahamas.

Dr. FRANKLIN, so lately the subject of the vilest and grossest abuse, had now the glory of signing this treaty on the part of the United States—the intelligence of which was received in America with emotions of exultation and rapture. The definitive treaty was not however signed till the following year, at the close of which New York, Charlestown, and Savannah, the only places in the possession of the English, were finally evacuated; and General Washington made his public entry into the first of these cities as soon as the royal army was withdrawn. The rejoicings on this occasion were celebrated with patriotic enthusiasm; after which an affecting leave was taken by the General of the friends and companions of his warfare, who accompanied him on his return to his own province, in silent and solemn procession, to the banks of the North River. When the barge quitted the shore, he waved his hat, bidding them for the last time adieu. To this valediction, fixing their regards on their beloved commander till they could no longer distinguish his person, they replied by acclamations intermingled with suppressed sobs and involuntary tears. In every town and village through

through which the General paſſed, he was received with the higheſt demonſtrations of gratitude and joy.

When he arrived at Annapolis, he ſignified to Congreſs his intention to reſign the command he had the honor to hold in their ſervice, referring to them the mode in which it ſhould be done. They reſolved it ſhould be in a public audience. When the day fixed for that purpoſe arrived, the hall of the Senate Houſe was crowded with perſonages of the higheſt merit and diſtinction; and General Waſhington, addreſſing the Preſident in a ſpeech remarkable only for its dignified ſimplicity, demanded leave to ſurrender into their hands the truſt committed to him, and, having finiſhed the work aſſigned him, to retire from the great theatre of action to the tranquil ſcenes of private life, earneſtly recommending to the protection of Almighty God the intereſts of his dear country, and thoſe who have the ſuperintendance of them to his holy keeping." To this addreſs the Preſident replied in words to the following purport:—" The United States in Congreſs aſſembled, receive with emotions too affecting for utterance the ſolemn reſignation of the authority under which you have led our troops with ſucceſs through a perilous and doubtful war. Called upon by your country to defend its invaded rights, you accepted the ſacred charge before it had formed alliances, and whilſt it was
without

without friends or a government to support you—you have conducted the great military contest with wisdom and fortitude, invariably regarding the rights of the civil power through all disasters and changes—you have, by the love and confidence of your fellow-citizens, enabled them to display their martial genius, and transmit their fame to posterity. Having defended the standard of liberty in this new world, having taught a lesson useful to those who inflict, and to those who feel oppression, you retire with the blessings of your country; but the glory of your virtues will not terminate with your military command, it will continue to animate remotest ages. May the Almighty foster a life so beloved with his peculiar care, and may your future days be as happy as your past have been illustrious!" The grand and interesting scenes which crowded upon the imagination of the General and the President, almost deprived them of the power of articulation; and the mingled emotions of joy, regret, and admiration, which agitated the minds of the spectators, were expressed more forcibly by looks and gestures than they could have been by words.

Immediately on this resignation, the late Commander "hastened," to use his own words, "with ineffable delight to his seat at Mount Vernon, on the banks of the Potowmac;" whence, at the powerful call of his country, he in a short time again emerged in order to assume the high station which

he

he now occupies as Prefident and Guardian of that new and noble Conftitution, which, by one of the happieft and moft extraordinary efforts of human virtue, wifdom, and ability, has been fubftituted in America to her former feeble, inefficient, and defective form of government.

In Great Britain, to the affairs of which we muft now revert, the feffion of Parliament commenced December 5, 1782, with a very excellent fpeech from the Throne, in which his Majefty, reverting after a long and inglorious feries of years to the genuine principles of Whig policy, declared, " that he had loft no time in giving the neceffary orders for prohibiting offenfive operations againft America, and had been directing his views to a cordial reconciliation with them. Such being his own inclination, and fuch the fenfe of his Parliament and people, he had not hefitated to conclude with them provifional Articles of Peace, by which they were acknowledged free and independent States. He deplored this difmemberment of the empire, which had become a matter both of policy and prudence; but teftified a hope that religion, language, intereft, and affection, would yet prove a permanent tie of union between the two countries. He fpoke with pride and fatisfaction of the late gallant defence of Gibraltar: he recommended an immediate attention to the great objects of public receipt and expenditure, and above all to the ftate of the national

tional debt. He applauded the liberal principles which had actuated the conduct of Parliament respecting Ireland: he pressed a revision of the whole system of trade with a view to its fullest extension; and, turning his attention to Asia, pointed out our vast possessions there as a most important object of regulation and care. He declared that the true spirit of the Constitution would be the invariable rule of his conduct, and called upon Parliament to exercise their temper, wisdom, and disinterestedness."

Loyal addresses were voted in both Houses without a division; but some severe remarks having been directed in the House of Peers against the inconsistency of the Minister, who had at a former period so strongly opposed the recognition of American Independence, his Lordship declared, " that he had exerted every effort to preserve America to this country;" and with great animation exclaimed, " that he had not voluntarily yielded up this independency; he had merely submitted to the controlling power of necessity and fate. It was not I, said he, that made this cession—it was the evil star of Britain—it was the blunders of a former Administration—it was the power of revolted subjects, and the mighty arms of the House of Bourbon."

Doubts having arisen whether the acknowledgement of Independency was absolute or conditional, and Lord Shelburne declining to communicate any particulars

particulars of a negotiation actually pending, Mr. Fox moved in the House of Commons an addrefs to the King, to lay before the House copies of such parts of the provifional articles as related to the fame; but this was oppofed as inexpedient and improper, not only by the Chancellor of the Exchequer Mr. Pitt, but by the late Minifter Lord North; and the queftion being put, Mr. Fox's motion was negatived by a majority of 219 againft 46—a divifion, perhaps, fatal to the Minifter, by infpiring him with high and lofty ideas of his own ftrength and fecurity.

On the 23d of December the Parliament, after voting one hundred thoufand feamen and marines for the fervice of the enfuing year, adjourned to the 21ft of January 1783—the day preceding which preliminary articles of peace were figned between Great Britain, France, and Spain, which immediately after the recefs were fubmitted to the confideration of the two Houfes. By this treaty Great Britain guarantied to France the ifland of Tobago, and reftored that of St. Lucia; alfo the fettlements of Goree and Senegal in Africa; and the city of Pondicherri, with her other conquefts in the eaft, accompanied by fome additions of territory. Laftly, the claims of Britain refpecting Dunkirk were exprefsly relinquifhed; and on her part, France agreed to reftore, Tobago excepted, all her valuable and important conquefts in the Weft Indies.

Indies. His Catholic Majesty was allowed to retain Minorca and West Florida, East Florida being also ceded in exchange for the Bahamas. Holland having rejected the former advances of the English Court towards an accommodation, it was resolved that she should not escape with total impunity; and the British Plenipotentiaries were directed to offer the restitution of the Dutch settlements in the possession of England, with the important exception of Trincomalee, which their High Mightinesses declared they could not reconcile with the professions of moderation on the part of his Britannic Majesty. On the other hand, Holland demanded an indemnification for the losses and expences of the war; a pretension which the English negotiators peremptorily rejected as totally inadmissible. These opposite claims for the present impeded the conclusion of the treaty with that power; but the preliminaries of peace actually signed were laid before the two Houses of Parliament, by the Secretaries of State, Lord Grantham and Mr. Townshend, on the 17th of February, and in both they met with a very violent and unexpected opposition.

An address of thanks and approbation being moved in the House of Peers by Lord Pembroke, and seconded by the Marquis of Carmarthen, a succession of able and eloquent speeches were made by the Lords Carlisle, Walsingham, Sackville, Stormont, and Loughborough, reprobating the
preliminaries

preliminaries of peace as derogatory from the dignity, and in the highest degree injurious to the interests, of the nation. " The dereliction of the Loyalists of America, and the Indians our allies, was said to be a baseness unexampled in the records of history. In the lowest ebb of distress we ought not to have subscribed to terms so ignominious. Francis I. when conquered and a captive, wrote, ' that all was lost except his honor;' and his magnanimity finally re-established his fortune. The folly of our negotiations was every where apparent. In Africa, our trade was surrendered to France by the cession of Senegal and Goree. In Asia, Pondicherri was not only given back, but, to render the boon more acceptable, a large territory was made to accompany it. In America, the prohibitions against fortifying St. Pierre and Miquelon were removed, and the limits of the French Fishery extended; and, under pretence of drawing a boundary line, the treaty grants to the United States an immense tract of country inhabited by more than twenty Indian nations. In the West Indies, St. Lucia was relinquished; which was of such military importance, that, so long as we retained this island in our hands, we might well have stood upon the *uti possidetis*, as the basis of negotiation in that quarter. The cession of East Florida to Spain was an extravagance for which it was impossible to find even the shadow of a pretence.—To complete the whole,

whole, France was allowed to repair and fortify the harbor of Dunkirk, which, in the event of a future war, might annoy our trade in its centre, and counteract all the advantage of our local situation for foreign commerce;—and, what is most wonderful, all these sacrifices are made on the professed ground of arranging matters on the principles of RECIPROCITY."

The Minister defended himself from these various attacks with great vigor and ability. His Lordship declared, "that PEACE was the object for which the nation at large had discovered the most unequivocal desire; the end he had in view was the advantage of his country, and he was certain that he had attained it. The vast uncultivated tract of land to the southward of the lakes," his Lordship said, "was of infinite consequence to America, and of none to England; and the retention of it, or even of the forts which commanded it, could only have laid the foundation of future hostility. If our liberality to Ireland was the subject of just applause, why act upon principles of illiberality to America? The refusal of the Newfoundland fishery would have been a direct manifestation of hostile intentions; and as it lay on their coasts, it was in reality impossible to exclude them from it by any restrictions; it is an advantage which nature has given them, and to attempt to wrest it from them would not only be unjust, but impracticable.

impracticable. Of one objection his Lordship acknowledged that he deeply felt the force. His regret and compassion for the situation of the unhappy Loyalists were as pungent as those of their warmest advocates. This objection admitted only of one answer, the answer which he had given to his own bleeding heart—' It is better that a part should suffer, rather than the whole empire perish.' He would have dashed from him the bitter cup which the adversities of his country held out to him, if peace had not been absolutely necessary—if it had not been called for with a unanimity and vigor that could not be resisted. No arts of address or negotiation had been neglected, but the American Commissioners had no power to concede farther. The Congress itself had not the power—for, by the Constitution of America, every State was supreme, including in itself the legislative and judicial powers; its jurisdiction, therefore, was not liable to control. In the mode of interposition, by recommendation alone could the Congress act. If after all the Loyalists should not be received into the bosom of their native country, Britain, penetrated with gratitude for their services, and warm with the feelings of humanity, would afford them an asylum; and it would doubtless be wiser to indemnify them for their losses, than to ruin the nation by a renewal or prolongation of the calamities of war. The cession of East Florida, his Lordship

ship said, was rendered unavoidable, by the mistaken and ruinous policy of those Ministers who had brought the nation under the miserable necessity of treating with its enemies on terms very different from those it could formerly have commanded. This province, detached from Western Florida, already conquered by the arms of Spain, was however of trivial value; and the amount of its imports and exports bore no proportion to the expence of its civil establishment. We had, nevertheless, obtained a compensation in the restitution of the Bahamas. Although the bounds of the French fishery were somewhat extended, by far the most eligible parts of the Newfoundland coast were left in possession of the English, and a source of future contention removed by the exact ascertainment of limits. In exchange for St. Lucia, France had restored six of the seven islands she had taken, and only retained Tobago—Senegal and Goree had been originally French settlements, but their commerce was inconsiderable; and the whole African trade was open to the English, by our settlements on the river Gambia, which were guarantied to us by this treaty. The restoration of Pondicherri, and our other conquests in the East, must be acknowledged not a measure of expediency so much as of absolute necessity, if the state of the East India Company were adverted to. Such had been the formidable confederacy against which they

were

were compelled to contend, such the wretched derangement of their finances, and so exposed to hazard were their vast and precarious possessions, that nothing but peace could recover to them their ascendency in Asia: in such a situation it was impossible to procure terms of accommodation more honorable. The removal of the restraints relative to the harbor of Dunkirk—restraints disgraceful to France, and of trifling advantage to England, was inveighed against without candor or reason. Dunkirk, as a port, was, as his Lordship asserted, far from possessing the consequence ascribed to it; it lies near a shoaly part of the channel; it cannot receive ships of a large size, and can never be a rendezvous for squadrons; it may indeed be a resort for privateers, but these we know by experience could easily issue from other ports. In fine, the confederacy formed against us was decidedly superior to our utmost exertions—our taxes were exorbitant—our debts, funded and unfunded, amounted to two hundred and forty-seven millions—our commerce was rapidly declining—our navy was overbalanced by the fleets of the combined powers, in the alarming proportion of more than fifty ships of the line. Peace was in these circumstances necessary to our existence as a nation. The best terms of accommodation which our situation would admit had been procured; and his Lordship ventured to affirm, that they could be decried or opposed only by ignorance, prejudice, or faction." On a division, the addreſs was carried by a majority of 72 to 59 voices.

A ſimilar addreſs in the Houſe of Commons was moved by Mr. Thomas Pitt, and ſeconded by Mr. Wilberforce, who urged in ſtriking and impreſſive language the expediency, the neceſſity, and advantages of peace. On which Lord John Cavendiſh roſe and declared, " that he alſo profeſſed himſelf an advocate for peace; but the queſtion was not whether a peace were neceſſary, but whether a better peace might not have been obtained—this was a queſtion which called for a ſerious deliberation. As the whole of the evidence proper to be produced was not before the Houſe, it was expedient to pauſe and heſitate. He propoſed therefore to annex to the addreſs the following words: " His Majeſty's faithful Commons will proceed to conſider of the treaties with that ſerious and faithful attention which a ſubject of ſo much importance to the preſent and future intereſts of his Majeſty's dominions deſerves, aſſuring his Majeſty, neverthelefs, of their firm and unalterable determination to adhere inviolably to the ſeveral articles for which the public faith is pledged."

This amendment was ſeconded by Mr. St. John, member for the county of Bedford, and ſupported with all the power of his eloquence by Lord North. "The addreſs," this Nobleman ſaid, "called for a vote

of

of approbation, and he had no such vote to give; for he considered the peace as dishonorable and destructive. His Lordship wished not, however, to set negotiations aside which had been concluded under the sanction of prerogative, nor to put those who advised them under PERIL of PUNISHMENT."

Such was the *candor* of the Noble Lord, and such his *indulgence* to those guilty of the crime of rescuing the nation from the ruin which impended over it, as the inevitable result of that fatal system patronised and supported by the Noble Lord and his colleagues, till the patience and credulity of an abused and exasperated people were at length exhausted. He who, by his own wretched misconduct, had created the necessity for making the sacrifices in question, ought surely in decency to have been the last man in the nation who should have suggested the profligate idea of putting those who advised them under PERIL of PUNISHMENT.

Mr. Fox now rose, and declared " his perfect concurrence with the sentiments expressed by the Noble Lord; and in still more bitter terms reprobated the peace as the most disastrous and humiliating that had ever disgraced any country. He had been accused, he said, of having formed an union with the Noble Lord, whose principles he had opposed for several years of his life; but the grounds of their opposition were removed, and he did not conceive it to be honorable to keep up animosities

mosities for ever. He was happy at all times to have a proper opportunity to bury his resentments, and it was the wish of his heart that his friendships should never die. The American war was the source of his disagreement with the Noble Lord; and that cause of enmity being now no more, it was wise and fit to put an end to the ill-will, the animosity, the feuds, and the rancor which it engendered. It was a satisfaction to him to apply the appellation of FRIEND to the Noble Lord; he had found him honorable as an adversary, and he had no doubt of his openness and sincerity as a friend."

By a very great and respectable part of the House, this declaration, which opened a perfectly new scene of things, was most indignantly received. Mr. Powys said, "This was the age of strange confederacies. The world had seen great and arbitrary despots stand forth the protectors of an infant Republic—France and Spain had combined to establish the rising liberties of America. The House now surveyed the counterpart of this picture—a MONSTROUS COALITION had taken place between a Noble Lord and an illustrious Commoner—the lofty assertor of the Prerogative had joined in alliance with the worshippers of the majesty of the People." On the division the effect of this *monstrous coalition* was immediately visible, there appearing for the amendment 224 against 208 voices.

On

On the 21st of February Lord John Cavendish moved a series of resolutions, importing—" 1. That in consideration of the public faith, his Majesty's faithful Commons will assist him in rendering the peace permanent. 2. That in concurrence with his Majesty, they will endeavor to improve the blessings of peace to the advantage of the nation. 3. That his Majesty, in acknowledging the Independency of America, has acted in conformity to the sense of Parliament, and to the powers vested in him by the act of the last session. 4. That the concessions made to the adversaries of Great Britain by the provisional treaty, and the preliminary articles, are greater than they were entitled to, either from the actual situation of their respective possessions, or from their comparative strength."

A vehement debate arose on the last of these resolutions; the merits of the peace were anew discussed; and the coalition, now openly avowed and gloried in, again underwent the severest crimination and the most poignant ridicule. Lord North, elated with the prospect not merely of perfect impunity, but of a re-admission to the power and emoluments of office, ventured to express, in high language, " his amazement at the reflections which had been thrown out against him. He did not, he said, repent of his conduct while a Minister; conscious of his own innocence, he bade defiance to censure or punishment. Proud as he was of the coalition to which he had been invited, it fhould be underftood that he was not difpofed to make any facrifice of his public principles. He dreaded no accufation, and he dared his enemies, whatever might be their abilities, their influence, and their character, to be decifive, and to proceed againft him"—expreffions furely thefe, confidering the calamities brought upon the nation by the grofs and flagrant mifconduct of the Minifter, in the higheft degree indecent and infolent. The queftion being put, was carried againft the Miniftry by a majority of 207 voices to 190.

From this time it was obvious that fome change in Adminiftration muft inevitably take place, but the Court hoped that a partial change might fuffice. Various conferences were held on the fubject of a new arrangement; but the COALITION, knowing their own ftrength, were determined not to deviate in any point from their preconcertéd plan. More than a month paffed in a kind of minifterial interregnum. At length Mr. Coke, member for Norfolk, moved an addrefs to the King, " that he would be gracioufly pleafed to take into confideration the diftracted and unfettled ftate of the empire, and condefcend to a compliance with the wifhes of this Houfe, by forming an Adminiftration entitled to the confidence of his people." This was unanimoufly carried, and prefented to the King by fuch Members of the Houfe as were

Privy

Privy Counfellors. His Majefty replied, " that it was his earneft defire to do every thing in his power to comply with the wifhes of his faithful Commons." This anfwer not giving fatisfaction, Lord Surry moved in a few days another addrefs, framed in very ftrong and pointed terms—" affuring his Majefty that all delays in a matter of this moment have an inevitable tendency to weaken the authority of his government; and *moft humbly entreating* his Majefty that he will take fuch meafures towards this object as may quiet the anxiety and apprehenfion of his faithful fubjects." But Mr. Pitt declaring that he had refigned his office of Chancellor of the Exchequer, and that any refolution or addrefs relative to a new arrangement of Adminiftration was unneceffary, Lord Surry confented to withdraw his motion: and the Minifters, who, reluctant to quit the luxury of power, had lingered in office to the laft moment, now gave place to their determined and victorious antagonifts.

The Duke of Portland was placed at the head of the Treafury; and Lord John Cavendifh was re-appointed Chancellor of the Exchequer; Lord NORTH and Mr. Fox were nominated JOINT SECRETARIES of STATE, the firft for the Home, the latter for the Foreign department; Lord Keppel, who had recently refigned on account of his difapprobation of the peace, was again placed at the head of the Admiralty; Lord Stormont was
created

created President of the Council; and Lord Carlisle was advanced to the post of Lord Privy Seal. The Great Seal was put into commission—the Chief Justice Loughborough, so distinguished for political versatility, " who could change and change and yet GO ON," being declared First Lord Commissioner; the Earl of Northington was appointed to the Government of Ireland; and Mr. Burke reinstated in his former post of Paymaster of the Forces. Of the seven Cabinet Ministers, the majority, who also occupied the most important posts of Administration, were of the Old Whig or Rockingham party;—Lord Stormont, Lord North, and Lord Carlisle, contenting themselves rather with a participation of honors and emoluments than of power.

Notwithstanding the admission of these Tory Lords therefore into the Ministry, it could not but be acknowledged, as to all the grand purposes of government, a WHIG Administration—more especially when the ability, the vigor, and the decision of its *efficient leader* were justly and impartially estimated. But, most unfortunately, no impartial estimate of the merits of this novel and heterogeneous arrangement could be hoped. The PUBLIC CONFIDENCE was lost, and universal experience confirms the observation of a celebrated writer, " that the public confidence once lost, is NEVER completely regained." The coalition was

the

the theme of univerſal and paſſionate execration. All thoſe bitter and opprobrious expreſſions of contumely and reproach againſt the late Miniſter Lord North, with which the ſpeeches of Mr. Fox and Mr. Burke had been for ſo many years filled, were now recalled to the general recollection, and excited a degree of anger, indignation, and amazement, which had not been equalled ſince the memorable and infamous defection of Mr. Pulteney. When Lord Chatham, in one of his laſt ſpeeches in Parliament, " wiſhed that the VENGEANCE of the NATION might fall HEAVY upon the MINISTERS;" when Mr. Fox declared, " that he would purſue even to the SCAFFOLD the authors of the PUBLIC RUIN;" and when Mr. Burke affirmed, " that he had articles of IMPEACHMENT actually framed againſt Lord North, whom he ſtigmatized as a STATE CRIMINAL;" great allowance ought doubtleſs to be made for that warmth and ardor of patriotic zeal, which might prompt them to exceed the too preciſe limits of a ſtrict and ſober diſcretion. The late Miniſters, it muſt be acknowledged, had done nothing for which they could juſtly incur legal puniſhment. But a parliamentary vote of cenſure and condemnation of thoſe meaſures and principles which had brought the nation to the brink of perdition, was eagerly wiſhed for by the independent and intelligent part of the public; and ſome ſatisfactory aſſurance anxiouſly expected,

expected, for the removal of men so unqualified for the talk of government, from his Majesty's person and councils FOR EVER;—sending them into ignominious retirement, with the CURSES of their COUNTRY upon their HEADS.

Lord Chatham, on receiving, not long before his decease, repeated and high-strained professions of amity and regard from Lord Bute, apparently intended to cover some insidious and political purpose, replied without hesitation, "that it was impossible for him to serve the King and Country either with Lord Bute or Lord North; and that if any thing could prevent the consummation of public ruin, it could only be new counsels and new counsellors—a real change, from a sincere conviction of past errors, and not a mere palliation, which must prove fruitless." There are no doubt situations of extraordinary difficulty and danger, which call for the united exertions of those who have been most opposite in sentiments and conduct: but the Nation was not at this time disposed to believe, that any peculiar danger to the country existed under the administration of the Earl of Shelburne, who, whether in or out of office, had uniformly shewn himself a friend to liberty. The terms of the peace were generally deemed as good as there was any previous reason, from the relative situation of the Belligerent Powers, to expect; and the COALITION of persons and principles radically hostile,

hostile, and which no effort of art or length of time could assimilate, was universally branded as a gross and palpable sacrifice of every sentiment of honor, consistency, and rectitude, on the altar of ambition, interest, and revenge.

One of the first measures of the new Ministry was to expedite the passing of a bill, before pending, " for the purpose of preventing any Writs of Error or Appeal from the kingdom of Ireland from being received by any of his Majesty's Courts in Great Britain; and of renouncing in express terms the legislative authority of the British Parliament in relation to Ireland." This was a necessary consequence of the general plan of Irish emancipation; for the mere repeal of the Declaratory Act did not, in the view of the common law, make any difference whatever in the relative situation of the two countries.

Soon after this, a bill was introduced by Sir Henry Fletcher, Chairman of the East India Company, " for suspending the payments of the Company now due to the Royal Exchequer, and for enabling them to borrow the sum of three hundred thousand pounds, for their farther relief."

Lord John Cavendish declared this bill to be only a branch of a larger plan; and that it was brought forward separately, in order to answer an exigency which did not admit of delay. His Lordship

Lordship viewed the territorial acquisitions of the Company as a fruitful source of grievance. " It would," he said, " have been more for their advantage, had they confined themselves to the character of merchants. As these acquisitions, however, had been made, they must be preserved, and it was his opinion that the relief necessary to the Company should be granted."

Lord Fitzwilliam, in the Upper House, dwelt on the almost desperate situation of the East India Company, and affirmed, " that, unless it passed, their bankruptcy would be inevitable. The expenditure of their settlements had far exceeded their revenue: bills had been drawn upon them which they were unable to answer without a temporary supply, so that the existence of the Company depended upon the success of the bill;" which accordingly passed both Houses with little difficulty or opposition.

In the month of April 1783, the Chancellor of the Exchequer brought forward his plan for raising twelve millions by loan. The most remarkable circumstance attending it was, that the money borrowed was funded at three per cent. at the extravagant rate of one hundred and fifty pounds stock for every hundred pounds sterling; so that an artificial capital of six millions was created beyond and above the sum actually paid into the Exchequer. This absurd and pernicious mode of funding was exposed and reprobated with much ability by Mr. Pitt in the Lower House, and the Earl of Shelburne in the Upper, but with no effect.

The former motion of Mr. Pitt for an Enquiry into the State of the Representation being negatived, he now brought forward, May 7, a specific plan for adding one hundred members to the counties, and abolishing a proportionable number of the burgage-tenure and other small and obnoxious boroughs. This plan, though supported by Mr. Fox, was negatived by a great majority; the numbers on the division being 293 to 149. As there must of course ever be a stronger opposition against any specific plan of reform in the first instance, than to a comprehensive and general motion of enquiry only, the latter is evidently the most politic as well as reasonable mode of introducing the question to the notice and discussion of the House; and had it been adopted by Mr. Pitt on this occasion, it could not have so egregiously failed of success. The motion was opposed in a very able speech by Lord North, who with an happy allusive pleasantry declared, " that while some with LEAR demanded an hundred knights, and others with Goneril were satisfied with fifty, he with Regan exclaimed, No, not ONE!" His Lordship, in a graver and more argumentative strain, said, " It was not true that the House of Commons had not its full and proper weight in the scale of government:—his political life was a proof that it had. It was Parliament that had made him a Minister. He came amongst them without connection. It was to them he was indebted for his rise, and they had pulled him down;—he had been the creature of their opinion and of their power;—his political career was consequently a proof of their independence;—the voice of the Commons was sufficient to remove whatever was displeasing to the sentiments and wishes of the country; and in such a situation to *parade* about a reformation was idle, unnecessary, inexpedient, and dangerous." This reasoning might perhaps have had some degree of weight, could it be lost to the public recollection, that the Noble Lord was originally advanced to the premiership by the *fiat* of the *Executive Power*, and was continued in office, during the first and last years of his administration at least, by the influence of the same power, in daring contrariety to the clear, unanimous, and decided sense of the Nation. His Lordship's compulsive resignation at the last, proved only that there are limits, beyond which even the complaisance of the representative body does not extend: and the infatuation of the Ministers became at length so notorious, that Parliament, alarmed at their rashness, and astonished at their folly, happily and critically interposed to save the nation from destruction.

A bill

A bill for regulating the trade of the African Company being introduced towards the close of the session, with a clause prohibiting the officers of the Company from *exporting negroes*, that humane, intelligent, and respectable class of citizens known by the appellation of Quakers, convened in their annual assembly in the metropolis, embraced this favorable occasion to petition the House of Commons, " That the clause in question might be extended to all persons whatsoever, professing themselves deeply affected with the consideration of the rapine, oppression, and blood attending this traffic :—Under the countenance of the laws of this country, say the petitioners, many thousands of these our fellow-creautres, entitled to the NATURAL RIGHTS OF MANKIND, are held as personal property in cruel bondage. Your petitioners regret, that a nation professing the Christian faith should so far counteract the principles of humanity and justice." This petition excited in a remarkable degree the attention of the House and of the Public; and laid the foundation of the subsequent noble and generous, though hitherto * unsuccessful efforts to effect a total abolition of this detestable and inhuman commerce—efforts which, however they may terminate, will, in the volume of the *recording angel*, " on leaves more durable than leaves of brass,"

* A. D. 1794.

enroll the names of WILBERFORCE, of SMITH, of DOLBEN, and many others, in the illuftrious catalogue of the friends and benefactors of mankind; and more particularly of that defpifed and unfortunate race of men born only to mifery, and to whofe wretched and moft compaffionable lot it has fallen " to plough the winter's wave, and reap defpair." Much bufinefs, comprehending details not fufficiently important to demand a place in general hiftory, having been completed, the Parliament was at length prorogued, July 16, by a fpeech, in which his Majefty intimated his intention of calling them together at an early period, in order to refume the confideration of the affairs of the Eaft Indies, which would demand their moft ferious and unintermitted attention.

In the courfe of the fummer, the King, as legally empowered by an act paffed for that purpofe, iffued an Order in Council, limiting the commerce between the Continent of America and the Britifh Weft India Iflands to fhips Britifh built. This was conformable to the grand principle on which the Act of Navigation was originally founded; and though this reftriction gave extreme offence to the inhabitants of the United States, they could not in reafon complain that they were precluded from enjoying the advantages of dependence and independence at one and the

fame

fame time. The definitive treaties with France, Spain, and America, were at this period signed with no material alteration: alſo preliminaries of peace with the States General, by which all the conqueſts of England were reſtored, except the town of Negapatnam on the coaſt of Coromandel, which their High Mightineſſes found themſelves, however reluctantly, at length compelled to cede.

During this interval of political repoſe in England, it will not be improper to caſt a tranſient view at the general poſture and relative ſituation of the great Continental Powers.

One of the moſt intereſting events which, ſince our laſt notice of foreign politics, had taken place in Europe, was the death of the Elector of Bavaria, December 30, 1777. This Prince was the laſt of the Ludovician line of Electors, which had been in poſſeſſion of the duchy and its appendages near five hundred years. Theſe dominions reverted to the heir general of the deceaſed, Charles Theodore, Elector Palatine; who being now himſelf advanced in life, and having no iſſue, both electorates ſeemed likely ſoon to fall into the poſſeſſion of the Duke of Deux-ponts, his neareſt relation in the male Palatine line. Scarcely, however, had the new Elector arrived at Munich, before he found that he was oppoſed by a rival of ſuch ſuperior force as to leave him no room to hope, however clear his right, for fuccefs in the competition.

This was no other than the Emperor, who advancing, on grounds of which it would be idle to examine into the validity, his imperial claim to the whole of the Lower Bavaria, and to all thofe diftricts of the Upper which had been formerly fiefs of the kingdom of Bohemia, caufed a vaft army to enter the electorate, notwithftanding the remonftrances of the regency, who in vain pleaded the laws of the empire and the rights of fovereignty.

The Elector Theodore, equally unable and unwilling to rifque the conteft, figned a convention with the Emperor in January 1778, in which all the pretended rights of the Court of Vienna were allowed and conceded in their fulleft extent. This tranfaction, however, could not fail to excite a general alarm throughout the empire.

The Duke of Deux-ponts formally protefted againft this invafion and dereliction of his rights, and called upon the princes and co-eftates of the empire, as members of the Germanic Body, and guarantees of the Treaty of Weftphalia, to interpofe for the prefervation of the Conftitution, thus openly violated.

The King of Pruffia, who regarded with a jealous eye whatever tended to the aggrandifement of the Houfe of Auftria, affumed, as well became him,

him, the lead in this important and common concern. His feveral memorials on this fubject to the Court of Vienna, and to the Diet of the Empire aſſembled at Ratifbon, were however extremely guarded and temperate, whilſt the replies of the Imperial Court were in the higheſt degree haughty and fupercilious.—" The Court of Vienna knew her own rights, and was the proper judge of them. An *amicable arrangement* had taken place, and his Imperial Majeſty did not think himſelf accountable to any Prince of the Empire for the meaſures he had purfued; and, being thoroughly fatisfied with the JUSTICE of his CAUSE, was refolved to fupport his pretenfions by force of arms."

The King of Pruſſia, who evidently appears to have been reluctant to proceed to extremities, at length propofed to the Emperor to guaranty to him in full right the ceſſion of two confiderable diſtricts of the duchy of Bavaria, contiguous to the Auſtrian territories, on condition that the Court of Vienna would relinquiſh her remaining claims. But this being refufed with difdain, his Pruſſian Majeſty publiſhed a manifeſto early in July 1778, ſtating " the unwarrantable and violent conduct of the Imperial Court, which, if fuffered to proceed without control, would effect the total overthrow of the whole Germanic fyſtem."

It was equally evident on the other hand, that the Emperor had from the firſt expected, and was prepared

prepared to rifque the event of a war for the fake of this great and moft defirable acquifition *.

With refpect to the Emperor, this was " the fpring of hope, and the fummer of the paffions;" but the Monarch of Pruffia, who had already attained the higheft feat in the temple of fame, and was now faft declining into the vale of years, would willingly have avoided a war which prefented no glorious or fplendid object, and which was impofed upon him by an unwelcome and imperious political neceffity.

Saxony, departing from its long and intimate union with the Imperial Houfe, now joined with all its forces the King of Pruffia, who in the beginning of July entered Bohemia at the head of a vaft army on the fide of Silefia, while another of nearly equal force, under his brother Prince Henry, penetrated the paffes of the mountains which feparate that kingdom from Saxony. Of the two Auftrian armies, the Emperor in perfon commanded one, and the famous Marechal Laudohn the other, or, to fpeak more properly, both; the

---

* " When the Emperor furveys the map of Germany," fays a moft agreeable and, though a Judge of the High Court of Jufticiary in Scotland, a moft LIBERAL writer, the late Lord Gardenftone, " he may well apply to the Electorate of Bavaria the words of the old rapacious neighbour in HORACE,—

————————O fi angulus ille
Proximus accedat qui nunc denormat agellum!"

whole

whole plan and conduct of this campaign, which on the part of the Austrians was entirely defensive, being ascribed to that justly celebrated General.

After a great variety of military movements and manœuvres unnecessary to particularize, and indeed almost unintelligible in the relation, but which were said on both sides to display uncommon proofs of skill, the King of Prussia, not being able to bring the Austrians to a general action, was finally compelled to evacuate Bohemia with great loss. Marechal Laudohn, in the whole of his operations, seemed closely to have adhered to the model of his renowned predecessor, Marechal Traun, whose defensive campaign of 1744 in Bohemia is so highly extolled by the Prussian monarch as a master-piece of professional judgment and ability.

Soon after the termination of the campaign, a negotiation for peace was set on foot by the Court of Vienna, whose counsels the Emperor could no longer influence. His mother, the Empress Queen, who possessed all the real and efficient power of the Austrian House, sighed for peace, while the Emperor her son was eager and ardent for the prosecution of the war, though nothing could be less encouraging than the prospects now presented to him. The whole empire was firmly united in opinion and interest in opposition to the Imperial claims. Russia openly declared, by her ambassador at Ratisbon, that if the usurpation of Bavaria was not relinquished, she should be under the necessity of furnishing to Prussia the auxiliary troops stipulated by treaty; and even France declared to the Diet her resolution in no respect to deviate from her guarantee of the Treaty of Westphalia.

There is moreover a possibility that the Empress Queen, who had in the latter years of her life become a religious devotee, might entertain some *slight scruples* of conscience at the sacrificing so many myriads of lives in support of an act of flagrant perfidy and injustice.

The motives for peace being thus urgent, the preliminary articles were signed at Teschen, May 13, 1779, in conformity to which the whole electorate was restored to its rightful possessor, the district of Burghausen excepted. The Empress did not long survive the pacification she so anxiously sought, dying November 12, 1780, much lamented by her subjects, whom she had governed for forty years with parental affection and indisputable ability.

Joseph II. her son early discovered that rage for innovation, without discrimination or judgment, which has in the sequel rendered his name so unfortunately memorable. His character was however as yet very imperfectly known, and Europe thought much better of this monarch, both in regard to the rectitude of his disposition

and

and the extent of his capacity, than TIME, the grand umpire of opinions, has eventually confirmed. " Ignorant of the sciences belonging to the art of government," says a writer who intimately knew both the man and the monarch, " his intercourse was with people still more ignorant than himself. His ideas were confused, and he attempted in vain to emancipate himself from vulgar prejudices. His pride would admit of no contradiction. He desired to appear infallible, and to impart this infallibility to all his officers. Flatterers and deceivers pressed round the throne, and, terming his obstinacy firmness, and his restlessness love of glory, steeled his heart, naturally obdurate, against noble and exalted sentiments; and assured him that he would become the greatest of princes, and obscure the glory of the great FREDERIC. Finding insurmountable obstacles to every innovation tending to good, he adopted measures of violence in preference to policy, and would have been in time the greatest of tyrants."

His reign nevertheless commenced with an act of beneficence, truly imperial, in the promulgation of letters patent, granting the free exercise of their religion to the protestants all over the Austrian dominions. By a second edict, he declared all religious foundations in the Austrian Netherlands exempt from all foreign ecclesiastical jurisdiction; and other regulations were adopted for the purpose

pose of reducing the number of religious houses, and of discountenancing all monastic institutions.

The Roman Pontiff, Pius VI. whose zeal for the church was very great, alarmed at these proceedings, declared to the Emperor his intention, notwithstanding his advanced age, to make in person a journey to Vienna, in order to confer with his Imperial Majesty on the subject of these recent and dangerous innovations. The Emperor in reply assured his Holiness, that his heart was truly catholic and apostolic; but that with regard to the late regulations, they had been made with due consideration and good advice; and that having already decided upon them, his Holiness's journey was in this view entirely superfluous.

The Pope however would not be deterred from the execution of his design, and on his actual arrival at Vienna he was treated by the Emperor with the highest demonstrations of respect and affection: but no alterations whatever as to public measures took place, as may easily be supposed, in consequence of this visit.

The good understanding of the Russian and Ottoman Empires had recently suffered great interruption, in consequence of the opposition of interests involved in the election of a Khan of the Tartars, with respect to which neither Power, agreeably to the terms of the late peace, had a right to interfere. An explanatory agreement at
length

length took place, by which the Khan Sahim Guerai, elected through the influence of Ruſſia, was acknowledged as lawful Khan of the Crimea by the Turkiſh Government.

In the year 1782, neverthelefs, theſe diſturbances were revived, and the Czarina entered into an alliance, offenſive and defenſive, with the Emperor, in the evident expectation of an immediate war with the Porte. And haughty memorials were delivered by the ambaſſadors of both the Imperial Courts at Conſtantinople, infifting that the Ottoman Court ſhould not henceforth interpoſe in the affairs of the Crimea; nor encroach upon the prerogatives of the Princes of Moldavia and Walachia; nor oppoſe the free navigation of the Euxine.

Soon after this the Khan of the Tartars, in conformity doubtleſs to the pre-concerted plan of the Imperial Courts, ſignified his reſolution to reſign his crown into the hands of the Czarina. After ſome affected heſitation, her Imperial Majeſty declared by a public manifeſto, dated April 1783, her acceptance of this reſignation, and her determination to take once for all the peninſula of the Crimea, together with the iſland of Taman, and the province of Cuban Tartary, on the other ſide of the Straits of Caffa, extending to Circaſſia, under her own immediate adminiſtration.

The Court of Conſtantinople, rouſed by this new

and unexpected attack, replied to the Ruffian manifefto with unufual animation and energy.— " What pretenfions of right (fay they) can her Imperial Majefty have to territories annexed for ages to the dominion of the Porte ? Would fuch claims on any part of the Ruffian empire not be inftantly refifted ? And can it be prefumed that the Sublime Porte, however defirous of peace, will acquiefce in what ambition may term policy, but juftice and equity would deem ufurpation? What Chriftian power has the Porte offended ? Whofe territories have the Ottoman troops invaded ? In the country of what prince is the Turkifh ftandard difplayed ? Content with the boundaries of empire affigned her by GOD and his Prophet, the wifhes of the Porte are for peace; but if the Court of Ruffia be determined in her claims, the Sublime Porte, appealing to the world for the juftice of her proceedings, muft prepare for war, relying on the decrees of Heaven, and confident of the interpofition of the Prophet of prophets, who will protect his faithful fervants in the hour of every difficulty."

The Ruffian Court however appeared no lefs refolute to maintain and fubftantiate, than that of Conftantinople to refift her claims; and Prince Potemkin, a nobleman of great influence and authority at the Court of Peterfburg, was delegated to take poffeffion of the countries in queftion, in the

the name of the Empreſs. A war now therefore appeared inevitable; but happily for the intereſts of humanity, the two leading kingdoms of Europe were at this period governed by wiſe and beneficent miniſters, who ſincerely wiſhed to ſecure to mankind the ineſtimable bleſſings of univerſal peace. From motives which reflected the higheſt honor on thoſe celebrated ſtateſmen, the Comte de Vergennes and Mr. Fox offered the mediation of their reſpective Sovereigns to effect an accommodation: and the Porte perceiving itſelf in a manner abandoned by France her antient ally, and wholly unable to contend againſt that tide of adverſe fortune which threatened to overwhelm the empire of the Ottomans in final and remedileſs ruin, at length reluctantly aſſented to the ceſſion of the provinces actually in the poſſeſſion of Ruſſia; and a treaty or convention to this purport was ſigned in the month of January 1784.

Thus did the Court of Peterſburg, with no expence of blood or treaſure, acquire an invaluable addition of territory, affording an unbounded ſcope for the aggrandizement of her commercial and maritime power; and which extended the limits of her empire from the Frozen Sea of Archangel to the utmoſt ſhores of the Euxine. A new city, called Cherſon, had been already founded by the Empreſs in the centre of her Turkiſh conqueſts, deſtined probably, at ſome future period, to become

come the emporium of wealth and the feat of power. The former defignations of the ceded countries were now by the Imperial mandate abolifhed. Thofe barbarous names fo offenfive to claffic faftidioufnefs were no longer heard, and the antient appellations, after the lapfe of a thoufand years, reftored. The Crimea became the Taurica—Actiar was changed to Sebaftopolis—Caffa was loft in Theodofia—and the Bog was happily fuperfeded by the Hypanis.

The political ftate of the remaining countries of Europe either requires no diftinct animadverfion, or would lead to difcuffions not within the limits of the prefent hiftory. It may however be tranfiently remarked, that an event very little to be lamented took place February 1777, in the death of Don Jofeph I. King of Portugal. His reign was marked in the records of hiftory only by weaknefs and calamity; it was deeply ftained with domeftic blood, and rendered deteftable by worfe than Dionyfian devices of cruelty. The earthquake of 1755 had laid his capital in ruins, and fhook the kingdom in a political as well as phyfical fenfe to its centre. The confpiracy of 1757 awakened all the malignity of ceafelefs fufpicion, and filled the dungeons of the ftate with the moft virtuous of her citizens. Saved from ruin in the enfuing war with Spain by the interpofition of England, this monarch could not forget

get nor forgive the magnitude of the obligation; and the commerce of the British merchants, under the arbitrary and capricious conduct of the Marquis de Pombal, his favorite minister, suffered under continual oppression.

He was succeeded by his eldest daughter, Donna Isabella, married by virtue of a papal dispensation to Don Pedro, brother to the late king. At her accession the prison doors were thrown open, and eight hundred perfons were set at liberty; but these were said to bear a very small proportion to the numbers who had perished in those regions of darkness and despair, under the sufferings and horrors of their confinement.

Pursuant to the intimation in the concluding speech of the last session, the Parliament of Great Britain was convened at an early period of the winter, November 11, 1783; and his Majesty stated, as a principal object of their consideration, the situation of the East India Company. "The utmost exertions of their wisdom (he said) would be required to maintain and improve the valuable advantages derived from our India possessions, and to promote and secure the happiness of the native inhabitants of those provinces."

The Address passed without opposition. Mr. Pitt in his speech on this occasion warned the Ministers, " that as to the affairs of India, it would not be enough to attempt measures of palliation,

liation, and of a temporary nature; that would only increafe the danger by removing it to a diftance, and he exprefled his furprife that this important bufinefs had been fo long poftponed."

Mr. Fox, well pleafed at this language, acknowledged " that the ftate of India was fuch as would ill brook delay in their deliberations, and he was happy to give notice that on that day fe'nnight he fhould be prepared to make a motion relative to India."

On the 18th of November, accordingly, Mr. Fox moved for leave to bring in a bill for vefting the affairs of the Eaft India Company in the hands of certain Commiffioners, for the benefit of the proprietary and the public. The plan propofed by Mr. Fox was marked with all the characteriftics of his ardent and daring mind. The total derangement of the finances of the Company, and their utter incompetency to govern the vaft territories of which they had, by very queftionable means, obtained the poffeffion, was too evident to admit of contradiction. The evil was notorious; the only difficulty was to devife an adequate remedy.

This famous bill propofed no lefs than to take from the directors and proprietors the entire adminiftration, not of their territorial merely, but of their commercial affairs, and to veft the management and direction of them in the hands of feven
Com-

Commiffioners named in the bill, and irremovable by the Crown, except in confequence of an addrefs of either Houfe of Parliament. Thefe were Earl Fitzwilliam, Prefident of the Board; Vifcount Lewifham, eldeft fon to the Earl of Dartmouth; the Right Honorable Frederic Montague, the Honorable George Auguftus North; Sir Gilbert Elliot, Sir Henry Fletcher, Baronets; and Robert Gregory, Efq. who, it could not fail to be remarked, were divided upon the model and in the fame proportion as the members of the Cabinet.— Thefe Commiffioners were to be affifted by a fubordinate board of nine Directors to be named in the firft inftance by Parliament, and afterwards chofen by the Proprietors. And the bill empowered thefe Commiffioners and Directors immediately to enter into poffeffion of all lands, tenements, books, records, veffels, goods, merchandize, and fecurities, in truft for the Company.

This act, by which the charter of the Company was entirely fuperfeded, was to continue in force four years, that is, till the year after the next general election;—and it was accompanied by a fecond bill, enacting very excellent, wife, and equitable regulations for the future government of the Britifh territories in Hindoftan. The aftonifhment excited by the difclofure of this plan was very great; and while it was on one fide of the Houfe extolled as a mafter-piece of genius, virtue, and ability, it was on the other reprobated as a deep and dangerous design, fraught with mischief and ruin. " INDIA, it was true," said Mr. Pitt, " wanted reform, but not such a reform as this;—it wanted a *constitutional* alteration, and not a *tyrannical* one that broke through every principle of equity and justice. By the bill before the House, an attack was made on the most solemn charters: it pointed a fatal blow against the faith and integrity of Parliament: it broke through every tie by which man was bound to man. The principle of this bill once established, what security had the other public companies of the kingdom? What security had the Bank of England? What security had the National Creditors, or the Public Corporations? Or, indeed, what assurance could we have for the GREAT CHARTER itself, the foundation of all our liberties? It would be folly in the extreme to suppose, that the principle, once admitted, would operate only on the present occasion. Good principles might sleep, but bad ones never. It was the curse of society, that when a bad principle was once established, bad men would always be found to give it its full effect. The bill under consideration included a confiscation of the property, and a disfranchisement of the members, of the East India Company; all the several articles of whose effects were transferred by violence to strangers. Imagination was at a loss to guess at the most insignificant trifle that had escaped the

harpy.

harpy jaws of A RAVENOUS COALITION. The power was pretended indeed to be given in trust for the benefit of the Proprietors; but in case of the grossest abuse of trust, to whom was the appeal? To the Proprietors? No:—to the majority of either House of Parliament, which the most contemptible Minister could not fail to secure, with the patronage of above two millions sterling given by this bill. The influence which would accrue from this bill—a new, enormous, and unexampled influence—was indeed in the highest degree alarming. Seven Commissioners chosen ostensibly by Parliament, but really by Administration, were to involve in the vortex of their authority the patronage and treasures of India. The Right Honorable Mover had acknowledged himself to be a man of ambition, and it now appeared that he was prepared to sacrifice the King, the Parliament, and the People, at the shrine of his ambition. He desired to elevate his present connections to a situation in which no political convulsions, and no variations of power, might be able to destroy their importance, and put an end to their ascendency."

These and similar arguments against the present extraordinary measure of the Minister were also ably and eloquently enforced by the Lord Advocate, Mr. Jenkinson, Mr. Grenville, and others.

On the other hand, it was with equal eloquence and ability vindicated by Mr. Fox, who with warmth declared, " that he would rifque upon the execution of this bill whatever was moſt dear to him—whatever men moſt valued: the character of integrity, of talents, of honor, of prefent reputation and future fame;—thefe he would ftake upon the conſtitutional ſafety, the enlarged policy, the equity and wifdom of this meaſure." While the bill was pending, a petition was preſented from the Company, repreſenting the meaſure as ſubverſive of their charter, and operating as a confifcation of their property, without charging againſt them any ſpecific delinquency, without trial, without conviction a proceeding contrary to the moſt ſacred privileges of Britiſh ſubjects and praying to be heard by counſel againſt the bill. The City of London alſo prefented a ſtrong petition to the ſame effect; but it was carried with rapidity through all its ſtages in the Houſe of Commons by deciſive majorities, the diviſion on the ſecond reading being 217 to 103 voices. And on the 9th of December, Mr. Fox, attended by a numerous train of Members, prefented the bill at the bar of the Houſe of Lords. On this occafion, Earl Temple declared, " that he was happy to embrace the firſt opportunity of entering his proteſt againſt ſo INFAMOUS a Bill; againſt a ſtretch

of

of power so truly alarming, and that went near to seize upon the most inestimable part of our Constitution—our CHARTERED RIGHTS."

The Duke of Richmond rose on the same side, and displayed in a striking manner the inconsistency of a part at least of the present Administration, by a view of the Protest entered by Lord Rockingham and other Noble Lords, on the Journals of that House, against the India Bill of 1773. This famous WHIG Protest concludes in the following remarkable words: " If the provisions and precedent of this bill should render the public faith of Great Britain of no estimation, the franchises, rights, and properties of Englishmen precarious; if the boundless fund of corruption furnished by this bill to the servants of the Crown should efface every idea of honor, public spirit, and independence, from every rank of people; after struggling vainly against these evils, we have nothing left but the satisfaction of recording our names to posterity, as those who resisted the whole of this iniquitous system, and as men who had no share in betraying to blind prejudices or sordid interest every thing that has hitherto been held sacred in this country." To this protest the signatures of the Duke of Portland, who held the highest post under the present Administration, and that of Lord Fitzwilliam, the future President of the new India Board, were affixed. Lord Thurlow declared

declared the prefent bill "to be a moft atrocious violation of private property, in juftification of which if the plea of political neceffity were urged, that neceffity muft be proved by evidence at the bar of the Houfe, and not by reports from a Committee, to which he fhould pay as much attention as to the romance of Robinfon Crufoe, They were told, that the finances of the Company were much deranged; but could Parliament in juftice forget that the Company were reftricted from employing that credit which refulted from its great and flourifhing fituation? and that if thofe reftrictions were taken off to-morrow, every demand to the State would be difcharged? Could Parliament forget that the politics of this country had involved the Company in an extenfive and ruinous war? and that while we encountered lofs, misfortune, and difgrace, in every other quarter of the globe, this delinquent Company had furmounted the moft aftonifhing difficulties in India? Would Parliament forget that when peace was reftored to this unfortunate country, the conquefts of this delinquent Company were given up to prevent farther facrifices of our more favorite poffeffions?"

The fecond reading of the bill took place on the 15th of December*, when counfel was heard

at

---

* During this interval, the regular bufinefs of the feffion was proceeding at the bar of the House in behalf of the Company. At eleven o'clock, the counsel requested of the House an adjournment for the conclusion of their evidence; and a motion being made, it was carried in opposition to the Ministers, by 87 to 79 voices.

On the 17th it was moved, That the bill be REJECTED. On this occasion, Lord Camden distinguished himself by a most able and eloquent speech, against a measure which his Lordship affirmed to be in the highest degree pernicious and unconstitutional. "To divest the Company of the management of their own property and commercial concerns was, his Lordship said, to treat them as IDEOTS; and

proceeding in the usual manner in the House of Commons; and on the 12th of December, amongst the ordinary estimates of the year, eighteen thousand pounds were charged for the purchase of the princely mansion of Sir Gregory Page, on Blackheath, as a royal military academy;— a sum not more than equal to the value of the materials. And as several thousand pounds would by this means be saved in the repair of the old incommodious building at Woolwich; and likewise an allowance of five hundred pounds per annum for lodgings to the Officers, who would henceforth be accommodated in the new academy, the expence was reduced to a mere nothing, whilst the purchase would have done honor to the taste and magnificence of the nation; yet was it opposed with most preposterous obstinacy by some weak and perverse Members of the House, as a wanton and scandalous waste of the public money; and the Chancellor of the Exchequer had the injudicious complaisance to consent to omit it on the report.

he regarded the bill not ſo much in the light of a commiſſion of bankruptcy as of lunacy. But as the means of throwing an enormous addition of weight into the ſcale, not of legal, but miniſterial influence, it was ſtill more alarming. Were this bill to paſs into a law, his Lordſhip forcibly declared, we ſhould ſee the King of England and the King of Bengal contending for ſuperiority in the Britiſh Parliament." After a vehement debate, the motion of rejection was carried by 95 againſt 76 voices. As the firſt diviſions in the Upper Houſe were favorable to this bill, it will readily be imagined that ſome powerful cauſe, adequate to the extraordinary and unexpected effect produced, muſt have intervened. The ſolution of the phænomenon was indeed ſufficiently obvious.

On the 11th of December, Earl Temple had held a conference with the KING, in the courſe of which his Lordſhip clearly and fully explained to his Majeſty the nature and tendency of a bill which had been hitherto honored with the King's entire approbation. The royal indignation was in conſequence of this diſcovery excited in a very high degree. The Monarch conſidered himſelf as having been DUPED and DECEIVED. A card was immediately written, ſtating, " That his Majeſty allowed Earl Temple to ſay, that whoever voted for the India Bill was not only not his friend, but would be conſidered by him as his enemy. And if theſe words

words were not ſtrong enough, Earl Temple might uſe whatever words he might deem ſtronger or more to the purpoſe." This interpoſition becoming a matter of public notoriety, Mr. William Baker, Member for Hertford, moved the Houſe of Com-mons on the very day the bill was rejected by the Lords, " That it was now neceſſary to declare, that to report any opinion or pretended opinion of the King upon any bill, or other proceeding, depending in either Houſe of Parliament, with a view to influence the votes of the Members, was an high crime and miſdemeanor." Mr. Pitt treated the motion lightly, and repreſented it as unworthy of the dignity of the Houſe to found any reſolutions upon rumors and hearſays.—But Earl Nugent, father-in-law to Earl Temple, with more ſeriouſneſs and firmneſs declared, " That the Reſolutions before them went to the utter annihilation of ſovereignty. What! Were not Peers by their rank and ſituation hereditary Counſellors of the Crown?—Would that Houſe dare to derogate from the high dignity which the Conſtitution had annexed to their ſtation? Every Peer, and indeed every Commoner, under certain reſtrictions, had a right to addreſs the Sovereign. But the tendency of theſe Reſolutions was to make the Monarch a kind of priſoner of ſtate; and to ſhut him up from every ſpecies of information unacceptable to the exiſting Adminiſtration. Were any relation of his, in a criſis

of

of difficulty and danger, to convey truths to his Sovereign of high importance to be known, though at the rifque of incurring the utmoſt puniſhment which the indignation of that Houſe could inflict, he ſhould conſider his conduct not merely as juſtifiable but tranſcendently meritorious; and ſuch as would tranſmit his name with honor to the lateſt poſterity." Other members acknowledged ſomething of irregularity in theſe proceedings, and wiſhed that a meaſure ſo dangerous might have been counteracted in a mode more open and conſtitutional: but a great good had been obtained, and in this caſe it were not wife to examine into the cauſe with too accurate a diſcrimination and too ſevere a ſcrutiny. The reſolution moved by Mr. Baker paſſed nevertheleſs by a great majority.

The quarrel between the Crown and the Miniſters, ſupported as they were by a decided majority of the Houſe of Commons, having now become public and palpable, an entire change of Adminiſtration was at all hazards determined upon. At midnight on the 18th of December, a royal meſſage was ſent to the Secretaries of State, demanding the Seals of their ſeveral departments; and early the next morning letters of difmiſſion, ſigned TEMPLE, were ſent to the other Members of the Cabinet.

In a few days Mr. Pitt was declared Firſt Lord of the Treaſury and Chancellor of the Exchequer; the Marquis of Carmarthen, and Mr. Thomas Townſhend,

Townshend, created Lord Sydney, were nominated Secretaries of State; Lord Thurlow was reinstated as Lord Chancellor; Earl Gower, created in the sequel Marquis of Stafford, as President of the Council; the Duke of Rutland was constituted Lord Privy Seal; Lord Howe placed at the head of the Admiralty, and the Duke of Richmond of the Ordnance. The Earl of Northington was recalled from his Government of Ireland, to which Lord Temple, who had retained the Seals of Secretary only three days, was again destined to succeed.

To the surprise, and unquestionably to the great eventual detriment of the public, the Earl of Shelburne was not included in the new arrangement of Administration. The intelligence of this change was, notwithstanding, received by the nation with transports of joy.

The INDIA BILL, concerning which the public judgment was at the first suspended, had now, by a multiplicity of able and popular tracts industriously circulated, been completely developed and explained*; and it was almost universally condemned as a measure in the highest degree arbi-

---

* Amongst these the publications of Mr. Pulteney and Mr. Rous were particularly distinguished, as the productions of men no less impartial than intelligent, truly attached to the principles of liberty, and writing not in the spirit of party or rhetorical exaggeration, but of calm and dispassionate enquiry—solely actuated by the love of TRUTH.

trary

trary and oppreffive, and with confummate artifice calculated to perpetuate the power of an Adminiftration who were the objects of the national deteftation. It is neverthelefs a fuppofition abfolutely inadmiffible, that fuch men as the Duke of Portland, Lord John Cavendifh, and Mr. Fox, had concerted a meafure infidioufly adapted to ferve their own purpofe—knowing or believing the fame to be inimical to the effential interefts of their country. In fact, no plan for the government of India could be framed which was not liable to very great objection. The bill of Mr. Fox was primarily and profeffedly defigned for the reformation of abufes in India; and as it was neceffary for this purpofe to eftablifh a new and extenfive fource of authority and influence at home, very plaufible, and to perfons interefted, doubtlefs, very convincing reafons might be adduced to prove it more fafe and conftitutional to entruft this power to Parliamentary Commiffioners than to the Crown, whofe influence it had been fo lately the grand and favorite object of all true patriots to diminifh. Nor was it poffible that the parliamentary rejection of this bill could have been attended with fuch fignal effects, had not the popularity of the Minifter with whom it originated been already completely and for ever annihilated by means of the fatal and ACCURSED COALITION.

On the 22d of December, the Houfe of Commons being in a Committee on the State of the Nation,

Nation, Mr. Erſkine moved, "that an addreſs be preſented to the King, ſtating, that alarming reports had gone forth of an intended diſſolution of Parliament, and humbly repreſenting to his Majeſty the inconveniences and dangers of a prorogation or diſſolution in the preſent conjuncture; and entreating the Sovereign to hearken to the advice of that Houſe, and not to the ſecret advice of particular perſons who might have private intereſts of their own ſeparate from the true intereſts of the King, and People."

This addreſs, which was of a complexion unknown in this country ſince the æra of the Revolution, was carried without a diviſion. The anſwer of the King was very diſcreet and temperate. His Majeſty ſaid, "It had been his conſtant object to employ the authority entruſted to him by the Conſtitution to its true and only end—the good of the people; and he was always happy in concurring with the wiſhes and opinions of his faithful Commons. He truſted they would proceed in the important matters mentioned in their addreſs with all convenient ſpeed, aſſuring them that he ſhould not interrupt their meeting after their adjournment by any exerciſe of his prerogative either of prorogation or diſſolution."

The Houſe now with tolerable ſatisfaction adjourned for the uſual Chriſtmas receſs to the 10th

of

of January 1784, on which day the Committee on the State of the Nation was refumed; and feveral refolutions were brought forward by Mr. Fox, and agreed to by the Houfe—prohibiting the Lords of the Treafury from affenting to the acceptance of the Company's bills from India—forbidding alfo the iffue of any of the public money after a prorogation or diffolution of Parliament, unlefs the Act of Appropriation fhall have previoufly paffed; and ordering accounts to be laid before the Houfe of the monies already iffued.

Thefe refolutions were followed by a motion from the Earl of Surry—" 1. That in the prefent fituation of his Majefty's dominions it was peculiarly neceffary that there fhould be an Adminiftration that had the confidence of the public. 2. That the late changes in his Majefty's Councils were accompanied by circumftances new and extraordinary, and fuch as did not conciliate the confidence of that Houfe." On this motion the Houfe divided, but it was carried in the affirmative by 196 to 142 voices.

On the 16th of January a refolution was moved by Lord Charles Spencer, " That the continuance of the prefent Minifters in trufts of the higheft importance and refpectability was contrary to the principles of the Conftitution, and injurious to the interefts of the King and People." Upon this queftion

tion the Houfe divided, ayes 205, noes 184; fo that the anti-minifterial majority was by an ominous defection reduced from 54 to 21 voices.

About this time the Chancellor of the Exchequer introduced into the Houfe a bill for the better government of India, on principles which left the commercial concerns of the Company in their own hands; and eftablifhed a Board of Control, confifting of certain Commiffioners appointed by the King, poffeffing a negative on the proceedings of the Company in all matters of government or politics. On the motion of commitment, this bill was loft by 222 voices againft 214—fo that the Oppofition majority was now diminifhed to 8.

A ftill more encouraging circumftance was, that addreffes of thanks and approbation to his Majefty for the removal of his late Minifters now began to flow in from every part of the kingdom; and became at length fo univerfal, that upon no occafion whatever was the fenfe of the people at large more clearly, ftrongly, and unequivocally afcertained. In this the City of LONDON had taken the lead, and in their addrefs they fay, " Your faithful Citizens lately beheld with infinite concern the progrefs of a meafure which equally tended to encroach on the rights of your Majefty's Crown—to annihilate the chartered rights of the Eaft India Company— and to raife a new power unknown to this free government, and highly inimical to its fafety. As this

this dangerous measure was warmly supported by your Majesty's late Ministers, we heartily rejoice in their dismission, and humbly thank your Majesty for exerting your prerogative in a manner so salutary and constitutional." And concluding in a manner very different from the usual tenor of their addresses in former times, they say, "Highly sensible of your Majesty's paternal care and affection for your people, WE pray the Almighty that you may long reign in peace over a free, an happy, and united nation."

The popularity acquired by the Monarch in consequence of this dismission was indeed so great as to efface all memory of former disagreements; and though originating in a cause merely accidental, and on the part of the Crown from a sudden and passionate resentment at a supposed invasion of the prerogative, yet has it not suffered in the sequel any diminution: on the contrary, from an extraordinary concurrence of circumstances, the loyalty of the people has been elevated to a pitch of ardor which court-flattery itself will scarcely hesitate to acknowledge at least commensurate with the merits of the Monarch.

Alarmed at the novel and dangerous circumstances of the nation, both parties seemed at length disposed to pause, and a judicious idea suggested by the independent interest in the House of Commons of a new Administration, founded upon the widest and

and moft comprehenfive bafis, was liftened to with approbation; Lord North, after all the mighty mifchiefs of which he had been the occafion or the inftrument, declaring himfelf willing to retire, if confidered as the obftacle to a general union.

The King, by a meffage to the Duke of Portland, expreffed his defire that an interview might take place between his Grace and Mr. Pitt, for the purpofe of arranging a new plan of Adminiftration on *fair* and *equal* terms. The Duke, previoufly to the interview, requefted to be informed in what fenfe he was to underftand the words *fair* and *equal;* and Mr. Pitt declining any previous explanation, the negotiation terminated. But it was fufficiently evident that the queftion had reference to the fuperiority of voices claimed by the Ex-Minifters in the Cabinet—a point which Mr. Fox ftill ftood upon ground too high to concede.

The Houfe of Lords, hitherto the filent and paffive fpectators of this extraordinary conteft, now thought proper to come forward; and at the motion of the Earl of Effingham their Lordfhips refolved, " 1. That an attempt in any one branch of the Legiflature to fufpend the execution of law by feparately affuming to itfelf the direction of a difcretionary power vefted by Act of Parliament, is unconftitutional"—alluding to the refolution of the Commons refpecting the non-acceptance of bills from India. " 2. That by the known principles of the Conſtitution the undoubted authority of appointing to the great offices of the Executive Government was ſolely veſted in the King, and that this Houſe had every reaſon to place the firmeſt reliance on his Majeſty's wiſdom in the exerciſe of this prerogative." Theſe reſolutions, in the form of an addreſs, were preſented to the King. In return, the Houſe of Commons (February 16) reſolved at the motion of Lord Beauchamp, "1. That the Houſe had not aſſumed to itſelf a right to ſuſpend the execution of law; and 2. That for them to declare their opinion reſpecting the exerciſe of any diſcretionary power was conſtitutional, and agreeable to eſtabliſhed uſage."

The Oppoſition, who were yet the majority of the Houſe of Commons, found themſelves daily in a more embarraſſing ſituation. The King, the Houſe of Peers, and the Nation at large, were now evidently and openly united in ſentiment againſt them; their numbers were continually diminiſhing, and there was good reaſon to believe they would ſoon dwindle into a minority. Unſupported by the voice of the People, the Houſe of Commons can never appear great or reſpectable; but when they are alſo unſupported by the power and influence of the Crown, they muſt become inſignificant and contemptible. Some farther efforts, however, to ſuſtain an apparently ſinking cauſe, were yet with unbroken ſpirit attempted.

On

On the 20th of February an addrefs, carried by a majority of 20 voices only, was prefented to the King by the Houfe, expreffive of " the reliance the Houfe had on the wifdom of the Sovereign, that he would take fuch meafures as might tend to give effect to the wifhes of his faithful Commons, by removing every obftacle to the formation of fuch an Adminiftration as the Houfe of Commons had declared to be requifite." To this the King again replied in terms happily adapted to the occafion— mentioning " his recent endeavors to unite in the public fervice, on a fair and equal footing, thofe whofe joint efforts might have a tendency to put an end to the unhappy divifions and diftractions of the country; obferving, neverthelefs, that there was no fpecific charge or complaint fuggefted againft his prefent Minifters, and that numbers of his fubjects had expreffed to him in the warmeft manner their fatisfaction at the late changes. Under thefe circumftances he trufted his faithful Commons would not wifh that the effential offices of Executive Government fhould be vacated until fuch a plan of union as he had called for, and they had pointed out, could be carried into effect."

On the 1ft day of March a yet ftronger addrefs was moved and carried, but by a ftill fmaller majority, in which the Houfe " humbly befought his Majefty that he would be gracioufly pleafed to lay the foundation of a ftrong and ftable Government, by the previous removal of his prefent Minifters." To this the King replied in the fame mild and firm language—repeating, that no charge had been brought againſt his prefent Minifters; and adding this remarkable obfervation, " that if there were any juſt ground for their removal, it ought to be equally a reafon for not admitting them as a part of that extended and united Adminiſtration which is ſtated to be requifite."

Addreſſes having been unavailingly tried, Mr. Fox in the following week moved a REPRESENTATION to the Crown, which at great length, and in energetic language, ſtated " the dangerous and pernicious tendency of thofe meafures and maxims by which a new fyſtem of Executive Government had been fet up; which wanting the confidence of that Houſe, and acting in defiance to their refolutions, muſt prove at once inadequate by its inefficacy to the neceſſary objects of Government, and dangerous by its example to the liberties of the people." The motion was carried by a MAJORITY of ONE. And here the conteſt may be faid to have terminated; for the Mutiny Bill being brought forward on the following day, March 9; Mr. Fox, perceiving himfelf deferted by many of his partifans, abandoned his original intention of moving its poſtponement, as a fecurity againſt a fudden and premature diffolution. The univerfal fenfe of the nation in favor of the new Miniſters, which could

no

no longer be denied, was afcribed to an *unparalleled delufion*; but Mr. Fox difclaiming any intention of obftructing the fupplies, a diffolution was faid to be in the higheft degree indefenfible. Little regard, however, was paid to the arguments of the Oppofition againft a meafure fo evidently to the advantage of the prefent Minifters; and on the 24th of March the Parliament was prorogued, and the next day diffolved by proclamation, and a new Parliament convened to meet on the 18th of May.

The influence of the Crown being now combined with the inclination and independent intereft of the country, at the general election the effect produced was prodigious. The COALITIONISTS, even thofe who once ftood higheft in the eftimation of the public, were almoft every where thrown out. Lord John Cavendifh for the city, Mr. Foljambe, the heir of Sir George Saville, for the county, of York; General Conway, for Bury; Mr. Coke, for Norfolk; Mr. Halfey, for Hertfordfhire; Mr. Townfhend, for Cambridge Univerfity; and Mr. Erfkine, for Portfmouth. Mr. Fox himfelf, to the furprife of all, had a clear and great majority on the poll for Weftminfter, though the High-Bailiff by a fcandalous partiality refufed to make the return in his favor—for which an action was fubfequently brought by Mr.

Mr. Fox, in the Court of King's Bench, and a verdict with large damages obtained.

The King in his opening speech expressed "great satisfaction at meeting his Parliament at this time, after having recurred in so important a moment to the sense of his people. He entertained a just and confident reliance that they were animated by the same sentiments of loyalty and attachment to the Constitution which had been so fully manifested in every part of the kingdom. He recommended to their most serious consideration to frame suitable provisions for the good government of our possessions in the East Indies. Upon this subject Parliament would not lose sight of the effect which the measures they adopted might have on our own Constitution, and our dearest interests at home." The address proposed on this occasion contained strong expressions of approbation respecting the late dissolution, which Lord Surry on the ground of unanimity moved to omit. But Mr. Pitt declared, " that much as he was convinced of the importance of unanimity, he would not purchase an hollow unanimity by passing over a great constitutional measure which the circumstances of the times had made necessary and wise, and which had given the most entire satisfaction to every part of the kingdom." On this point, therefore, the House divided, and the amendment of the Earl of Surry was rejected by a majority of 76 voices; so that the dissolution appeared to have completely answered its intended purpose, and from this period Mr. Pitt may be regarded as the constitutional and efficient Minister of the Nation.

END OF THE THIRD VOLUME.

www.ingramcontent.com/pod-product-compliance
Lightning Source LLC
Chambersburg PA
CBHW020306240426
43673CB00039B/723